NEWS LIMITED

WHY YOU CAN'T READ ALL ABOUT IT

Brian Whitaker

preface by Tom Hopkinson

MINORITY
PRESS·GROUP

9 Poland Street · London W1V 3DG · Tel.01-439-2059

The **Minority Press Group** was set up to investigate and monitor the radical and alternative press in Britain and abroad today. The aim of the project is to provide basic information, investigate problems areas, share the experiences of those working within the radical press and to encourage debate about its future development.

Other titles in this Minority Press Group series are:

No.1 *Here is the Other News*
Challenges to the local commercial press £1.25/£3.50
No.2 *Where is the Other News?*
The newstrade and the radical press £1.25/£4.50
No.3 *The Other Secret Service*
Press distributors and press censorship 60p
No.4 *Rolling Our Own*
Women in printing, publishing and distribution £2.25/£7.50

First published in 1981 by
Minority Press Group, 9 Poland Street, London W1V 3DG
Telephone: 01-439 2059

© Brian Whitaker, Liverpool Free Press
   and Minority Press Group

ISBN 0 906890 04 7 (Hardback)
ISBN 0 906890 03 9 (Paperback)

Reprinted in 1984

Designed & photoset by
Redesign, 9 London Lane, London E8 (01-533 2631)

Cover illustration by Peter Kennard and photographed by Ed Barber

Printed in Great Britain by
The Russell Press, 45 Gamble Street, Nottingham NG7 4ET
(0602 784505)

Trade Distribution: Marion Boyars, 24, Lacy Road, London.
SW15.

Distributed in USA by Marion Boyars and the Scribner Book Companies.

Distributed in Canada by DEC, 427, Bloor Street West, Toronto, Ontario M5S 1X7.

Distributed in Australia by Second Back Row Press, 50 Govett Street, Katoomba, NSW 2780.

Contents

Preface

by Tom Hopkinson

Are the men who have seized this plane and are threatening us with machine-pistols 'terrorists' or 'freedom fighters'?

Is the fat cat on his way to establish residence in the Bahamas 'evading taxes' or 'protecting his legitimate earnings'? And did he acquire that fortune through 'the long overdue reorganisation of British industry' or by 'depriving workers of their livelihoods'?

Define the terms 'scrounger', 'exploitation', 'in the national interest'; and state under what circumstances 'defensive missiles' can be used in a 'preemptive strike'.

Every journalist knows that there are certain assumptions taken for granted by his own and every other newspaper, as well as by radio and television. These assumptions — that the view of the world as seen from these islands is the 'true' one; that certain nations are our 'friends' and certain others traditionally hostile; that laws are just and apply equally to everyone; and that capitalism is the only basis for democratic freedom — colour the way all news is selected, written up and presented, including, of course, the way in which it is photographed.

Nor is this confined to political issues and great events. Financial and industrial developments are reported in terms of 'us' and 'them'. We 'export'; other countries 'dump', particularly the developing countries which are trying to break into the manufacturers' club. Employers 'make offers'; unions 'reject'. Similar, if less obvious, assumptions underlie most writing about art and literature, and even sports reporting.

Those of us who have worked for some time in the media take these assumptions for granted, just as we take it for granted that we produce our copy in English, not in Arabic or Russian.

The value of a minority or alternative press is that is exposes these assumptions. In so doing it is likely to introduce assumptions of its own, which may be as liable to criticism as those it challenges. But at least the public is offered a choice and the conventions given a shake-up.

Being in opposition to the established press — particularly the popular press, whose hallmarks are complacency, servility, triviality and the avoidance of controversial issues — the minority press tends to be suspicious, investigative, denunciatory. It is also always struggling, since it can expect neither financial backing nor advertising support from the establishment it attacks; usually, too it experiences great difficulty in securing distribution.

What has made a minority press possible — and even allowed some growth and expansion in the last decade — is, first, the new technology whereby a few thousand copies can be printed cheaply. Second, the readership, minority papers can attract by focussing on important local issues — such as corruption in high places — which the established press is unwilling or afraid to touch. And, thirdly, the readiness of young journalists, men and women, to renounce or postpone their own chances of advancement in order to work for minimal pay on small-scale publications which may last only a few months, but which can achieve something worth-while in their short lifetime.

The small radical newspaper in this country is the heir to a great tradition, and it is very much to the good that this tradition has been revived. Those who make sacrifices to carry it on are in no need of lectures on journalistic ethics from establishment figures who have made a very good thing out of not seeing further than which side their bread is buttered.

In my opinion, however, it is a mistake for minority press writers to attack objectivity and impartiality on the grounds that objectivity is a "a recent invention, a pseudo-scientific myth, and not even the most diligent journalist can hope to be objective". I understand the resistance some feel to a word which has been so much abused as 'objectivity'. But dislike of a word does not justify abandoning the principle it denotes.

'Commitment journalism', 'advocacy journalism', 'knowing which side we're on' are no substitute for the effort to produce honest journalism; and the fact that so many journalists are unconsciously half-blind does not give others the right to be deliberately one-eyed.

I am wholly in favour of the struggle to establish newspapers, magazines and radio stations which will give the public news and information which they are not getting from the established press. But the news has to be true, and the reporting of it factual. The strength of many minority papers is precisely that their reporting has been more true, more factual, more *objective* than that done by newspapers with fifty times their staff and fifty thousand times their resources.

Tom Hopkinson was formerly editor of Picture Post *and Founder-Director of the Centre for Journalism studies in Cardiff.*

1. News as propaganda

L ATE one night in 1944 a woman told police in Mattoon, Illinois, that she and her daughter had been victims of a strange attack. Someone, she said, had opened her bedroom window and sprayed a sickly-sweet smelling gas that partly paralysed her legs and made her ill. The police found nothing. Next day Mattoon's evening paper, the Daily Gazette-Journal, reported the incident with the headline: ANAESTHETIC PROWLER ON LOOSE.

The following day a man said that he and his wife had been attacked. He had woken up sick and asked his wife if the gas had been left on. On waking, his wife had been unable to walk. Before hearing about the prowler, the couple had blamed their symptoms on eating hot dogs. About the same time another man told the Press his daughter had woken up coughing. When his wife got up to attend to the girl, she could hardly walk. They had not suspected gas until they read the papers.

On the evening after these two accounts were published, a woman arrived home and found a cloth in the porch. She picked it up and sniffed it. The fumes, she said, burned her mouth and lips and made them bleed. Meanwhile, a man who worked nights said his wife had heard someone at the bedroom window, had smelled gas and had been partly paralysed by it. In the next six days 20 further cases were reported. Many more people thought they had heard or seen the mad gasser (as he became known) and calls to the police reporting prowlers more than doubled[1]. Bands of men and boys armed with shotguns patrolled the streets or laid wait on doorsteps. State police with radio cars moved in and joined the hunt. But despite these efforts no-one was caught. Police were baffled by the apparent lack of a motive. Nothing was stolen and there was no evidence to suggest the culprit was a Peeping Tom.

Scientists, too, were puzzled. Symptoms described by the victims were nausea and vomiting, palpitations, paralysis of the legs, dryness of the mouth and throat and, in one case, burns to the mouth. All recovered quickly. Some said the gas smelled musty or like cheap perfume. Others said there was no smell. A major problem was identifying the gas. It must be strong enough to produce vomiting and paralysis quickly, and yet weak enough to disperse rapidly, leaving no traces and no noticeable after-effects in its victims. Scientifically, it had to be both stable and unstable — which was a contradiction. No gas fitting the description could be found in books on anaesthetics and war gases, and chemists at the University of Illinois doubted that such a gas could exist.

Eventually the police began to talk of "imagination" and insisted on victims being seen by doctors. Some newspapers then spoke of "mass hysteria". Abruptly, the "gassings" stopped. In most victims symptoms had disappeared before doctors could examine them. Of the four who were examined, all were diagnosed as suffering from hysteria. Shortly afterwards, Donald M Johnson of the University of Illinois investigated and concluded that the whole affair could be explained as hysteria[2].

He also found that the hysteria had been spread by the Press. The cases were widely scattered throughout the town. Apart from those who lived together and were 'attacked' at the same time, the victims were not in direct contact with each other. Rumour and gossip take time to travel, but the hysteria spread rapidly. The main source of news was the Daily Gazette-Journal which, according to surveys, was read by 97 per cent of families in the town. (There was no local radio station and no-one interviewed by Johnson mentioned radio reports of the affair.) It was probably the Gazette-Journal that informed most people of the first incident. Its unsceptical first report ensured that many people took the case seriously. But it went even further. Its headline announcing a "prowler on loose" and its description of the mother and daughter as "first victims" suggested more attacks would follow. More 'attacks' did follow, and the reports of them led to yet more 'attacks'. After a day free from 'attacks', the paper began its report:

> Mattoon's "mad anaesthetist" apparently took a respite from his forays Thursday night and while many terror-stricken people were some-what relieved they were inclined to hold their breath and wonder when and where he might strike next.

The 'attacks' started again the same night.

EARLY in 1954, the United States tested its first H-bombs. Beginning on March 23, newspapers in Seattle carried reports of damage to car windscreens in a town 80 miles away. Police blamed vandals but could not prove it. On April 14, papers reported similar damage in another town 65 miles away. Later the same day cars at an air base only 45 miles from Seattle were "peppered". Hours later, Seattle itself was "hit". 242 people called the police, reporting damage to more than 3,000 cars (many of the calls came from car park attendants and garage staff). Usually the damage was described as pitting marks on windscreens. Some windscreens were said to be splattered with tiny, metallic-looking particles. Various explanations were offered — the most popular was that it was fallout from the H-bomb tests. The mayor of Seattle dramatically announced that the damage was no longer a police matter, and called on the President for help. Many people covered their windscreens or kept their cars in the garage.

In fact the damage was probably nothing more than normal wear and tear which was spotted only when the Press reports caused people to look *at* their windscreens instead of *through* them. A chemist from Washington University's Environmental Research Laboratory, asked by the Governor to investigate, concluded: "The number of pits increases with the age and mileage of the car". There was no scientific evidence that the windscreens were pitted by some mysterious cause in the space of a few minutes or hours. Later, a random survey of 1,000 people in Seattle, conducted by two university researchers[3], showed 93 per cent of those interviewed had heard reports of windscreen damage. When asked how they first heard the news, 51 per cent said from newspapers, 19 per cent from other people, 18 per cent from the radio, 6 per cent from television and 6 per cent from direct experience. They were then asked whether they believed there had been unusual damage with an unusual cause. The results were: Believers 50 per cent, undecided 26 per cent, sceptical 21 per cent, no reply 3 per cent.

There are numerous examples of strange effects induced by the media. Probably the most famous was the panic caused by an American radio dramatisation of H G Wells' "The War of the Worlds" in 1938. But that was the result of people mistaking the play for reality. On another occasion, as an experiment, British astronomer Patrick Moore pretended to have seen an Unidentified Flying Object near his home. The story he told to his local paper was entirely fictitious but when it was published several 'witnesses' came forward to confirm the 'sighting'[4]. At a more down-to-earth level, a British newspaper once warned of the possibility of a salt shortage within a few months. The prophecy was fulfilled immediately as people rushed to the shops to stock up. At a conference organised by the British Psychological Society in 1980, Dr Roger Ingham, who has made a special study of football violence, pinned some of the blame on the Press. He gave an example of a match between Southampton and Chelsea, where newspapers had predicted trouble. "A lot of Southampton supporters who do not usually carry knives took them to that particular game because they had been told how violent Chelsea was. So the prediction had an effect on the actual game," he said. He added that reports of violence also affect the public's behaviour. Faced with groups of supporters wearing team scarves, people tend to keep their distance and be fearful. The fans sense this reaction and eventually assume the role people expect of them[5].

NO self-respecting person admits to being easily influenced. If you were asked: "Do you believe everything you read in the newspapers?" the only sensible answer would be "No". Answer "Yes" and you could end up looking silly. And yet what alternative have we but to believe? We all rely very heavily on newspapers and television for our knowledge of what is going on in the world. So how do we decide what to believe and what not to believe? Partly, it is a question of credibility: Does it seem likely that an event has actually happened in the way it is reported? Also, it is a question of reputation: We regard some sources as more reliable than others — often without any good reason. A survey in 1973 showed that only 27 per cent of people who said newspapers were their main source of news also believed newspapers were the most accurate and trustworthy source of news[6].

Also — rather illogically — we tend to become less sceptical about news reports the further they are removed from our personal experience. So factory workers may dismiss newspaper reports of a dispute in their own factory as a load of rubbish, but not question stories in the same paper that say the Social Security provides a life of luxury for immigrants. Evidence from several surveys supports this view. In Seattle, for instance, car ownership was 10 per cent higher among those who were sceptical about the windscreen damage — suggesting that those without a chance of personal experience were more willing to believe in it. And a survey of racial attitudes among school children[7] found that children in areas of low immigration are more likely to think of race relations in terms of conflict than children in high immigration areas.

Stories about "scroungers" and Social Security fiddlers, for example, are common in the popular Press. These papers are read by vast numbers of ordinary people, and they influence ordinary people. Stories about "scroungers" can be effective in several ways. They can:

(a) make people more willing to accept work for low wages rather than stay on the dole;

(b) get popular support for keeping state benefits at a low level;

(c) create divisions between the employed "taxpayers" and the unemployed;

(d) encourage people to inform on fiddlers.

And by the sinple repitition of such stories, the public begin to accept that "scroungers" are a major drain on public resources. But if the papers' real purpose was to save money, they would concentrate on the much more serious problem of tax evasion.

Not only is the agenda for debate pre-determined. The very language in which it is conducted can be decided for us. Words, Humpty Dumpty said, meant whatever he wanted them to mean. Their meaning is in the hands of the media and those who speak through the media. And once we lose control of our own words, we lose control of our own thoughts. George Orwell, in "1984" foresaw language as so controlled by the authorities that opposition became linguistically impossible. As an example, the American Declaration of Independence could be translated into the new language, Newspeak, in two ways: It could be condensed into one word — "crimethink" — or be given a full ideological translation, turning it into a panegyric for absolute government. Much of journalism involves reporting the words of those who are considered important. This gives "newsworthy" people a great deal of power to manipulate language for their own ends. The point was noticed by The Sunday Times when Italian politician Aldo Moro was kidnapped by an organisation called the Red Brigades. A leading article said:

> One of the sickening aspects of the Red Brigade crisis in Italy is the way the terrorists borrow the language of civilised institutions — and the way the media round the world regurgitate it. We are told the Red Brigade has issued a "communique" threatening the "execution" of Signor Moro, who is being held in a "people's jail" pending being "brought to justice" in a "trial". The reality is that a gang of murderers in a secret hideout has sent a message saying it is going to kill its victim. There cannot be a proper trial unless there is a recognised law and a procedure acknowledged to be fair by all reasonable men.
>
> Wrong or questionable acts are often obfuscated by words — the bombing raids in Vietnam that were referred to as "pacification missions" is a classic example . . . Newspapers and television should report what the Red Brigades say and the words they use, but they should handle them as a biologist handles toxic matter.
>
> To endorse them by transmitting them neutrally as if the words represented something valid is itself an act of corruption[8].

While a reluctant Britain was being dragged into the Common Market, the unattractively-named Common Market was suddenly renamed. Supporters of entry constantly referred to it as "Europe" or "the Community" and were themselves described in the Press as "passionate Europeans". Giving the Common Market a more acceptable name was the sort of trick any smart public relations firm would recommend. It also confused the geographical Europe to which Britain has always belonged with the political "Europe" which it had only recently joined. (In this case, the change to a more appealing name was not entirely successful because the popular Press continued using "market", which was already well understood by readers.)

Another technique used by politicians — and one with a distinctly Orwellian character — is to take ordinary, well understood words and give them a technical meaning that is somewhat different. One was the concept of "fair" rents. Under the Heath Government's Housing Finance Act, for example, rents were to rise to a "fair" level — fairer, that was, to landlords. Another was "peaceful" picketing. The Heath Government's view of "peaceful" picketing was extremely narrow. This meant that picketing which might be peaceful in the ordinary sense was not necessarily peaceful in the legal sense. Trade unionists soon realised that "peaceful" picketing meant ineffective picketing. The effect of changing the meaning of these words was to make opposition linguistically difficult. What reasonable, sensible person would object either to a fair rent or to peaceful pickets?

One of the most noticeable things about newspaper language is the scarcity of adjectives. You cannot get very far with adjectives before someone challenges their appropriateness. Everyone may agree that the Queen's dress is pink — or perhaps rose-coloured — but you only have to say it has been a good summer and someone questions it. Novelists, of course, can use adjectives as much as they like because they are writing fiction. It may be that one of the unconscious ways that readers distinguish "fact" from "fiction" is by the free or unrestricted use of adjectives. More consciously, readers may suspect adjectives of being used to influence them. Nouns, on the other hand, are much more acceptable. People believe that a noun states what something *is*, not what the writer thinks it is. And a popular newspaper technique is to turn words which were originally adjectives (eg moderate) into nouns (a moderate).

Being in a position to decide what to call someone or something is by no means unimportant. Orwell's state had ministries of peace, plenty, truth and love, each dealing in the opposition of what its name implied. (The dreaded Ministry of Love was the thought police.) Most modern British Government ministries are named according to the same principle. The War Office has been re-organised into the Ministry of Defence, implying we would never start a fight. The Departments of Health and Employment deal with sickness and unemployment, while their names suggest they are doing something positive. Numerous companies have given themselves names which have an obvious meaning — Supasave, Gainmore, etc — so that no-one can talk about them without paying them a compliment. Others pay to have sports tournaments named after them (eg the Gillette Cup and the John Player League in cricket) to get a mention on the sports pages and also on the BBC where trade names are normally banned. Political groups also choose their own names, and this causes the papers problems when a name implies something the papers do not want to imply. The Times, for example, refers to Ulster Loyalists with inverted commas, presumably to avoid suggesting it regards them as loyal.

On the other hand, newspapers sometimes choose their own names to describe people. "Activist" has the innocent meaning of someone who believes in action. By repeatedly using it in a certain context, newspapers have made it mean someone who stirs up trouble. Approved troublemakers in Communist countries used to be called "intellectuals". That has now gone out of fashion, perhaps because "left-wing intellectuals" in the West were confusing readers. They are now known as "dissidents" and newspapers have to be careful not to use the word to describe troublemakers on this side of the Iron Curtain. Words can be given added force by frequent association with other words. Most people will, at some time, have heard the phrase "mindless militants". It is used by columnists and politicians in a general way, not referring to identifiable individuals, and so avoiding the risk of a libel action. If the two words are associated often enough, when papers refer to "Joe Smith, a militant", readers will associate him with mindlessness, but the courts will not.

Much of the same effects can be achieved by judicious selection of photographs. Photographs are the visual equivalent of nouns: We trust them because the camera does not lie. But what the camera reveals is a moment of truth, nothing more. We cannot see what happened before the split-second when the picture was taken, nor what happened afterwards. Context is all-important. A newspaper picture freezes an action or expression and gives it permanence. We may see Roy Jenkins, one of the darlings of the press, photographed with an amiable smile and think better of him as a result, not knowing that it was the sort of amiability bestowed by a four-course lunch at the Savoy served with the finest claret. There are times — so they say — when Tony Benn, the demon of the left, also looks amiable. But try finding the pictures to prove it. More often, he is shown at an instant during a speech, looking wild, dangerous and slightly batty: mouth open, arms flailing, eyes flashing with the light of the photographer's own flashgun. Such pictures convey what a lot of papers would like to say in words, if only the law of libel would let them.

So far we have looked at ways the news media can influence people's attitudes and beliefs. But more important than beliefs is behaviour. Mr W R Pitt, Vice-Chancellor of Reading University expressed a typical view from the top in 1970 when he complained:

> There are certain people, both inside and outside the university, who hold views positively destructive of national institutions. They are tolerated because a university should be a place where people can read, write and think freely. We must draw the line, however, when these people think their ideas should be put into action.

In the West generally, there is more concern with what people do than with what they think. And if we return to the odd events in Mattoon, we can see that the largest number of people affected were not those who believed they had been gassed, but those whose behaviour was influenced. What is more, behaviour can sometimes be influenced without belief being affected. Much of the behaviour at Mattoon was sensible or reasonable: Some checked for prowlers or made sure their windows were locked — just in case. And the police, believing or not, had to react to the reports and beliefs of others and to restrain the vigilantes. In Seattle, no doubt, there were sceptics who checked their car windscreens out of curiosity.

The effects of the news media in Mattoon and in Seattle were produced accidentally. And they were undesirable, causing disruption and inconvenience, particularly to the authorities. But the media can also have the opposite effect, helping the authorities and powerful interest groups to maintain control and govern smoothly. And that is when news becomes propaganda.

Journalists by and large recognise that they are under pressure from various quarters to present the news in ways they may disagree with — to make propaganda on behalf of others. Alternatively, they may be tempted to slant the news in ways they do agree with — to make their own propaganda. Their response is to employ certain safeguards —

ethical and professional principles — in their work. Of these, the most important principle is objectivity.

A dictionary definition of objectivity is "Concern with outward things, not thoughts and feelings". Journalists attempt to exclude their own thoughts and feelings from news reports so they can say to readers: "Look! I haven't been bribed, intimidated, cajoled or influenced by anybody". Thus, to journalists, objectivity has come to mean impartiality, neutrality, lack of bias. In a more particular sense, objectivity describes a method of working and presenting information that is designed to ensure impartiality, neutrality, etc. There are, as we shall see, some serious practical difficulties in achieving this. Many journalists accept there are problems but usually fall back on a second line of defence, arguing that objectivity is an ideal to be aimed at, and calling for higher professional standards, better training and so on.

Despite the problems, objectivity is regarded — almost universally by western journalists — as a fundamental of good journalism. Its desirability is hardly ever questioned. And yet a closer look at the origins of objectivity shows it is not the purely ethical principle it is widely believed to be. The separation of fact and comment which is the basis of objective journalism developed to meet a specific need of the Press in its transition from the small, radical, non-commercial journals of the 17th, 18th and early 19th centuries to the large, pro-establishment, commercial newspapers of today. What is more, the practice of objectivity provides no safeguard against a supply of news that is — as we shall see later — largely shaped by forces outside journalists' control. Indeed, as long as journalists believe that by giving that supply an objective presentation they ensure impartiality, objectivity can be positively dangerous.

Until the present century it was very difficult to argue that the main function of the Press was anything but propaganda. Very quickly after the arrival of printing in Britain, the subversive possibilities of journalism were recognised and a flourishing radical Press developed, at first in the form of pamphlets rather than newspapers. Governments recognised the threat, too. Between 1500 and 1700 there were numerous attempts to restrict the number of printers, without success. Between 1700 and 1820 they tried instead to control what was printed. Journalists were imprisoned or — where more appropriate — bribed. Walpole, for example, spent £50,000 on bribing newspapers. One paper set up as a counterweight to the radical Press was The Times, which received a Government "subsidy" of £300 a year. Advertisements were taxed and a stamp duty was imposed on every page. The declared purpose was not to raise money but to "suppress libels". By 1815 stamp duty had reached 4d — quite a hefty sum. A red seal on the page showed that duty had been paid. Some publishers designed their own stamps to use instead. In 1831 the Poor Man's Guardian carried a drawing of a printing press and the slogan "Knowledge is Power". Beneath it were the words: "published in defiance of the Law, to try the power of Might with Right". Its statement of aims simply quoted a list from the Act of Parliament saying what was forbidden:

> News, intelligence, occurrences and remarks and observations thereon tending to excite hatred and contempt of the government and constitution . . . and also to vilify the abuses of religion.

Stamp duty actually had the opposite effect to what was intended. Radical papers continued to be sold — but more cheaply than the law-abiding ones. The radical papers were by far the more important. Early in 1836 the combined circulation of the leading six unstamped journals was about 200,000 — compared with just over 7,000 for The Times and less than 6,000 for the Morning Chronicle. And there were other (legal) radical papers like the Weekly Dispatch, which combined reports on the wicked deeds of the nobility with attacks on the Government. (In 1836 it was selling 30,000.) It was illegal to sell unstamped papers — but there were ways around that. One shop in London in the early 19th century had what was probably the first slot machine in history. Customers turned a pointer on a dial to the name of the paper they wanted and put their money in a slot. Then someone hiding behind a partition sent the paper down a chute. This meant that informers could not identify the sellers and have them prosecuted. Most of the prosecutions up to this stage had been done privately, by societies set up for the purpose. But the cost was enormous. One society, the "Constitutional", spent £30,000 on prosecutions and went bust in 1823. And soon after, what was known as the Vice Society (Society for the Suppression of Vice, Blasphemy and Profaneness) also ran out of cash. The Government then stepped in briefly, but eventually gave up.

Pressure to abolish stamp duty grew. It came not only from thew radical press but also from the "responsible" papers who realised that once it had gone they would be able to compete on more than equal terms. The more perceptive politicians also saw the value in abolition. In 1834 Lord Brougham, the Lord Chancellor, argued that it was no longer a question of whether people should be allowed to read or not, but what they should read. He said: "The only question to answer . . . is how they shall read in the best manner; how they shall be instructed politically and have political habits formed the most safe for the constitution of the country." In 1836 stamp duty was reduced to 1d and in 1855 it was abolished.

The 1830s also brought the steepest rise in production costs since newspapers began. Access to newspaper ownership became more restricted as the amount of capital and size of organisation needed to run a competitive newspaper grew. To meet higher costs, larger circulations became necessary and distribution became more formalised. Papers began to be sold in shops rather than only in the streets.

In the 1840s Samuel Morse was developing the telegraph, which was to have an important effect on the content of newspapers. It was this invention that began the separation of fact from comment that is so familiar today. Telegrams were expensive; they had to be kept as short as possible and confined to the bare essentials — the facts. The managing editor of The Times, Mobberley Bell, told correspondents: "Telegrams are for facts. Background and comment must come by post"[9]. Previously, accounts and interpretations of events had arrived simultaneously. But from then on there were likely to be delays between reporting news and commenting on it.

Improved communications brought an enormous increase in the volume of news. If newspapers used their own staff alone to provide it, the cost would be too great. Economies were possible, however, if correspondents supplied more than one newspaper. This was how the news agencies began. But agency reporters could not work in the old way, mixing facts with comment. That was fine for reporters who wrote for their own newspaper and knew its policies. Agency news had to be acceptable to any newspaper. The agency provided the hard facts and the newspaper used them in whatever way it liked. In practice agency news was not quite acceptable to *any* newspaper; it often had a strong national bias. American newspapers, for example, found Havas and Reuters provided material they did not want[10]. But certainly within individual countries, and between countries with political ties, the agencies did become a universal source of news.

Newspapers were still seen as organs of propaganda. But an important change had taken place: The concept of "pure" news had arrived. Where once propaganda had been the raw material of newspapers, the raw material was now facts — The News. Propaganda was something newspapers imposed on the news by their selection, interpretation and comment. But from there it was only a small step to say: Let the readers impose their own propaganda on the news; let newspapers provide the facts and let readers draw their own conclusions. This was the idea expounded in grandiose form by C P Scott, the revered Manchester Guardian editor in 1926:

> The newspaper is of necessity something of a monopoly, and its first duty is to shun the temptations of monopoly. Its primary office is the gathering of news. At the peril of its soul it must see that the supply is not tainted. Neither in what it gives, nor what it does not give, nor in the mode of presentation, must the unclouded face of truth suffer wrong. Comment is free but facts are sacred[11].

Scott's doctrine did not preclude a newspaper from holding opinions and making them known, as long as it did so in the right place. But a year later, in 1927, the BBC's charter went a step further and forbade the BBC to express any opinions of its own. The charter freed the BBC from direct Government control (though it is still controlled indirectly because Parliament votes on its licence fees). In return for this "freedom", the BBC had to be balanced, unbiased, impartial and neutral.

Arguments that "pure" news cannot be propaganda are, however, untenable. Propaganda is most effective when it is unrecognised, and when people come across a factual, informative statement they are off guard and believe it cannot be propaganda. And if they can be made to think that the views they hold are their own, arrived at without outside interference, so much the better. Propaganda is no longer a simple matter of praising oneself or hurling abuse at opponents. Separation of fact from comment, or the exclusion of explicit comment altogether, is entirely compatible with modern forms of propaganda.

This sort of propaganda can be hard to distinguish from pure information. The difference was perhaps best summed up by the Nazi propagandist, Goebbels, when he said: "We do not talk to say something, but to obtain a certain effect". The need for factual — and truthful — propaganda has become widely recognised in the last forty or fifty years. In the United States accuracy is the Number One rule (except for unbelievable or harmful truths). One American propaganda manual says:

> When there is no compelling reason to suppress a fact, tell it . . . Aside from considerations of military security, the only reason to suppress a piece of news is if it is unbelievable . . . When the listener catches you in a lie, your power diminishes . . . For this reason never tell a lie which can be discovered[12].

On the Communist side, Lenin recognised the need for propaganda to be factually accurate. Writing on "The Character of Our Newspapers", he called for

> the gathering, *careful checking* and study of the facts of the actual organisation of the new life. Have *real* successes been achieved by the big factories, agricultural communes, the Poor Peasants' Committees, the local Economic Councils in building up the new economy? . . . Have they been verified? . . . Where is the blacklist with the names of lagging factories which since nationalisation have remained models of disorder, disintegration, dirt, hooliganism and parasitism? Nowhere to be found. But there *are* such factories[13].

French propagandists have discovered that it is better to announce bad news yourself than to wait for it to be revealed by enemies. Goebbels — despite being nicknamed The Big Liar by the allies — usually insisted on accuracy. American and neutral opinion between 1939 and 1942 was that German communiques were on the whole more truthful than the Allied ones[14]. Also, the Germans liked to get in first, publishing the news two or three days before the Allies. Goebbels did approve of lying where there was no danger of contradiction. For example, only the captain of a U-boat knew whether he had sunk a ship or not. This meant the Germans could safely go into great detail about fictitious U-boat successes. Goebbels also understood the danger of telling the truth when it is too improbable for people to believe. A good example was in 1942 when Montgomery had a decisive victory in North Africa and thought he had beaten Rommel. In fact Rommel was in Germany because the attack was not expected. Goebbels gave orders to keep this secret — because no-one would believe it was not Rommel who had been defeated . . . they would think the Germans were making excuses.

It should be clear from these examples that the emphasis on truthful propaganda is not for moral reasons — it simply pays to tell the truth. To be caught in a lie casts doubt on everything else you say. Silence also has its dangers; keep quite about the bad news and you lose people's confidence if an opponent reveals it. Be first with the bad news and you gain people's confidence.

Belief in "pure" news rests on the premise that fact and comment can actually be separated. At a very basic level this is not difficult to do. Anyone can describe a meal they have eaten without saying whether they thought it enjoyable or well-cooked. A comment is a way of conveying personal feelings about something. But feelings can also be conveyed indirectly, using only facts. A person who says the meal included fresh peaches and real cream will convey a much more favourable impression than someone who speaks of canned peaches and artificial cream. Of course the impression may be conveyed accidentally or deliberately.

Let us now take a very ordinary, uncomplicated occurrence to illustrate the problem facing would-be objective journalists. An egg lies broken on the floor. What happened? Witnesses give their accounts — all factual, but all different:

The egg broke.
Joe broke the egg.
The egg fell.
Joe dropped the egg.
Joe dropped the egg and broke it.
Joe dropped the egg and it broke.
The egg fell and broke.
The egg rolled from Joe's hand and broke.
The egg hit the floor and broke.
When the egg and the floor met, the floor broke the egg.

All the accounts are objective, in that they contain only facts, not openly-expressed opinions. And yet they are not pure description — they are all interpretations. In these interpretations, two processes are at work: Selection and organisation.

Selection: Facts are selected by time, relevance and the observation of witnesses. *Time:* The event is isolated in time from the continuous chain of events to which it belongs. The event is created by the accounts, which impose on it a beginning and an end. We are not told, for instance, how the egg came to be in Joe's hand because that is not considered part of the event — it is something that happened before the "event". Several accounts make no mention of Joe and begin the event with the egg already falling. *Relevance:* Some accounts include more information than others. Most do not mention the floor. None tell us what time of day it was, whether Joe had anything else in his hand, whether he slipped and lost his balance. The reason we are not told is probably because none of the observers thought it relevant. So we may assume Joe was not groping in the dark, that his hands were not full and he did not slip. *Observation:* Some information may have been excluded because witnesses did not notice. This is unlikely in the case of the broken egg, but it is a serious problem for journalists. Relevant information may be omitted because someone is withholding it or because no-one can be found to describe what happened.

Organisation: Witnesses must select and organise words to describe what they have seen in a way that seems to them satisfactory. Some versions of the broken egg differ only in nuances, others differ greatly. Some choose Joe as the subject of the sentence, others choose the egg. In some there are hints that Joe, either deliberately or through carelessness, was the cause of the egg's fall. Others imply it was the fault of the egg for rolling or being fragile.

Neither of these processes is truly objective: The observers must use their judgment and opinion in deciding what the "event" is, what is relevant, and in using language to describe it. Of course, if the observers were asked to discuss their different versions they might eventually agree on a single account of what they had seen. But that would still be an interpretation — an interpretation based on collective judgment and agreed opinion.

Objectivity insists on facts, not opinion. But facts are nothing more than observations that are — in the general opinion — accepted. So the problem for objective journalists is to determine which "facts" are acceptable as facts and which are not. Those which are not must either be rejected as "opinion" or supported by evidence (ie more acceptable "facts"). Gaye Tuchman, in an American study of newspaper objectivity, gives two examples of borderline facts:

> One evening the assistant managing editor asked for "more objective obituaries" after reading an obituary which described the deceased as a "master musician". He asked: "How do we know" the deceased was a "master musician" as opposed to a "two-bit musician" playing with the town band? He was told that, several paragraphs into the story, one learns that the deceased had played with John Philip Sousa [an American bandmaster and composer who died in 1932]. The additional "fact", the editor agreed, justified the term "master musician".

Of course that was not really a fact at all. Whether or not readers would be convinced that the man was really a master musician would depend on how highly they regarded Sousa. Tuchman continues:

> Similarly, a reporter criticised the news editors for "bad" non-objective editing, when a published story referred to "Communist propaganda" seen at a specific location. He claimed the article should have included more

"facts", such as titles of specific observed works. While recognising that the label "Communist propaganda" might not be an accurate characterisation of each individual piece of literature, he insisted that such a presentation would be more "objective". It would offer "facts" (titles) supporting the initial truth-claim. Furthermore, the titles would presumably enable the reader to assess the degree to which the description "Communist propaganda" was accurate and thus "factual".

If the disputed article had listed Das Kapital as a publication seen at the scene of the story, the term "Communist" would supposedly have been justified. Das Kapital is commonly associated with communism and is not generally viewed as a text concerning the theory of economics[15].

Unproven or unprovable statements can very easily be made into "facts" by attributing them to someone. Thus a journalist would not normally write: "Unemployment will fall next year" because it is unlikely he can prove it. But if he writes: "The Prime Minister said unemployment would fall next year", that is a fact. The fact is that the Prime Minister said this. Of course there is a danger here; the reporter may be accused of bias by accepting that what the Prime Minister said was true. So he may balance the statement with another from the opposition party saying the Prime Minister is talking rubbish. The reporter may have a strong suspicion that one side or the other is lying, but objectivity prevents him evaluating the statements. The result is that readers are perplexed by two equally weighted but opposite views.

The BBC has long prided itself on its balance. But even this sort of objectivity starts from certain assumptions. It has to be interpreted in the eyes of right-thinking citizens. And what right-thinking citizens see as fair treatment for Members of Parliament is very different from the "fair" treatment meted out to those who threaten the fabric of society. As Lord Reith, the father of the BBC, noted in his diary in 1926: "They know they can trust us not to be really impartial". These double standards were accepted by a majority of the public until quite recently. According to the BBC's own surveys, in 1962, 62 per cent thought BBC television "always impartial". A repeat survey in 1970 showed a sharp drop to 47 per cent. A few of the younger people questioned thought lack of coverage given to IRA and Vietcong points of view was a sign of bias. Even if the BBC could dismiss these people as extremists, it could not get away from the fact that more than half the population now thought the BBC was not always impartial[16]. In 1976 a research team at Glasgow University showed that BBC bias was not limited to the IRA and Vietcong but extended to quite ordinary British trade unionists[17].

From a philosophical standpoint, objectivity has been summarised like this:

Objectivity is what is commonly received as objectively valid, all the attitudes, presuppositions, unquestioned assumptions typical of any given society. Objectivity implies the acceptance of the dominant social, ethical and religious views of the society. Objectivity is, for all practical purposes,

the totality of what is taken to be the case, believed to be the case, af-
firmed to be the case. Objectivity is the totality of received opinion on what
is acceptable/not acceptable, desirable/not desirable, good/not good, etc.
Objectivity in any given society in fact gets defined as the political and social
status quo[18].

And from a journalistic standpoint it has been summarised like this:

[To journalists] a finite number of things "really happen", of which the most
special, interesting or important are to be selected. The typical conception
of the media's role, then, at least in western, formally uncensored societies,
is that the media stand as reporter-reflector indicators of an objective
reality "out there", consisting of knowably "important" events of the world.
Armed with time and money, an expert with a "nose for news" will be led to
occurrences which do, indeed, index that reality. Any departure from this
ideal tends to be treated as "bias" or some other pathological circum-
stance . . .

Because western conceptions of news rely on the assumption that there is a
reality-out-there-to-be-described, the product of any system which denies
this premise is termed "propaganda". Thus, in the western mind, the
distinction between news and propaganda lies in a premise seen to be em-
bodied in the assemblers' [journalists'] work: Those with purposes produce
propaganda; those whose only purpose is to reflect reality, produce
news[19].

In virtually any other profession, such a narrow attitude would at least be
questioned. In education, for example, few teachers see their task as
purely to impart knowledge, regardless of whether it equips children for
life after school. And few medical researchers study diseases with no
intention of discovering a cure. Journalism is surely the only profession
where a lack of purpose is so highly esteemed, where belief in it is so
deeply rooted and yet so patently absurd. Thus the function of
objectivity is to deny that news has a purpose: to transform the selection
and processing of news from an essentially subjective business into a
technical one; and to disguise a narrow, highly filtered and regulated
picture of the world as reality. How that picture of the world is obtained
we shall see in succeeding chapters.

NOTES

1. A prowler case is one where someone reports seeing or hearing something
   suspicious but there is no evidence of damage or a break-in.
2. Donald M. Johnson: The "Phantom Anaesthetist" of Mattoon — a field
   study of mass hysteria. Journal of Abnormal and Social Psychology, Vol
   40, April 1945.
3. Nahum Z Medalia/Otto N Larsen: Diffusion and belief in a collective de-
   lusion. American Sociological Review, Vol 23, No. 2.
4. Disclosed by Moore during a television discussion of flying saucers.
5. The Times, 11 January, 1980.
6. Annual Review of BBC Audience Research Findings, 1973-74.

7. Paul Hartmann/Charles Husband: The mass media and racial conflict. Race, Vol 12, 1970-71. Reprinted in The Sociology of Mass Communications, Penguin, 1972.
8. The Sunday Times, 23 April, 1978.
9. Anthony Smith: The Politics of Information. Macmillan, 1978.
10. Anthony Smith: *op. cit.*
11. Manchester Guardian, 6 May, 1926.
12. Quoted in Jacques Ellul: Propaganda — the Formation of Men's Attitudes. Vintage/Wildwood House, 1973.
13. V I Lenin: Pravda, 20 September, 1918. Reprinted in Lenin: Where to Begin. Progress Publishers, Moscow, 1971.
14. Jacques Ellul: *op. cit.*
15. Gaye Tuchmann: Objectivity as strategic ritual. American Journal of Sociology, No. 77, 1972.
16. Glasgow University Media Research Group: Bad News. Routledge & Kegan Paul, 1976.
17. *ibid.*
18. Roger Poole: Towards Deep Subjectivity. Allen Lane, 1972.
19. Harvey Molotch/Marilyn Lester: News as purposive behaviour. American Sociological Review, Vol 39, February 1974.

2. News limited

THERE is no limit to what might be reported. The number of observable, describable events is infinite. Every event is a series of smaller events, which in turn consists of still smaller events. The wave of an arm is — to the eye — one movement, one event. To the cine camera it is a number of small jerks. To the scientist, the arm consists of cells, molecules, atoms, electrons, all contributing to that one movement. A scientist could spend years observing and describing the thousands of minute events involved in waving an arm. While few newspaper readers would want journalists to go to such lengths, we often fail to realise what a very, very limited selection of events is that it appears on our table at breakfast time. On some days, whole continents do not rate a mention. So what makes some events become news?

When asked what news is, journalists usually offer replies like "News is what you find in newspapers", "News is what fills the space left by the adverts", or "News is what somebody doesn't want you to know". It may seem surprising that journalists, usually so adept at compressing everything into a few short sentences, are at a loss to provide a simple, adequate definition of news. In fact there is a very good reason why they are unable to do so: News, by its nature, cannot be defined. It is futile to seek an infallible formula that will predict what events will become news because the circumstances governing the selection are never constant; what is news at nine o'clock may be nothing at ten. Therefore, in order to understand what news is, we must approach the problem from a different angle. We must examine the process by which events are transformed into news, and the forces that influence that process. The process can be considered in four parts:
1. Hearing about the event.
2. Assessing its 'newsworthiness'.
3. Preparing the story for publication, taking into account:
    (a) practicalities (eg time available, feasibility of checking information);
    (b) internal constraints (eg editorial policy);
    (c) external constraints (eg the law);
4. Printing and distributing the paper.
The first of these is the subject of this chapter. The remaining parts of the process are discussed in turn in the next three chapters.

To say that journalists must hear of an event before they can report it sounds obvious — which probably explains why this aspect of the Press is so often overlooked. Most studies of the Press employ, in one form or another, the "gatekeeper" theory. This was originally devised in 1943 to study food marketing[1] and was first applied to news around 1950[2]. Essentially it treats news as a crop which is harvested by reporters and then passes through a series of gatekeepers (editors, sub-editors, etc) who sift, select and refine it until a small quantity eventually reaches the consumers (readers). However, in transferring the concept from food to news, two important differences are ignored. Firstly, news — unlike farm produce — does not grow naturally; it has to be created. Events occur, but news does not occur unless it is reported. The gatekeeper theory starts with the "harvest" — piles of reports gathered into the office ready for selecting and editing — but in doing so it ignores the all-important first stage, the transition from events to reports of events. Secondly, news-gathering cannot be compared with harvesting. Harvesting is not selective; a farmer gathers his entire crop and the produce is sifted and graded later. That is possible because the crop is a finite quantity. News-gathering, on the other hand, must be selective because the number of events is infinite. Selection cannot be delayed — it begins with the events themselves, not with reports of events; it begins when journalists decide where to look for the events they will report, when they decide who they will talk to and who they will listen to.

Unfortunately the notion that news exists as an unrefined raw material pervades most articles and books on the Press — even those that do not explicitly adopt the gatekeeper theory. This inevitably focuses attention on what happens to news reports after they reach the newspaper office. It highlights the essentially destructive parts of news production, the work of sub-editors who cross out what they do not need or do not want and who can add little more than polish or a different slant. Meanwhile the earlier, creative part of the process remains in the shadows. The result is to emphasise differences in presentation in different newspapers and to make the differences seem significant. But more important and more significant than the differences are the similarities.

Newspaper offices are factories producing a product: News. All but a handful of newspapers are in business to make money (not all succeed but that at least is the intention). And the product is shaped less by events than by economic and market forces. Readers of the evening papers, for example, might get the impression that a lot happens on Thursdays and Fridays because that is when there is most news in the papers. But they would be wrong. The *amount* of news is governed not by events but by the amount of advertising. Thursdays and Fridays are the days when people have full pay packets and firms want to advertise, and the number of pages is increased to accommodate the ads. In a similar way economics influence the *type* of news and the sources that supply it.

The basic sources used by journalists can be seen most clearly at the offices of the local paper. A typical day's mail brings a variety of information: A Press release from a local firm which has appointed a new manager, another about a marathon walk for charity . . . the result of a darts tournament . . . a couple of parish magazines . . . the annual report of the Townswomen's Guild and a handful of wedding photographs. Some of this will be published in more or less the state in which it arrives. On an evening paper, press releases may be rewritten or followed up by a reporter if there is time; often on a weekly paper, they will go straight to the printer, perhaps shortened a little or with a few words changed. There will also be letters and notices about forthcoming events, with requests to send a reporter and photographer. If they sound interesting the details will be entered in the office diary for coverage later. The parish magazine and annual report will be given to a reporter to skim through for possible stories.

If there is too much material it takes a minimum of editorial judgment to decide what to use. Anything that needs a lot of work to get it into printable form will be the first to be rejected. Next, perhaps, news from organisations that have had more than their fair share of publicity in recent issues. Apart from that, whatever happens to be the right length to fill a hole in a page will be shovelled in. It's the easiest form of news there is: No trouble to get, little trouble when it arrives — and it costs next to nothing.

During the day there are phone calls from people suggesting stories; people with problems and grievances: "You should see the rubbish on that spare ground at the end of our street," or "The council says I'll have to wait 10 years for a house". There will probably be a few visitors, too. Perhaps someone looking for a long-lost relative or the local gossip popping in for a chat.

These, then, are the paper's casual sources. The paper does not seek them out; they make the first approach. Some may be in contact frequently, others only once in a lifetime. They are a mixed bunch, ranging from those who just want to see their name in print to those who hope to benefit in some way from publicity. As sources of news they are entirely self-appointed. They perform the first stage in the selection process themselves when they decide what to tell the Press. The decision is not entirely their own, however. People do not contact the Press unless they think there is at least a chance of their story being published. What they offer is not simply the news that they would like to see printed. It is also the news that — from their reading of newspapers — they expect the paper will want to print. This is one of the ways news becomes self-sustaining, one of the reasons why the sort of stories that were written years ago are still written today and will be written again in the future.

Casual sources can be useful but they are also erratic. The supply tends to dry up at holiday times and the sources cannot be relied on to provide anything approaching comprehensive coverage. If journalists did nothing more than wait for the news to come to them, the result would not be the steady, predictable flow of news that is required. The most effective way is to have regular sources that can be relied on, come what may. So reporters make regular calls to the police and fire brigade — at least once a day — to find out what has been happening. (If there is a big fire the brigade will probably phone the paper straight away so they can send a photographer.) Then there are the courts and council meetings — always something to report there. Together, these four regular sources fill many — if not most — of the columns of the average local paper. Take these examples which all appeared on the same night in the Liverpool Echo:

Chair Blaze: An armchair in a joiner's shop in Walton Lane, Anfield, Liverpool was damaged by fire . . .

Light Blaze: Liverpool firemen dealt with a small fire which damaged a flourescent light fitting in the Ear, Nose and Throat Hospital . . .

Bedding Fire: Liverpool firemen were called to a house in Garth Avenue, Allerton, today, when bedding caught fire. No-one was hurt.

Gorse Fire: Bebington firemen dealt with a blaze involving gorse and undergrowth at Eastham Ferry last night.

House Blaze: Fire damaged a first floor rear room of a house in Lumley Street, Grassendale, Liverpool . . .

Works Blaze: A compressor was damaged in a fire at the Monsanto Chemical Works at Acrefield, near Wrexham at the weekend.

Theatre Fire: Southport fireman tackled a blaze in a store room at the Little Theatre, Hoghton Street, Southport yesterday. Only slight damage was caused.

Oil Blaze at Shell Plant: Firemen from Cheshire County and the Shell fire service fought a fire in No. 2 Auxiliary Pumping Station at the Shell Mex Ellesmere Port plant last night . . .

Fires can, of course, provide stories of drama, tragedy, even heroism, but these were of no conceivable interest or importance to anybody. We have to presume that it was a "thin" night for news and that when all else failed the fire brigade came to the rescue. The fire brigade is an easy, dependable and economical source of news. And because it is such a useful source its activities have become incorporated into local papers' conception of news to the extent that even a small fire in an armchair or a light fitting can be considered newsworthy.

With the police it is much more of a two-way relationship. The paper needs the police and the police need the paper. The police know the sort of stories reporters like and do their best to provide them: toddlers saved from drowning by elder sisters, babies delivered by unmarried constables, armed robbers foiled by 70-year-old postmistresses. In return they expect the paper to make their task easier. Publicity can help them to identify bodies or track down wanted men. Occasionally there may be a tactful request to say more in a story than is journalistically necessary: "It would be particularly helpful if you could give a full description of the stolen property in this case". At other times a paper may be told that "publicity at this stage could hamper our inquiries".

This relationship sets the overall tone of local papers' police coverage: respectful, co-operative and admiring. In peaceful market towns where the police are less acquainted with the ways of The Sweeney or Starsky and Hutch there is probably no reason to take a different attitude. But in big cities, where allegations of brutality and corruption usually arise, it is a rare paper which steps out of line to report them. The general feeling is that such stories are best left to the national papers, or perhaps "alternative" papers: the local paper has to live with the local police force. On a weekly paper, probably all the reporters have almost daily dealings with the police; on an evening paper there may be a specialist crime reporter who spends hours in police stations. Business is conducted on a very personal level, whereas a national paper can send in a reporter to do a critical story, with no need to return to the area again. Like any source, the police, if offended, can make life very difficult for reporters who regularly seek information from them. And the police are not just *any* source — they are a vital source.

Court reports are another easy way to fill a local paper. The fact that outsiders find them extremely boring does not really matter: the interest for local readers is in checking the names and addresses to see if any neighbours have been up to no good. In small towns, where magistrates normally sit for perhaps two days a week, virtually every case will be reported. The cases are usually short and it is a very productive way for reporters to spend their time. In cities, however, many courts may be in session at the same time — say, six or seven magistrates' courts and similar numbers of Crown and County courts. All these may be "covered" by as few as two or three reporters who cover them selectively, relying on tips about "good" cases from police, solicitors, court officials, etc.

Whereas cases in the magistrates' courts normally last only a few minutes, trials by jury in the Crown courts can go on for days or even weeks — and that makes them a very expensive source of news. This problem is neatly solved, however, if papers pay for stories according to the number of words they print rather than according to the time spent on them by reporters. In at least one major city, court reports are normally bought from a small freelance agency and staff reporters only attend for especially newsworthy cases. Freelancing is notoriously precarious work and in order to succeed you have to be as much a businessman as a journalist. So freelances who do court reporting naturally organise their work in a businesslike fashion. There are several ways to cut corners. In the Crown courts, a reporter can "keep an eye" on several trials at once. Common practice is to ignore most of the evidence and report only opening statements by prosecution and defence, the judge's summing up and the verdict.

A freelance who spends a whole day on one story in the Crown court may find only 10 or a dozen paragraphs are published, while another could earn the same amount of money by spending a couple of hours in the magistrates' court and producing half a dozen simple, short reports: name, offence, punishment and perhaps a few pertinent words of reproach from the magistrate. Of course the national Press are more likely to be interested in Crown court cases, and they pay at a higher rate than local papers, but a freelance who sends them reports on spec is taking a chance. On the other hand, reports to local papers from the magistrates' courts can provide a steady income. And the one- or two-paragraph stories that magistrates' courts so readily produce are very popular with local papers: they are ideal for filling awkward spaces.

The constitutional role of the Press in the courts is an important one — the same as that of the public. Nowadays few members of the public attend, apart from relatives and friends of those involved in cases, so the Press must take their place. The purpose of holding trials in public is to let justice be seen to be done — and the Press has a duty to ensure that the public see it.

There are two senses in which justice can be seen to be done: one can see that a person who has committed a crime is suitably punished, and one can see whether the accused is fairly convicted or acquitted on the basis of the evidence. The first of these functions is more than amply performed: The Press not only reports the punishment but in doing so, adds to it. Indeed, the odium of seeing a case reported is probably much worse for the accused than a £50 fine. There are also times when papers seem less concerned with justice than with social control. Some papers deliberately give prominence to shoplifting offences just before Christmas — the period when shoplifters cause most problems for the stores. Others help to enforce the TV licence regulations by printing long lists of licence dodgers. Meanwhile that other function of the Press in the courts — as a watchdog — is almost wholly ignored. Any doubts or inconsistencies in particular cases, and any injustices, are ironed out along with the bulk of the evidence to meet the needs of efficient reporting.

It is in coverage of council affairs that local papers are usually at their worst. You have only to read the papers to learn that councillors are as public-spirited, well-informed, thoughtful, eloquent, dedicated and high-principled a body as you could ever hope to meet — but then a paper does have to be responsible. To reprint verbatim the speech of Councillor X, a former mayor who has served the borough for nigh on 50 years, would let the world know that the old boy has completely lost his marbles — and that would be cruel. To record the number of times the mayor has to be corrected on procedural matters by the clerk would imply that he is not fit for his office — and that would be disrespectful. To list the financial interests of all the members who get business from the council would suggest that they are out to feather their own nests — and that would be a slur. In short, to tell the truth, the whole truth and nothing but the truth about the council would be nothing less than to embark on a campaign to discredit the whole of local government — and that would be grossly irresponsible.

The reasons for the gross "responsibility" on the part of local papers are several. Many of them are family-owned and the proprietor, as a person of some standing in the community, probably knows most of the councillors socially. Some papers may fear reprisals if they offend the council, though such fears are largely unfounded since journalists have a legal right to attend council meetings. Individual councillors who run substantial businesses might be able to hit back, however, by withdrawing advertising. Then there is the fear of libel. Unlike national papers, most local papers do not have lawyers on hand to give advice. In addition, their financial resources are smaller and many of them would probably be closed by one major libel action.[3]

But above all, there is just no reason to cause trouble. For a start, local papers generally have no competitors in their own field, and there is no point in getting scoops if there is no opposition to be scooped. The reporting staff is usually small. Allowing one reporter to go digging for scandals can mean (to a weekly paper) having a sixth or even a quarter of the workforce engaged in unproductive work for weeks, with no certainty of a publishable story at the end of it. Also, the reporters on local papers tend to be young and inexperienced; the editor must never forget the possibility of them getting carried away with themselves.

There is no doubt that a good exposé can increase sales, but is it worth it? It takes time and money and can upset influential people. And there are other ways to put up sales. A picture of 40 faces on a pensioners' outing will sell 40 papers for sure — at a fraction of the cost and with none of the risk.

The local evening papers are, of course, much larger than the weeklies. They cover a bigger area, have more readers, more staff, and usually more money. Together with the handful of regional morning papers they serve as a halfway stage between the weeklies and the national dailies, carrying a mixture of local, national and international news. Their sources of local news are basically the same as those of weekly papers and, despite their greater resources, the greater pressure on space leads to more sketchy, more selective coverage. There are, for instance, several councils in any evening paper's circulation area, not just one, and covering them all means reporting them in less detail. Outside its own circulation area, a typical morning or evening paper has one or two reporters based in London and none elsewhere. Papers which belong to newspaper groups may have larger, shared facilities in London and from time to time they also exchange stories with other papers in the group. Most of the national news, however, comes over the teleprinter from the Press Association.

PA is the nearest thing Britain has got to George Orwell's Ministry of Truth. In the words of the New Statesman:[4]

Staple news is pumped out to every substantial newspaper in the country, *and* the BBC, and ITN, and Independent Radio News. Much of the "diversity" of the British media consists of re-packaging this ubiquitous material, with application of suitable glosses for up-market, down-market and across — though not very far across — the political spectrum. And even the re-packing operation is likely to be no more than vestigial.

PA is owned by the regional newspapers, though anyone can subscribe to its service. The general news service gets about 63 per cent of its income from regional papers and most of the rest from radio and television news and the national papers. It is also very cheap. A provincial daily selling 15,000 copies can get the full general news service, plus Reuter's international service, for under £25,000 a year — no more than the cost of employing two fulltime reporters (allowing for overheads like phone calls and travelling expenses).

But at a price like that there is no room for probing or sceptical stories. Essentially it is journalism of the lowest common denominator: the stories most likely to be used by the largest number of papers. PA has an estimated 150 active reporters, aided by freelances around the country, churning out 200,000 words a day. And as any reporter knows, sustaining an average output of 1,300 words per person per day takes some doing. The emphasis is on a fast, basic service of straightforward stories — which naturally leads to a heavy reliance on easily available material: sources like company press handouts and officially approved accounts of events. It also means that certain stories — often many of the stories — in all the papers and on radio and television are the work of the same reporter. To quote the New Statesman again:

There is something curious about the idea that a single organisation can produce "news" which is more accurate than the product of a number of independent organisations. Implicit here is the idea of news as an objective commodity, centrally generated and dispensed (if there is only one version, it must inevitably be the most "accurate").

It is easy to dismiss local papers as unimportant, but they *are* important. There are major areas of local affairs which they alone can cover; stories which concern their readers and no other paper's readers. Local papers are also important for another reason: They are a crucial link in the news-gathering chain and a basic source for news for the national papers and television. Thus the deficiencies in local paper's coverage tend to be perpetuated (rather than compensated for) in other sections of the news media.

The nationals use local papers as a source in two ways: By reading the papers and following up stories which seem particularly significant or likely to interest their readers, and by direct contact with the reporters. Any local reporter with an eye on a future job in Fleet Street is eager to become known to national news editors and occasionally offer stories. On some local papers the staff provide national papers with stories more systematically through a linage pool (linage is payment according to the number of lines of type printed). The money earned is then divided among them to supplement their income.

The national papers do have regional offices and a few locally-based reporters but their resources are spread thinly. These reporters have large areas to cover so they leave a lot of the routine groundwork to local papers and freelances. Much of their time is spent getting regional angles on national stories and finding news that is especially suited to their own paper's market, whether sexy stories for the Sun and Daily Star or reds-under-the-bed stories for the Express and Mail.

To a great extent the national papers depend on the same regular sources as local papers, though they often use them rather differently. For instance, the court stories in popular dailies usually either involve celebrities (eg a racing car driver charged with a motoring offence) or have a spicy flavour ("interesting" rapes and murders, schoolteachers having sexual relations with pupils, etc). Court stories are particularly useful in this latter respect because they are "privileged" — anything said in open court can be reported with complete safety. The evidence can be quoted in all its lurid detail; there is no risk of libel and no need to substantiate the allegations before printing them. Apart from these, national papers have some additional regular sources: Parliament, for example. There are also regular checks on the engagements of the Royal Family and a specialist agency in London airport keeps permanent watch for VIPs entering and leaving the country. Although journalists make a point of not naming confidential sources, it is actually quite easy, from a careful reading of any newspaper story to make a good guess at the *type* of source which is most likely to have been the reporter's starting point. The range of possibilities is in fact fairly small:

1. Sources monitored routinely
   a. Parliament
   b. Councils
   c. Police (and the army in northern Ireland)
   d. Other emergency services
   e. Courts (including inquests and tribunals)
   f. Royalty
   g. "Diary" events (eg annual events like Ascot or conferences known about in advance)

    h. Airports
    i. Other news media

2. Organisations issuing statements and holding Press conferences

    a. Government departments
    b. Local authority departments
    c. Public services (transport authorities, electricity boards, etc)
    d. Companies
    e. Trade unions
    f. Non-commercial organisations (pressure groups, charities, etc)
    g. Political parties
    h. Army, Navy, Air Force.

3. Individuals making statements, seeking publicity, etc.

    a. Prominent people (eg bishops and film stars)
    b. Members of the public.

There are enough clues in any daily paper to fit almost all the stories into the first 18 of these 19 categories. Of those that are left, some will have come from members of the public. (There are also stories which might be described as creative journalism, such as the stunts arranged by some popular papers purely to get a picture).

    What an examination of published stories and their sources reveals is that news — certainly the serious news — is mainly a one-way traffic: "Them" telling "us" what they want us to know. Any senior politician, company, trade union leader, "personality", or even a bishop can get their message over to the masses simply by issuing a statement, giving an interview or holding a Press conference. The Press, being "objective", faithfully reproduces the message, even if it is a pack of lies, or just plain daft. What matters is that we pay attention to the right people. There are occasions, however, when these people are so plainly out of touch that papers have to edit their words to make them seem more sensible. Keith Waterhouse, in his Daily Mirror column, noted one example:[5]

> Judges who sound off about the need to put young thugs in glasshouses, or chop off their ears or whatever, are as much a feature of old England as church bells or thick-cut marmalade. So I will say nothing that might discourage Lord Justice Lawton from making foolish speeches about law'n'order. But one little comment of his Lordship's did intrigue me slightly. Paying tribute to his own experience of life, the good judge went on to recommend that youngsters in his short, sharp shock camps should be deprived of television on Saturday afternoons so that they would not be able to look at Sacha Distel . . .
> How, out of all the names that could be grabbed from thin air, did he happen to fix on Sacha Distel? . . . Tory papers which carried reports of Lord Justice

Lawton's ramblings by the yard omitted this baffling reference. Probably because they sensed that for most young hooligans, an afternoon with Sacha Distel would be a more nightmarish experience than an afternoon without him.

Over the years the regular suppliers of news have learned how to use the Press for their own benefit. The Government, big firms and other large organisations employ people specially to deal with the media. Press officers are often former journalists or people with experience in advertising or publicity. Their job is both defensive and offensive: (a) to protect the public reputation of their employers and (b) to promote the interests of their employers.

An example will show the sort of effect this has: At the beginning of 1976 the British army had over 40 Press officers in northern Ireland, with 100 back-up staff. The Royal Ulster Constabulary had twelve full-time Press officers. And the Government had another 20 civil servants there briefed to deal with the media.

This makes it very easy for journalists to get the official version of events in northern Ireland. The result has been described by Guardian reporter Simon Hoggart:[6]

Most journalists working in northern Ireland are almost completely dependent on this (the army's) information service (and the smaller one run by the police), simply because there is no other source for news of day-to-day violence. This means that the army has the immense advantage of getting in the first word, and it is left to the integrity of the journalist to check that Word One. Some do, some don't. Most only check when there is time or the incident looks like becoming controversial and a few hardly bother at all. When the British Press prints an account of an incident as if it were an established fact, and it is clear that the reporter himself was not on the spot, it is a 99 per cent certainty that it is the army's version that is being given.

And how do the army arrive at their version of events? Hoggart continues:

Information about incidents has to be passed on to the Press as soon as possible — often within 20 minutes of its happening. This means that the first account is always the unchecked word of the soldier on the spot. He may be mistaken, or he may be lying in order to avoid a possible charge (army discipline is so draconian — up to a year for a soldier who loses a rifle, for example — that men must inevitably present their side of the case as forcefully as possible) . . .

Once the army version has been established, virtually every officer believes it implicitly. If a man is shot for carrying a gun, and locals say he was not, the army has no doubts at all. I believe that the army has been mistaken on several occasions, and its genuine belief that it is right must look exactly like deliberate lying to people who were on the spot.

HOW THE PRESS SEE THEMSELVES: Above — The Daily Mirror . . . a sugary pill for the masses. Below — The Times . . . serious information for those in power.

Hoggart quotes an army Press officer as saying: "Our job is to tell the truth at all times and to correct deliberate misinformation put out by the other side. Occasionally we make mistakes, but we always correct them wherever possible. I have no objection to newspapers printing what the other side says, but I do get angry when they suggest that they are right." Some army officers go even further and object to reporters using phrases like "the army states" and "troops claim" as these imply they might be mistaken.

The trouble is that when an incorrect version is given it takes time to be corrected and gets little publicity because by then the story is cold. Simon Winchester, also a Guardian journalist at the time, describes such as incident:

> The gunfire that began around 8.30 p.m. went on and on, and it invited the inevitable reply by the army. To anyone who experienced the battle it was perfectly obvious that hundreds and hundreds of bullets were being fired by both sides — and yet the army had the gall, when asked by reporters later in the weekend, to say that its soldiers had fired only 15 shots in sum. The official figures were to be published later: Soldiers in the Falls that weekend fired no less than 1,457 rounds . . .
> Ever since those later figures were quietly published, many reporters found it terribly hard to accept contemporary accounts from the army public relations men. Never, since then, have I found myself able to take the army's explanations about any single incident with any less a pinch of salt than I would take any other explanation.

Anyone who persistently takes that pinch of salt has everything to lose and nothing to gain. A journalist in northern Ireland has to stay on speaking terms with the army or risk missing important stories. And because army statements have the backing of the state, it's safe to take them as gospel whether they're true or not.

To taine uncooperative reporters, the army uses carrot-and-stick techniques. One method is an approach to the reporter's employers. This happened to Times correspondent Robert Fisk. He refused to accept the army's interpretation of a confidential document he had got hold of. Peter Broderick, the civilian head of army public relations sent a message to the Times describing Fisk as a "hostile reporter". Once, the Guardian printed three anti-army pieces by Winchester and Hoggart within a week. They appeared close together by accident, but the army took this as a sign of deliberate aggression . . .

> For about a fortnight we were given 'minimal co-operation' by Lisburn — curt, unwilling accounts of violence, and no background or extra information at all. It was an inconvenience, but no more, since we got the information from helpful colleagues, and it ended after a fortnight, following discussions at the Ministry of Defence.

A few months later, the army tried the "buttering-up" technique. Hoggart had suggested the army had been unnecessarily brutal in putting down a Protestant riot . . .

> I was invited to Lisburn for lunch and drinks, and shown papers which suggested that the soldiers might, to some extent, have been justified, I am sure the lunch and drinks had nothing to do with it, but, if I am completely honest, I think the approach might have made me a little more cautious, when writing about the army. This may or may not be a good thing, but I am quite certain that the opposite would have happened after another spell of "minimal co-operation".

In another report, Hoggart told how the army had blackmailed an innocent young man into spying on his neighbours. Even Lord Carrington admitted the story was true, and Hoggart expected some hostility.

> In the event, a week later, I was given an excellent exclusive story by an army major, which also turned out to be true. This is the smartest approach of all, for in spite of journalists' reputations, any reporter would prefer a good story to a free drink. Drinks with information, after all, come on expenses.

Probably few reporters would admit to having been strongly influenced by this sort of treatment. Nevertheless, the results can be seen in the Press. "On balance," Hoggart concludes, "the public relations operation remains a considerable success. Hardly a word is breathed against the army in the popular papers or on radio and television in Britain. If criticism is made, it is invariably in the mouths of others, and always hedged with a full account of the army's position — however sceptical the reporter himself might be."

Very occasionally much more sinister examples of news management come to light. (When they do, it is usually because they have misfired. The successful ones, by their very nature, do not become public). In 1979, Dr Robert Irwin, a highly respectable police surgeon in Northern Ireland appeared on television and complained that suspects under interrogation at Castlereagh barracks were frequently beaten. Over the next few days the RUC's Press officers hinted that Dr Irwin's action had been inspired by some grudge. Finally one of the Press officers — a Chief Inspector spelled out what they meant: The doctor's wife had been raped and he was angry with the RUC for not tracing the suspect. The smear was then repeated by other Press officers and ordinary police officers, and the so-called Community Relations Unit provided graphic details.

When Dr Irwin was asked about this he said that his wife had indeed been raped — shortly *after* he made his first (private) protest about brutality to the authorities. Far from feeling bitter against the police, he said they had acted promptly and had in fact traced the rapist (who turned out to be in the Army). Reporters in Belfast discussed the story and agreed not to publish the allegation or Irwin's denial. Private Eye observed:[7]

> They concluded that the way the story had been leaked . . . in a manner which was clearly concerted with other efforts throughout the police force and government, proved beyond doubt that the smear had been authorised from above.

The silence was eventually broken by the Daily Telegraph, despite the well-established rule that rape victims are not identified. Private Eye continued:

> The effect of the story was, first, to circulate the smear. But the intention of the smear in the first place was to sow suspicions in the minds of journalists, rather than to have it published. Publication of it boomeranged on the authorities. So vile was the suggestion that Dr Irwin had made his allegations because his wife had been raped that public sympathy suddenly swung round to his side.

Journalists who are regularly critical of the police can land in serious trouble. Whereas the army has to rely on its ingenuity, the police can actually put the boot in, for they have powers of arrest. In the last resort, unpopular journalists can be — and sometimes are — arrested, either on charges connected with their work or on unrelated charges.

In 1975, freelance crime reporter Thomas Bryant faced 47 charges, including dishonestly handling the Police Gazette and confidential police information and photographs and inciting an officer to commit a breach of discipline. The charges were eventually dismissed. Bryant believed he was hounded because he had "never been afraid to write stories which have often upset the police".[8]

In 1974, during an investigation into arms trafficking, Sunday People reporter Trevor Aspinall was arrested and charged with conspiring to obtain firearms and inciting others to sell them without a certificate. The conspiracy charge was later dropped and he was acquitted of incitement. The People, of course, has a reputation for exposing police deviance.

The same year, David May of Time Out bought a French residence permit belonging to a kidnapped Spanish banker and photographs of the banker in captivity. When May refused to identify his contact to the police he was charged with dishonestly handling the permit — and later acquitted. The photographs were sold to the Sunday Mirror through John Rodgers, the proprietor of a Fleet Street news agency. Rodgers was cautioned twice over possession of photographs which the police claimed were stolen from police files. Rodgers described the result:

They effectively put you out of business, at least for a while. Your contacts are afraid to talk to you in case the police are watching and you think twice before handling a story which might land you in a lengthy legal battle.

IN THE FACE of such highly organised news sources, it is small wonder that ordinary, *unorganised* people hardly get a look in. The reason is that ordinary people are difficult, expensive and inefficient sources.

Communications between the Press and organised bodies are deliberately made easy. The channels of communication work efficiently. Often a telephone call is all that is needed. Members of the public who have no telephone — and this includes particularly those with problems — start at a disadvantage; if their story is to be used, expensive, time-consuming journeys by reporters are necessary. Interviews with regular sources are also generally quicker and easier. Regular sources know what information the Press are likely to want and organise the facts beforehand. The reporter's work is already half-done. Casual callers to the Press often fail to "sell' a story by not presenting the facts in the readily usuable form that reporters are accustomed to. Sensing that the reporter is confused or bored, the caller may then try and compensate by exaggerating the facts. The reporter then becomes sceptical of the whole story and gets rid of the caller as politely and quickly as possible.

There is also a feeling that ordinary people are unreliable sources. This is due, not so much to any belief that individuals deliberately give false information, as to a realisation that if what they say is contradicted by more powerful voices there is nothing to fall back on. The Press are protected when dealing with organisations because representatives who speak to the Press are under the discipline of the body that employs or appoints them. Individuals are responsible to no-one. If something does go wrong, the Press can say, for example: "The information we were given was incorrect, due to a misunderstanding between two police officers." That sounds excusable and lets the Press off the hook. But to say: "Betty Smith of 45 Sycamore Grove got it wrong" begs the question: Why didn't they check the facts? Some newspapers take this even further and refuse to trust the observations of their own reporters. Staff of the Liverpool Daily Post and Echo, for example, are urged not to estimate the numbers of people in demonstrations themselves, but to get a figure from a "reliable source" (ie the police).

What is said matters less than who says it. If tenants complain that the council is neglecting their flats the Press will tread warily. If the story is used at all it will be carefully balanced with a full rebuttal from the council. An aggrieved council is articulate and influential enough to hit back where it hurts. On the other hand, if the council accuses tenants and their children of wrecking their flats and keeping them in a filthy state, anonymous, unorganised tenants probably won't be asked for a comment. They may grumble or even phone the paper to complain. But before long they'll get tired. They'll even carry on buying the paper, if only for the racing results and job adverts. It's a question of which side knows how to shout loudest. We have already seen how, in northern Ireland, it pays to go along with the army's version of events. Even if that version is wildly wrong, it's still safe to print. The army is backed by the Government and you can't play safer than that.

Bureaucracies — Government departments, councils, law enforcement agencies — interpret problems in bureaucratic terms. Problems are shaped to fit the organisations. Those that won't fit are either forgotten about or shuffled off somewhere else. Paul Rock, in his essay, "News as eternal recurrence", sees newspaper offices as bureaucracies, too:[9]

> The business of any bureaucracy is the routine production of sequences of activity that are anticipated and guided by formal rules. Those rules can never be exhaustive. They explicitly and implicitly define the limits of variation in the material that can be processed by the bureaucracy. When an organisation does not exercise total control over that material, there is always the possibility that it will fall outside the defined limits of variation . . . An organisation can respond by attempting to force the obdurate materials into a workable form; it may modify some of its practices; it may destroy the materials; or it may simply refuse to handle them.

Stories about people's problems are especially difficult to fit into the mould. Often they are complex, containing situations without any single completed event to make them newsworthy. The only way to get these published is to arrange an event to suit the situation — like persuading an MP to ask a Parliamentary question.

When ordinary people do make the news it is often to provide light relief from "serious" figures like politicians. Take Joyce McKinney And The Manacled Mormon. Or the woman who collected her dogs' fur, spun it into wool and knitted a bikini. That story had almost everything — human interest, animal, a hint of sex . . . what a pity the dogs weren't the Royal corgis. Sometimes the "ordinary" people in the papers aren't quite as ordinary as they seem. Remember the craze for streaking (running about naked) that swept the country — or did it? Wasn't it too much of a coicidence that streakers only seemed to appear when newsmen were around? Like the lucky photographer who just happened to be standing on Westminster Bridge, facing Big Ben, with his camera focused at a few yards when a naked woman popped into his viewfinder. A freelance agency in Liverpool noticed British Rail's offer of reduced tickets to London for pairs of women travelling together. What a wheeze, they thought, if two men dressed up in drag to claim the cheap tickets? So they hired two male models to do just that.

When ordinary people appear in a more serious context the purpose is often social control. They are held up as examples to be followed or shunned. In a six-month study of welfare and social security stories in 1976, two researchers found that 30.8 per cent of all the stories dealt in some way or other with abuse of the system, and no fewer than 12.6 per cent of these dealt with legal proceedings.[10] Many newspapers, of course, have a deliberate policy of making an example of "scroungers". But the tendency to highlight prosecutions is also reinforced by the papers' use of courts as a major news source. There is no comparable, well-established channel by which journalists hear of claimants who are hounded by snooping officials or unjustly refused benefits.

Along with the stick comes the carrot: For encouragement, moments of triumph at pianoforte, elocution and flower arranging all rate a mention; while victories over landlords, employers, gas boards and bureaucrats go unrecorded. And there's always praise for a man who is happy in his work . . .

Joe Waring, the man who loves every minute of his job as a dustman with St Helens Council failed in London yesterday in his bid to be "Best Refuse Collector of the Year". The award went instead to last year's winner, Brian Hammond, of Southwick, Sussex, an employee of Adur District Council. He won £100 and a holiday in the sun for two.[11]

We have seen how influential people can say the craziest things, with rarely a hint from the Press that their words are anything but rational. But what happens when ordinary people try to make a point? This:

A woman disrupted a university graduation ceremony attended by the Queen Mother yesterday when she ran on to the platform shouting: "When will this mockery end?" Watched by 2,000 students from Dundee University, the woman, wife of a lecturer, shouted: "I plead with Your Majesty to let me speak."
Detectives ushered her from the hall and the ceremony continued with the Queen Mother conferring honorary degrees.[12]

No reason is offered for this protest; no leader writers are moved to question this suppression of free speech; and as the Queen Mother recovers her dignity and the woman is "ushered" out, we are left with the distinct impression that she is slightly dotty.

On Merseyside, one night in 1976, a group of people entered bus depots and stuck these official-looking notices inside the buses: "EXPERIMENTAL FREE TRAVEL: Due to the sharp rise in administration and collection costs the Executive are introducing free bus travel for an experimental period of 14 days. No fares will be collected on any MPTE services from Monday 3 May to Sunday 16 May 1976,"

The point, presumably, was to draw attention to the main reason for high fares: The high cost of collecting them. But when the papers reported the "hoax" they quoted only the second part of the notice — the part announcing free transport. They omitted the first part explaining the reason for it.

Pressed to explain how the notices had gone into the buses, the transport executive had to conceal the fact that their depots were unguarded at night. So they invented this story: Someone with inside knowledge had put the notices in the place where notices were usually left for the cleaners to stick up. The cleaners, not knowing any better, had stuck them up. It was a plausible tale and the Press, assuming as always that people like cleaners are stupid, fell for it.[13]

Industrial disputes get similar treatment. News media concentrate on the effects of the action and neglect the reasons for it. If no reason is offered, people naturally get the idea that no reason exists. The result is that what may well be a perfectly understandable action by strikers appears stupid or even sinister.

An example from television, described in detail in the book Bad News,[14] was the "Glasgow Rubbish Strike" of 1975. Actually it was a strike by corporation drivers with Heavy Goods licences (only half of them dustcart drivers). It lasted more than three months and was one of the biggest television news stories in the first half of the year.

In all fourteen people were interviewed on national bulletins during the strike. They were: The Secretary of State for Scotland (four times), a university professor (three times), the Lord Provost of Glasgow (twice), a Member of Parliament, a councillor, a fire officer, a Lieutenant-Colonel (twice), a 2nd Lieutenant, four soldiers and two union officials (four times). No-one taking part in the strike was interviewed, and since the strike was unofficial, the union could hardly be expected to speak for the men.

On the day the strike ended one man did appear on ITN. He said the drivers were prepared to go on strike again "if it comes to the cause again, and it's a justful cause." The book comments: "The public hardly had a chance to discover from the bulletins what this "justful cause" was." Out of 102 reports on all channels, 67 gave no indication what the dispute was about. Where the cause was mentioned, generally it was made out to be a simple pay claim. Only 14 reports mentioned "parity" or "regrading".

Much was made of the fact that this was the drivers' second strike within three months, leaving the impression that the men were strike-happy. In fact there was a rational explanation: The drivers had gone on strike the previous autumn, wanting parity with HGV drivers in other industries. They went back after four weeks on the understanding the corporation would negotiate a local agreement of national talks (still in progress at the time) failed to produce a satisfactory settlement.

The second strike started when the corporation went back on their promise to negotiate a local agreement. This was the central issue, yet it was only reported on local programmes in Scotland and in fifteen words on one national BBC bulletin.

NOTES

1. Kurt Lewin: Forces behind food habits. Bulletin of the National Research Council, 1943.
2. Kurt Lewin: Channels of group life. Human Relations, Vol 1, No. 2. See also D White: The gatekeeper — a case-study in the selection of news. Journalism Quarterly, Vol 27, 1950.
3. For a detailed study of the local press and politics see David Murphy: The Silent Watchdog. Constable, 1976.
4. New Statesman, 29 February, 1980.
5. Daily Mirror, 4 September, 1978.
6. Quoted in Steve Chibnall: Law-and-order News. Tavistock, 1977.
7. Private Eye No. 451, 30 March, 1979.
8. Steve Chibnall: *op. cit.*
9. S Cohen/Jock Young (eds): The Manufacture of News, Constable, 1973.
10. Media, Culture and Society, Vol 1, No. 1, January, 1979.
11. Liverpool Daily Post, 12 May, 1977.
12. Daily Mirror, 13 July, 1973.
13. Liverpool Free Press, June, 1976.
14. Glasgow University Media Research Group: *op. cit.*

3. All the news that fits

WHEN journalists receive information they must decide whether it is newsworthy — that is, whether it will make a newspaper "story". They must also decide how it is likely to fare in competition with other stories for space. No story is intrinsically newsworthy. The meaning of "news" varies from place to place, from moment to moment, from paper to paper. While disasters and crimes make big news in the west, in the east it is the Ukrainian grain harvest. And the biggest news in Peking one morning was the dicovery of a new way to prove that Pythagoras got his theorem right.

The meaning of "news" is determined by the function of newspapers. In the Soviet Union, for instance, the Press has three clearly-defined tasks: It is a collective propagandist, collective agitator and collective organiser[1]. These principles, laid down by Lenin before the revolution, are still in use today and young journalists are trained to interpret and apply them. News, in the Soviet Press, is whatever fits these principles. The purpose of the Soviet Press is, above all, political. Stalin wrote:

> The Press is the strongest instrument with which, day by day, hour by hour, the party speaks to the masses in their own essential language. There is no other means so flexible for establishing spiritual links between the party and the working class[2].

Newspapers in Britain — and the west generally — have a very different function. It is often said they exist to inform and entertain. But that only explains why they are bought and read, not why they are produced and sold. Most newspapers are produced with the intention of making money — and in this respect the Press is no different from any other private industry. News is whatever is good for business. However, there is one important difference which distinguishes a newspaper from, say, a firm canning beans. Newspaper ownership confers on the owner a certain political status; the ability to use the product to influence events and the attitudes of readers — in a word, power.

The purpose of this chapter is to show how these twin functions — the pursuit of profit and the exercise of power — influence western concepts of news.

It must be understood at the outset that commercial newspapers, unlike the Soviet Press, have no fixed news values. Newcomers to journalism do not learn formal rules for measuring newsworthiness. Professional mystique speaks of people having "news sense" or "a nose for a story". Some, supposedly, are born with it. Most acquire it from colleagues or by experience. There have been many attempts to define "newsworthy" — and as many failures. This is partly because the selection process includes many practical considerations as well as purely journalistic criteria, and partly because commercial necessities require news values that are highly flexible. For example, editorial space in a newspaper is decided by advertisement bookings, often days in advance of the events to be reported. News then has to be compressed or expanded to fit — and the criteria for newsworthiness adjusted accordingly. So it would be futile to search for rules governing the selection process and then attempt to predict accurately what news would or would not be selected. However, if we examine stories which have passed through the selection process and been published, certain common elements can usually be found. They are:

1. An event;
2. Interest;
3. Importance.

Let us now look at these in turn:

1. The event

When a river burst its banks, killing 145 people and devastating parts of Kiev, the Soviet Press took 18 days to announce that it had happened. And when storms hit the coast of Poland, newspapers in the affected towns waited for confirmation of the obvious. Then they reported: "The Polish Press Agency informs us from Warsaw that the day before yesterday a heavy storm raged on our coast[3]."

To western journalists such delays in reporting the news are unthinkable. But to journalists in Communist countries, western haste can seem equally strange. Why alarm people with bad news, they ask. Why not wait — as happened in Kiev — until the cause of the disaster has been found and the negligent engineers responsible have been arrested? The usual explanation for the slowness of the Communist Press is that it is controlled by the authorities. Some news is suppressed, some is delayed as the bureaucracy mulls over the consequences of publishing and picks its words carefully. Speed is subordinated to political correctness. So, when Kruschev fell in 1964, Pravda failed to appear — delayed, presumably while the new bosses decided how the story should be told. Such behaviour seems to us abnormal. Western newspapers know big stories are good for sales; they change their front pages and rush off extra copies even if there is only time to prepare the briefest and sketchiest report. That does not strike us as odd. We assume that the western Press, with its breathless urgency, follows some natural law that would apply to all newspapers if some of them were not enslaved. But the behaviour of the western Press is not necessarily any more "natural" or "normal". For just as Communist news values are determined by the Party from principles laid down by Lenin, western news values are determined by the capitalist nature of the Press and the system the Press both supports and depends on.

The western attitude to up-to-date news provides a revealing example of commmercial forces at work. The events most likely to be reported are those that occur on a similar time scale to the production of newspapers. The building of a ship is not newsworthy because it takes too long. But incidents within the building process may be newsworthy — awarding the contract, the launching, work stoppages, announcements of sharp rises in costs, and so on. Running stories, like court cases lasting days or weeks, are broken down into a series of completed daily incidents: Each report contains an event (such as an allegation by the prosecution or the retirement of the jury), though other material may be worked into the story. The event provides what journalists call a news "peg". It justifies the inclusion of the story in a particular issue of the newspaper and shows why the story could not have been published earlier. In the morning papers all the news happened "yesterday".

The origin of the news peg can be traced to times when news travelled more slowly; when, using ingenuity and the wonders of the telegraph, it was possible to get the news ahead of rivals and thereby gain commercially. Even if two papers had the same news simultaneously, readers could still marvel at how soon after the event the report had been published. Today readers are probably less impressed, but the practice continues. Newspapers will not abandon it, for fear of losing ground to competitors or simply appearing inefficient in news-gathering. In addition, they are reluctant to concede the battle for "instant" news to television and radio.

Carrying up-to-date news is considered enormously important. Readers are made aware of especially late page changes by labels like "3am NEWS". Some papers go to extraordinary lengths. One newly-appointed editor of a provincial paper objected to the heading "LATE NEWS" in the late news panel because it implied the rest of the paper was full of early news. So he had "LATE NEWS" re-named "LATEST NEWS". The effect on sales can be substantial. In 1978 the Sun's circulation rose above the Mirror's for the first time. But in the north, the Mirror — despite its higher price — continued to outsell the Sun. The most likely reason was that the Sun was printed in London while the Mirror was printed in both London and Manchester. This meant that northern readers of the Sun got earlier editions than readers of the Mirror — sometimes with unfortunate consequences for the Sun. For instance, when Pope Paul VI died, the Mirror and other Manchester-printed papers splashed the news on the front page. But the main story in northern editions of the Sun was a typical silly-season gossip story about Princess Margaret, printed before news of the Pope's death broke. Sun readers who did not know the paper's problems would doubtless think the Sun had not heard to big news or thought the Pope unimportant. The Sun had particular difficulties during the Soccer season, because it was unable to carry results of late mid-week matches in the north. The Mirror gleefully hammered this home with a slogan on its sports pages: "IF IT'S LATE — TELL YOUR MATE IT'S IN THE MIRROR".

The timing of events can be crucial in determining whether they become news. Events close to a newspaper's deadline get priority. So a story of uncertain value which breaks just before edition time may replace an earlier — but stronger — story. A late story has a momentum of its own; journalists know time is short and rise to the challenge. This extra effort can increase commitment to using a story and may also exaggerate its importance. One example in my own experience was a "mystery blast" on an overnight train. The train was stopped and fire engines, police and Army bomb experts were called. There was just time to get the story in the final edition. Space was made by dropping an earlier story. Then, as the type was about to go into the page, the mystery was solved: a fire extinguisher in the guard's van had fallen on to the floor and gone off with a bang. That greatly weakened the story, but all that could be done at that stage was to change the words "train blast" in the heading to a non-committal "bomb alert" and add a final paragraph explaining that it was a false alarm.

Where news pegs do not occur naturally they may have to be created. Here is a typical example:

> Dance hall Romeo Tom Flay, 70, was waltzing on air last night. For the sprightly pensioner's 22-year-old partner, Carolyn, is going to make him a dad next month[4].

Does this mean sprightly Tom's wife has been pregnant for eight months without him noticing? Of course not. It means the Press have not noticed until now. Tom was waltzing on air *last night* because that was when the reporter spoke to him. The fact that it is an old story is disguised. The real story is that a man of 70 is to be a father — but that is old news. So his feelings last night become the news peg instead. However, up-dating of this sort is usually only done when an old story is thought too good to miss. Another example of disguising old news can be seen on Monday mornings, when there is often a shortage of fresh news because of the weekend. Events that happened on Sunday happened "yesterday". But rather than admit that some happened "on Saturday", the phrase "at the weekend" is preferred.

With scoops and exposés the act of publishing sometimes provides a news peg: "Now at last the story can be told". . . "The Daily X today reveals". . . etc. The public relations industry provides them too — by creating pseudo-events which can be reported. Not only are ships launched (a physical necessity), sales campaigns and new products are also "launched" (a necessity only to get free publicity). Press conferences where manufacturers display their new product and ply thirsty journalists with drink are often the only "event" that is needed. Some non-commercial organisations now copy this practice. Well-organised bodies like Shelter and the Child Poverty Action Group get in the news by issuing reports and Press releases and holding Press conferences. Publication of their report does often provide a news peg. But the difficulties remain for the less articulate, less formal and less professionally-organised pressure groups who want publicity but do not stage stunts and contrive "events".

When Londoner George Davis was jailed for armed robbery, his friends maintained he had been wrongly convicted, on identification evidence that was suspect. But their doubts about his conviction were not "newsworthy" and the way their campaign was ignored forced them into increasingly desperate measures. Damaging the Daily Express building and ramming the gates of Buckingham Palace got them nowhere. Finally, in August 1975, they attacked a sacred institution — cricket — by digging up the pitch at Headingly the night before a Test Match. The game had to be abandoned and that was a newsworthy event. Most papers then agreed that the campaign had a point about the Davis case, but complained that it should have used reasonable argument instead of wrecking the match. It was, of course, precisely because reasonable argument had not been newsworthy earlier that the match was wrecked. A few months later, Davis was released.

The news media's obsession with events has severely narrowed the range of reportable news. Situations which are static or developing slowly — such as social trends and problems — often go unreported. Newspapers must demonstrate that something significant has happened between editions, and happenings which do not fit into the timetable for newspaper production are likely to pass unrecognised as events. This partly explains why the problems of industry — almost exclusively in the popular Press and on television — are portrayed in terms of strikes. We are all familiar with stories like: "STRIKE THREATENS FIRM'S FUTURE" but not at all familiar with others like: "MANAGEMENT BLUNDERS THREATEN FIRM'S FUTURE". In 1975, the Ryder report on British Leyland pointed to lack of investment as the key to the car firm's decline. It noted that between 1968 and 1972 only five per cent of the profits had been re-invested. The rest had gone on dividends to shareholders. This meant that much of the machinery was out of date and often broke down. In one period shortly before the report was published, more than half the company's production losses had nothing to do with disputes. And yet journalists happily accept mismanagement and equipment failures as part of the normal pattern of industrial life. So the absence of strikes is equated with "normal" or even "full" production:

For the moment at least, *normal* production of cars — Maxis and Marinas (12,000 of which, worth about £1¾ million, were lost yesterday) — was possible[5].

With the engine-tuners back at work, at least for the time being, the Austin-Morris plant . . . was also back in *full production*[6].

The engine-tuners at British Leyland's Cowley works have ended their strike and the plant is back in *full production*[7].

Undoubtedly there are often political motives behind this kind of picture; news media intended for mass consumption feel obliged to educate the masses into not going on strike. But even if their intentions were different, there would still be problems. Strikes are eminently newsworthy: They involve action and their effects can be dramatic and immediate. The gradual run-down of a company is a less tangible "event": There is only inaction and it may be years before there is a noticeable effect.

The limitations of events-related news might be overcome if newspapers wanted to do so. There is certainly ample space. A look at any newspaper shows that only part of the content is "news" and a large part consists of "features" — television guides, motoring columns, fashion articles, cartoons, crosswords and so on. One reason for the existence of features is cost: Inch for inch, they are generally cheaper to produce than news. But the most important reason is ease of production. A paper which contained only the latest news would need an enormous production staff who might be occupied for as little as three hours a day. The function of features is to smooth out this rush. Features are produced early, thus spreading production over a longer period and reducing the number of staff required. So in practice, the conflicting commercial needs of up-to-date news and efficient production have to be balanced against each other. This does provide the opportunity to broaden the scope of news, but the opportunity is rarely taken. Instead, feature pages are used to broaden the market for advertisers. In the early days of newspapers, features were often directed at women because it was thought women were not interested in the affairs of the world. That is less true of features today, though specially-titled "women's pages" persist in many papers, and most of the others devote a lot of space to fashion articles and pictures and housekeeping hints. And these attract advertisements from supermarkets and chain stores. Other sections, like gardening and motoring columns are also accompanied by related advertising. Even the lists of television programmes have a function in extending the useful life of morning papers. They help ensure that papers are left lying about the house until evening, giving the whole family a chance to read them, or that a husband who buys the paper on his way to work takes it home with him.

2. Interest

Sir Max Aitken, Chairman of Beaverbrook Newspapers, wrote in 1966: "The Fleet Street newspapers today offer the public a complete range of opinion and expression." He would have been nearer the mark if he had said they offered advertisers a complete range of likely customers. For it is the advertising market, as much as anything, that governs the range of opinion and expression in the newspapers. Obviously, newspapers want to sell as many copies as possible, but they must also sell them to the right people.

Nobody tries to sell newspapers to old age pensioners because their spending power is small. Young people searching for homes, furniture, washing machines, cars and better jobs make a much more attractive audience for advertisers. During the final months of Beaver-brook rule at the Daily Express, management became very alarmed at the death rate among their readers who were older, on average, than those of competitors. So the paper changed to tabloid size from the more old-fashioned broadsheet and made strenuous efforts to include stories to interest young people.

Not all newspapers chase after the same readers. The Times, for instance, would be most unwise to print pictures of "Good Times Girls" on page three in the hope of winning more readers: They would be the wrong sort of readers. This is because the requirements of advertisers vary. They want their message where it will be most effective. Obviously a manufacturer of cheap, mass-produced furniture would be looking for the mass market of the popular Press. But a vacancy for the post of university professor would not be advertised in the Sun because suitably qualified people would be unlikely to see it. The needs of some advertisers are altogether too specialised for the Fleet Street papers. There is no point in a shopkeeper in Devon, for example, advertising in a paper that circulates as far afield as Ireland and Scotland when an advertisement in the local paper is cheaper and reaches all the likely customers. Few pop records are advertised in the national Press because many of the readers have no interest in buying them. There are pop music papers to cater for this market. Other papers cater for hi-fi fanatics, amateur photographers, railway enthusiasts, etc. Most of them are owned by firms who publish Fleet Street newspapers — with the aim of soaking up as many different kinds of advertising as possible.

The variety of advertising markets largely explains the differences between newspapers (the other important factor — politics — is discussed later). It also explains why some papers thrive with relatively small circulations while others with much larger circulations sometimes have difficulties. Large circulations are more important to papers at the lower end of the market. A newspaper attracting "high quality" readers is more likely to succeed because rich people are more attractive to advertisers. So, the Financial Times is viable with a circulation of only a few hundred thousand while some popular papers like the Daily Sketch, selling more than a million copies, have gone to the wall.

The aim of each paper is to find a gap in the market, exploit it and keep others out. Attracting the right sort of readers for the market means news is not necessarily selected because of any intrinsic merit. In local papers, for example, a particular district (usually one with a growing population) may suddenly seem to have become very newsworthy. It is a safe bet that the paper is having a sales drive in that area. Apart from specific instances like this, the range of news has to be tailored to meet the varied interests of readers. Stories are selected or rejected to balance the various categories of news as the supposed demands of readers, rather than events, dictate. Too much industrial or political news on one day could put some readers off. On a day when there is a lot of overseas news, for example, some good-quality overseas news that would normally have been published may be left out in favour of some less significant home news in order to balance the content of the paper.

We have already seen that the first essential for newsworthy news is newness in the sense of time: There must be a recent event. But news must also be new in another sense: It must tell readers something they did not already know or surprise them with something unexpected. In the popular Press, news is primarily for entertainment. Like films, plays, novels, television, it can be exciting, sentimental, amusing, even tragic — with the added attraction that the drama is about real people and set in the present.

We have also seen, in discussing events, that stories are internally justified — that is, the reason for publishing a story at a particular time can be found within the story. This not only justifies the story to readers, but to editors and sub-editors assessing the story's "strength". The elements of interest in a story are internally justified in the same way. For example, a report that a prominent Member of Parliament is to send his son to a public school would probably be rejected as boring by most newspapers. But perhaps the reporter has omitted to mention that the man has frequently advocated abolishing public schools. Once that element is included the story becomes interesting. It is the contrast between the man's private and public stance that creates the interest. If only one aspect is mentioned, the story falls flat.

Interest is provided by inter-play between the familiar and the unfamiliar, the commonplace and the extraordinary, the good and the bad, the expected and the unexpected, the happy and the sad, the normal and the abnormal. So, it is not news if an old man dies in bed (unless he happens to be a former Prime Minister), but it is news if a bride dies on the way to the altar; it is not news if a woman takes her clothes off for a living, but it is if she is also a Sunday school teacher.

Some news, of course, is selected for reasons other than interest. It may be dull but important, or it may be published because of editorial policy. Journalists may try to brighten dull news by highlighting the most interesting points — and the ability to do so is regarded as a professional skill. Subjects outside readers' experience are made relevant and interesting by introducing a familiar element, or one readers can readily sympathise with. Islamic law, for instance, was a topic rarely mentioned in the British Press until 1978. Then two Britons in Saudi Arabia were flogged in public for drinking alcoholic liquor. The clash of cultures made all the difference, and the story became big news. The victims were interviewed at length and received almost a heroes' welcome from thirsty newsmen when they arrived back in Britain. Background articles on strange Islamic punishments followed, together with another report (which proved false) that a Briton and an unmarried Arab girl were to be executed for being found alone together. Similarly, "deviant" groups like Punks, Hell's Angels, Hippies and Teddy Boys make more interesting news when it can be shown that they interfere with "normal" life by frightening old ladies, disturbing peaceful Sunday afternoons, etc. But this is only effective if readers are "normal" and do not amuse themselves by frightening old ladies and livening up Sunday afternoons. "Interesting" presentation of a story relies on readers sharing the values of newspapers. When these values are not shared, "interesting" stories may simply strike readers as ludicrous or biased. One very common practice is to report political demonstrations as traffic jams — a technique parodied by the Morning Star when, under the heading: "TRAFFIC DISRUPTED", it reported the chaos in central London caused by a Royal wedding. Here is a real, non-satirical example from the News of the World:

> RALLY JAMS CITY CENTRE
> More than 10,000 chanting demonstrators brought the centre of Manchester to a halt for two hours yesterday in an anti-Nazi rally.
> They marched from Strangeways jail to Alexandra Park for an open-air concert after speakers told them: "This is our answer to the National Front"[8].

While this says little about the demonstration, it says a lot about what the News of the World thinks of its readers: They are not interested in demonstrations and do not take part in them. So the event is presented in terms that make it "relevant" to readers' own experience — traffic congestion. Probably only a handful of readers were caught up in this particular jam, but it is something familiar — a situation they can all imagine themselves being in. At the same time, the contrast between the familiar and unfamiliar is heightened by words like "chanting" and "marched". This ensures the alienating technique is still effective for readers who have anti-Nazi feelings but do not march around chanting about them. However, it would be wrong to assume that the reporter concerned rationalised the story in this way. The story follows such a well-established formula with so many precedents that the reporter probably just copied the pattern of other stories he had read, or even some he had written himself.

A more straightforward approach (and, perhaps, to non-journalists, the obvious approach) would be a simple who-what-when-where-why account of the demonstration. But that raises problems. A traffic jam with an unusual cause meets the requirements of interesting news. It is apolitical and, above all, self-justifying: Readers do not have to be told why it is news. A straight report of the demonstration does not meet those requirements because the paper believes a demonstration is not interesting in itself. If it is to be news it has to be justified in some other way. A straight report would, at the very least, signify the paper ascribed some importance to the demonstration, if not approval. So to escape the question of politics and a possible conflict with editorial policy; the journalist opts for the "professional" approach — the traffic jam. But though that is the safe, approved course it is not neutral — it removes the politics from what is essentially a political event. With this particular story, the News of the World apparently recognised the dilemma and in later editions of the same paper the story was re-written like this:

ANTI-NAZI FOLK CALL THE TUNE
More than 25,000 people voted with their feet yesterday against the National Front. Thousands of demonstrators from all over the north converged on Manchester for the Anti-Nazi League's march through the city.
Fear of violent clashes with Front sympathisers never materialised as the marchers paraded to Alexandra Park for a pop concert. More than 500 police were on duty.

Presumably this more sympathetic version was intended to bring the story into line with the paper's policy of opposing the National Front — and in the process the estimated number of demonstrators was more than doubled. (The report appeared some weeks before the News of the World denounced the Anti-Nazi League as a Troskyist front.) To prevent this straight report boring readers, a familiar technique for creating interest is employed: "Violent clashes" are introduced by saying they did not occur.

Industrial disputes are made "interesting" in much the same way. Stories about "ordinary citizens" who suffer inconvenience and hardship caused by strikes are "interesting", while those about ordinary citizens who suffer the inconvenience of low wages and bad employers are apparently less interesting. The reason seems to be that those who work in the mass media see themselves and their audience as consumers rather than workers (and potential strikers). This also helps to explain why strikes in certain industries are more newsworthy than others.

The Glasgow University Media Research Group, in their study of television news[9], confirmed what many people had long suspected — that television is obsessed with the motor industry. During the study period the motor industry featured in 255 bulletins and took up 28 per cent of all television strike reporting. Actually, strikes in the car factories accounted for less than seven per cent of total days lost through strikes. Engineering was more seriously affected. 24.9 per cent of days lost were in engineering and there were 260 stoppages (compared with only 38 in the motor industry). Engineering strikes featured in only 43 bulletins and took up 5.3 per cent of strike reporting. Out of the Government's list of the "Top Twenty" strikes, nine were completely ignored by television. Six of these were major disputes in engineering. Only one was reported by television, and even then the issue seemed to be how far it would affect the motor industry. The team concluded that there was no direct relationship between the severity of strikes and the amount of coverage they got. The car, as the supreme symbol of the consumer society, naturally gets the most attention. The book pointed to other strikes reported from a consumer's point of view:

> A strike that grounds aircraft is highly inconvenient to the holidaymakers and businessmen, a railway strike is very troublesome to the commuter, a doctors' work-to-rule or hospital workers' boycotting of private patients is distressing to the consumer of health services and a strike of dustcart drivers is a growing difficulty for the consumer wishing to dispose of his unconsumed leftovers. Given this emphasis, it is difficult to structure news in a way that does not, implicitly at least, blame those groups or individuals who precipitate action that, in one way or another, is defined as "disruptive"[10].

1978 saw the birth of a new national paper, the Daily Star, with its sights set unashamedly on a working-class readership. The editor, Peter Grimsditch, promised that the paper would be different and said he aimed to interest readers by covering "the kind of situations we all imagine we could find ourselves in"[11]. So did that herald a long-waited change? Not a bit of it. Grimsditch explained what he meant with examples of stories other papers had published in the past: The couple making love in a field when a farmhand, mistaking them for rabbits, blasted them with a shot-gun; and the wife who scalped her husband's teenage mistress. After all, he did say situations we *imagine*. He did not say the real, everyday situations that actually happen frequently — like having the gas cut off or losing your job. His new product on offer was just like the old ones — not reality but real-life fantasy; the fascinating things that happen in life to a few, but to most of us only in the world of dreams.

3. Importance

The commodity called news is a mixture of entertainment and information. The proportions are varied to suit the intended market; some newspapers provide mainly information, others mainly entertainment. Some news may be for entertainment only, some a combination of both.

News which is primarily informative is published because the information is considered important. That raises the question: In what ways is it important, and to whom is it important? As there are no formalised principles for assessing news, the relative importance of different events might be the subject of endless debates in newspaper offices. But news must be produced at speed — so delays have to be eliminated as far as possible. This is achieved partly by employing a hierarchy of decision-makers and partly by reducing the need for decisions, by processing events in the way that arouses the least controversy and raises the fewest complications within the news machine. There are, therefore, a number of points of reference against which journalists can check their judgment. These are: (a) tradition, precedent and their own past experience, (b) the judgment of their colleagues in other news media and (c) the expectations of their superiors.

(a) Tradition, precedent and experience: The most efficiently processed events are repetitive events. Once the importance of an event has been established, any repetition of the event is more easily dealt with because precedents can be used as a guide. Thus an event may be justified as important by showing its similarity to an event that was held to be important in the past, or its relationship to the earlier event (for example, that one is a consequence of the other).

It follows that repetitive events are preferred, while those that journalists have no experience of processing are difficult to handle and may be rejected outright as unimportant or "not news". In this sense, news is really "olds". Crimes, strikes, accidents, elections, Soccer matches, inquests, riots, wars, blizzards and heatwaves are reported routinely. Time after time the events are the same, the cliches and headlines are the same. Only the names of people and places change. And happily, this is exactly the sort of news that institutionalised sources like the courts, police and emergency services are best suited to provide. In addition, other, less regular sources may themselves be guided by precedent in deciding whether or not to inform the Press; they are more likely to tip off the Press if they know similar stories have been used in the past.

Reporters are also affected. It is very tempting, when starting work on a story, not to treat it as unique but to seek — and find — similarities with stories that have been published before. And reporters are well aware that sub-editors will be looking out for these pointers to assess the story. This influences not only the selection of the story itself but also the selection of detail within the story. Once on familiar ground, the reporter can quickly eliminate unwanted angles. He knows from experience which angles will be liked back at the office; he knows which of the many possible lines of inquiry are likely to be fruitful in the time allowed.

(b) Judgment of colleagues: The popular image of reporters perpetually hunting "scoops" is an exaggeration. Certainly newspapers like the occasional scoop to boost their reputation and sales. But scoops are not the bread and butter of journalism. It is far more important not to be caught napping and miss a story, because that can damage a paper's reputation and actually lose sales. The result is a tendency for newspapers to copy each other rather than try to be different. Journalists feel there is something wrong if their own paper is out of step with the others — if they miss a story the others feature prominently, or attach much more or much less importance to a story than their rivals. Of course, allowances have to be made for different types of reader. The Sun, for example, would not be worried if The Times had a big front story about international diplomacy which it had overlooked. But it would be

worried if it missed a big story in the Mirror. When one paper does get a scoop the others do their utmost to weaken its impact. This happened in 1978 when Joyce McKinney, an American, was accused of kidnapping Kirk Anderson, a Mormon missionary in Britain. The Mirror checked into her past and found she had been a nude model. The Mirror's exclusive story ran for several days. It quoted Joyce McKinney as saying she loved Anderson so much she was prepared to ski naked down Mount Everest with a carnation up her nose for him. The Sun seized the opportunity to get in on the story and, with the aid of an artist and a picture of Joyce McKinney's face, produced a "composite" picture for the front page showing what she would look like skiing down Mount Everest with a carnation up her nose. The Mail, on the other hand, conceded defeat but nevertheless tried to devalue the Mirror's scoop by advertising itself as "The paper WITHOUT Joyce McKinney".

Although it might be expected that competition between papers would lead to greater diversity, in practice the opposite happens: It leads to standardisation. On the whole, the differences between papers are not so much in content as in presentation. Most papers start the day with basically similar material and the competition is to make the best use of it — pick the best angles, think up the cleverest headlines, and so on.

Standardisation takes place in several ways. First, as we have already seen, newspapers have similar sources for their news and all receive the same stories from the Press Association and other agencies. In London particularly, journalists from competing newspapers work together in packs, often comparing notes. This is usually for self-protection — a safeguard against complaints of mis-reporting or mis-quoting. If all the papers say the same thing no-one will believe they have all got it wrong. But self-protection is not the only reason. Sometimes it is a way of "improving" a story. Once, when President De Gaulle of France was visiting Ireland, several papers carried graphic descriptions of his bedroom. In fact, no journalist had been allowed to see it; they had simply agreed amongst themselves on what they would say it looked like. Besides working with colleagues from other papers and socialising with them, journalists frequently swop places. There is a steady interchange of staff, and moving from one paper to another is the way many journalists get promotion. This mobility helps to standardise attitudes and working practices.

When the first copies of the Fleet Street papers come off the presses, messengers rush from office to office, exchanging copies. Reporters then have an hour or so to check out any stories from rival papers they have missed and get them into the second edition. The Press Association also sends out a list of main headlines from all the papers and follows up any major stories it has missed. Newspapers usually have a reporter watching the evening news bulletins on television and taking notes. When commercial radio started, at least one provincial paper (which had previously had no local competition) made a reporter take down the hourly radio bulletins in shorthand. Changes are not only made to include new stories. After studying the opposition, editors often revise their assessment of their own stories to give them more or less prominence — usually bringing the paper more into line with the others. Rumours spread rapidly if a paper is planning a big exclusive story. The first sign is usually the preparations for printing extra copies, like arranging overtime for the press operators. Once the word is out, reporters from rival papers head for the drinking haunts to find out what the story is about. Sometimes they succeed. Some papers take the precaution of not including scoops in their first editions so that competitors will have less time to catch up. But the danger is that competitors may already be on to the story and may have it in *their* first editions.

(c) **Expectations of superiors:** Britain's colonial wars of the late nineteenth century worked wonders for newspaper sales. Across the Atlantic, newspaper boss William Randolph Hearst looked enviously at the British Press and decided America must have a war of her own. Hearst's New York Journal was in the midst of a circulation battle and he knew a war would help. For two years the Journal reported Cuban struggles for independence in Spain in the hope of getting America to intervene on the Cuban side. Then Hearst sent an artist to Cuba to produce drawings of the action. The artist cabled back: "Everything is quiet. There is no trouble here. There will be no war. I wish to return." Hearst is said to have replied: "Please remain. You furnish pictures. I will furnish war"[12]. Shortly afterwards an American battleship blew up in Havana harbour. Spain insisted it was an accident but Hearst, without a shred of evidence, blamed "an enemy's secret infernal machine". In the public outcry that followed, Hearst got his war and sales of his papers soared. Hearst's aim was political power and he pursued it ruthlessly, exposing some corrupt politicians while corrupting others with his own money. With the aid of his papers he won a seat in Congress and in 1904 came close to winning the Democratic nomination for the presidency.

In Britain during the first half of this century, newspaper ownership was very much a family affair. Most of the national papers (and many provincial ones) at some stage belonged to one of four families — the Aitkens, the Astors, the Berrys and the Harmsworths.

Alfred Harmsworth began with a successful magazine, Answers. In 1894 he bought the London Evening News and rapidly expanded its circulation. Then, following the American example of Hearst, he stood for Parliament as a Unionist in Portsmouth. To ensure good coverage of his campaign he bought up the local paper. But despite that the voters failed to elect him and he abandoned democratic politics with the words: "My place is in the House of Lords, where they don't fight elections". He got his place a few years later and became Lord Northcliffe. In 1896 he founded the Daily Mail, which soon achieved a circulation of almost a million. In 1903 he bought the Daily Mirror, an unsuccessful paper for women and turned it into a popular picture paper which he sold to his younger brother, Harold (later Lord Rothermere). In 1908 he bought The Times. At the peak of his power, Northcliffe controlled half Britain's national newspaper sales. Northcliffe has been described as a man who "began as a journalist and finished as a propagandist seduced by his own headlines"[13]. A megalomaniac, he believed he bore a striking resemblance to Napoleon. He inundated his staff with daily instructions and sacked so many that he had to avoid Ludgate Circus (at the end of Fleet Street) for fear of meeting them again. Whether his whim of the day was for building battleships or eating brown bread, his readers were sure to know about it. Eventually he became insane and died in 1922. His brother, Rothermere, took over and attacked both the Labour Party and the Conservative Party under Stanley Baldwin. He attempted to form his own party, the United Empire Party, composed of MPs nominated by himself. He also apparently believed he had a right to help choose Tory Cabinets (a role that traditionally belongs to the Prime Minister alone) and once wrote: "Under no circumstances whatsoever will I support Mr Baldwin unless I know exactly what his policy is going to be, unless I have complete guarantees that such policy will be carried out if his party achieves office, and unless I am acquainted with the names of at least eight or ten of his most prominent colleagues in the next ministry." This led to Baldwin's famous denunciation of Rothermere as seeking "power without responsibility". By the time he died in 1940, Rothermere had become a defender of Mosley, Mussolini and Hitler.

Max Aitken, a wealthy Canadian, came to Britain in 1910 and almost immediately became a Tory MP. His first involvement with newspapers came when he loaned £36,000 to the Daily Express in return for its support for his friend, Bonar Law (the future Prime Minister). The Express continued to have financial problems until he bought it outright in 1916. His intention was to use it to topple Asquith and replace him with Lloyd George. He expected Lloyd George to reward him with a Cabinet post, but he got a peerage instead and took the title Lord Beaverbrook. Later, he bought the London Evening Standard and founded the Sunday Express. Beaverbrook eventually controlled a quarter of British national newspaper sales[14].

Welsh brothers William and Gomer Berry (later Lord Kemsley and Lord Camrose) began with two magazines and built up an empire that included The Sunday Times, the Financial Times, the Daily Telegraph and a host of magazines and provincial papers.

In 1893 William Waldorf Astor, an American immigrant and Tory politician, bought the Pall Mall Gazette, a Liberal evening paper. The editor, who was on holiday at the time, returned to find himself expected to edit a Tory paper. He resigned. In 1911 Astor bought the Observer from Northcliffe. Then his brother, Colonel J J Astor (later Lord Astor of Hever) bought The Times from Northcliffe's brother, Lord Rothermere.

The era of individual proprietors has now almost ended. Only two national newspapers remain entirely in private hands — the Guardian, owned by a trust, and the Daily Telegraph, whose principal shareholder and editor-in-chief is Lord Hartwell (one of the Berry family). However, it should not be forgotten that a handful of men dominated the national daily Press (and particularly the popular Press) in its formative years and shaped its news values — values which have been handed down largely intact to today's journalists.

Most newspapers now belong to large public companies like Reed International (Daily and Sunday Mirror, Sunday People, etc.) or Trafalgar House (Daily and Sunday Express, Daily Star). To these companies, newspapers are only a part (sometimes a minute part) of their business and their main concern is with profit rather than political power. And contrary to popular belief, most newspapers do make profits. Managements, like farmers, moan loudly during the lean years and reap quietly during the fat ones.

Modern corporate owners do not use their papers for Parliamentary intrigue, nor do they usually meddle in the day-to-day content — though they do often direct policy in a general way. When Trafalgar House bought the Express, the new boss, Victor Matthews, appeared to continue the Beaverbrook tradition when he announced: "We have not got an Empire any more, but we have got Britain... If believing in Britain means being Conservative, then that is what we will be." "I find some of the Labour Party principles completely offensive, so we could not be a pro-Labour paper." And he added: "We want good news. The newspapers of today seem always to be looking for bad news... I would not discount the Nixon/Watergate story if it had happened here, but it would have been a dilemma for me." On the other hand, the late Lord Thomson[15], head of the Thomson Organisation, maintained news was simply the stuff filling "the space between the adverts" and prided himself on not interfering with editorial content provided his papers made money. There was one well-publicised incident when The Sunday Times attacked the Macmillan Government, from whom Thomson was expecting a peerage. Thomson declared he would have "bitten my tongue off" rather than reprimand the editor. However, that was no real sacrifice: He got the peerage and also enhanced the "independent" reputation of his papers.

Giving editors the "freedom" to edit can be a wise policy for large companies — especially those based overseas or with large interests outside newspapers. Editors understand the technicalities of news production better than businessmen and are more familiar with local conditions. Editors can safely be left to their own devices because they are trusted. "Responsibility" is a qualification for editorship. As Victor Matthews put it: "By and large the editors will have complete freedom as long as they agree with the policy I have laid down"[16].

But it is not only editors who know what they must do. The humble reporters, too, read the signs. They can write whatever they want, but there is no guarantee it will appear in print. It is very disheartening to write stories that are not used, so they study their paper and take hints. They soon learn what sort of stories will be given a good show — then they go out and find them. Journalist Eamonn McCann summed it up like this:

> Reporters who know what is expected of them; news editors and sub-editors trained to recognise and eliminate "unhelpful" references; editors appointed with "sound" attitudes; boards of management composed of substantial businessmen: The whole sprawling machinery of news gathering and publication automatically filters, refines and packages the information fed in and works to ensure that the news, as printed, is fit to print. The general picture is enlivened by occasional bursts of maverick radicalism. A "fearless exposé" every now and then helps to maintain the official myth of the independent Press (and can be good for circulation) but does not alter significantly the pattern which emerges[17].

And ultimately everyone knows where the wages come from. Even if newspapers no longer further the political ambitions of their owners in print, they are still ready to be used to safeguard the company profits. The lorry drivers' strike of 1979 saw particularly ferocious reports of "crippling" effects and editorials urging the drivers back to work (at less than half the pay of a Fleet Street leader writer). At the same time, papers were turning away advertisers and printing small-sized editions because supplies of newsprint were not being delivered.

Here is another example, from the provincial Press: One of the planners' dreams of the 1960s was a motorway around the centre of Liverpool. By the end of 1970 the scheme, which was expected to cost £22 million a mile, looked like being abandoned as too expensive. At the Liverpool Daily Post and Echo, management, editors and selected writers met for a conference to discuss the threatened road. The result was a full page article in the Daily Post with the emotional headline: "FAIL TO BUILD THIS ROAD AND THE CITY WILL DECAY"[18]. The leader column pronounced: "The inner motorway and associated works must go ahead, even if it means pruning the money off other departments" — the other departments being, presumably, housing, education and welfare services. And the article charted every reason (except one) in favour of the motorway and not a single reason against. The one reason in favour that was not mentioned was this: The motorway would be ideal for sending vans full of newspapers whizzing round the city. The motorway had been a crucial factor in choosing the site for the company's new offices and printing works. A year earlier the company's internal newspaper had said: "The building is within the line of the proposed urban motorway, to which all principal traffic routes in the city centre will be linked." And it published a map showing the building right beside the motorway. The importance of this location was shown in a letter from the company's chairman to Liverpool Corporation outlining the need to move to a new building. It said: "The traffic factor alone may make removal urgent".

The new pattern of ownership may have increased the freedom of editors but in a sense it has also lessened the independence of newspapers as a whole. The old proprietors could, if they chose, go out on a limb to fight their own personal vendettas and wage their own private wars — with only their own individual fortunes at stake. Today's newspaper companies spread their roots much more deeply into the country's economic system. They depend on that system and in turn must support it. They may criticise it in order to make it work more efficiently but they cannot afford to challenge it.

NOTES

1. Antony Buzek: How the Communist Press Works. Pall Mall Press, 1964.
2. *ibid.*
3. *ibid.*
4. Daily Star, 4 January, 1979.
5. Peter Beharrell/Greg Philo (eds): Trade Unions and the Media. Macmillan, 1977.
6. *ibid.*
7. *ibid.*
8. News of the World, 16 July, 1978.
9. Glasgow University Media Research Group: *op. cit.*
10. *ibid.*
11. New Manchester Review, No. 67. October 20-November 2, 1978.
12. L Snyder/R Morris (eds): A Treasury of Great Reporting. Simon & Schuster, New York, 1962.
13. Quoted in Simon Jenkins: Newspapers — The Power and The Money. Faber, 1979.
14. Simon Jenkins: *op. cit.*
15. For more on Lord Thomson, see John Whale: The Politics of the Media. Fontana/Collins, 1977 and Simon Jenkins: *op. cit.*
16. Simon Jenkins: *op. cit.*
17. S Cohen/Jock Young: The Manufacture of News. Constable, 1973.
18. Liverpool Daily Post, 4 December, 1970.

4. Publish and be jailed

IN PREVIOUS chapters we have looked mainly at the internal forces shaping news. We have seen how the need for an efficient, dependable, cheap supply of news influences the choice of sources, and how information from these sources is processed into a product that serves the interests of a commercial Press. But this still leaves a large area of news that the Press, even by their own standards, might like to publish — but do not.

Having heard of a story and decided that at first sight it is newsworthy, editors and news editors must decide on its feasibility and legality. Feasibility raises the practical question: Will the story "stand up"? By that, they mean not only "is it true?", but what checks must be made, what additional information is needed and — most important — whether this can be done. *Can* the story be checked? *Can* the necessary information be obtained? *Will* the people essential to the story be willing to speak? It is here that the public relations industry, usually so ready to deluge the Press with unsolicited information, jerks sharply into reverse gear to protect business or officialdom. "The information you're asking for would take weeks to sort out." "It might invite unfair comparisons/be open to misinterpretation/be misunderstood by your readers." "We can't possibly let our competitors know *that*," and so on. Unlike colleagues in some countries, notably the United States and parts of Scandinavia, British journalists have no constitutional right to information.

Legality raises the question of the relationship between the Press and the state. In the past, newspapers have sometimes chosen to ignore the law. We saw in Chapter One how the radical, unstamped Press thrived, even though its very existence was illegal. Today's commercial Press has to operate more openly to stay in business — and that means it has to obey the law. Not only that; it has to play safe. In some hazy areas of the law, for example, a newspaper may be advised that what it proposes to publish is probably lawful, but it may nevertheless hold back for fear that the cost of proving the point in the courts will be too great.

In the present century, the struggle between the Press and the state has been less apparent, giving the impression, perhaps, that the battle for Press freedom has been won. But the battle is far from won.

In part, the change is due to the changed nature of the Press. In the twentieth century, when newspapers became big business, they found they had everything to lose and nothing to gain by rocking the boat. The rise of the commercial Press brought a corresponding decline in the radical Press, the traditional pacemakers in the fight for free speech. Commercial constraints have made Government attempts at control less necessary than in the past. In 1938, for example, newspapers were under pressure from advertisers to stay cheerful and play down international tension, because if people thought a war was coming it would be bad for business. So, just before the war the Daily Express used to carry on its front page the blithe message: THERE WILL BE NO WAR THIS YEAR NOR NEXT YEAR EITHER. In 1956, the Guardian was the only big national newspaper to oppose the invasion of Suez. It paid for its independent stand with a 40 per cent drop in advertising revenue.[1] The Communist Daily Worker had few advertisers to worry about but it too suffered financially when in 1930 it urged workers not to handle munitions for India. The Government was urged to have the editor arrested. The Government did nothing, but the paper's distributors began a boycott that lasted 12 years.[2]

To some extent attitudes of Governments towards their opponents have also changed. The state's main weapons used against the Press in the past were conduct likely to cause a breach of the peace (an easy one to prove because no actual breach of the peace is necessary) and two forms of criminal libel: Blasphemy and sedition. The law of blasphemous libel was supposed to protect God and religion from scurrilous attacks, but could sometimes be used to protect politicians. In one case, a crippled newspaper seller in Exeter got nine months for blasphemy and six months for sedition and had his entire stock burned for selling this parody of the Lord's Prayer:

> Our Lord who art in the Treasury, Whatsoever by thy name. Thy power be prolonged, thy will be done throughout the Empire, as it is in each session. Give us our usual sops, and forgive us our occasional absences on divisions, as we promise to forgive them that divide against us. Turn us not out of our places; but keep us in the House of Commons, the land of Pensions and Plenty; and deliver us from the people. Amen.

Seditious libel is anything that brings the Royal family into "hatred or contempt", "excites disaffection" against the sovereign or constitution, encourages people to "take the law into their own hands" to change "any matter in Church or state by law established", or stirs up public "discontent or disaffection" or "feelings of ill-will and hostility between different classes".[3] In 1704 Lord Chief Justice Holt spelled out the purpose of the law in this no-nonsense fashion:

> If persons should not be called to account for possessing the people of an ill opinion of the government, no government can subsist; for it is very necessary for all governments that the people should have a good opinion of it.

And in 1804 Lord Ellenborough said:

> If publication be calculated to alienate the affections of the people, by bringing the government into disrepute, whether the expedient be by ridicule or obloquy . . . it is a crime.

Such sweeping definitions of sedition conflict with what many people have long regarded as normal political activity. Twentieth century judges have generally held that merely promoting class hostility is not sedition. In 1947 Mr Justice Birkett took the view that "Sedition has always had implicit in the word, public disorder, tumult, insurrection or matters of that kind." On the other hand, Mr Justice Rigby Swift in 1925 interpreted sedition in a way that could include both violent and peaceful attempts at change. Summing up at the trial of Communist leaders, he said the defendants should be found guilty if their *"language* tended to subvert the Government and the laws of the Empire".

   The lack of any recent prosecutions for sedition is no guarantee for the future, however. The conviction of Gay News for blasphemy in 1977 shows how easily archaic laws can be revived. (The paper published a poem which described a Roman centurion's devotion to Christ in sexual terms.) Moreover, in both blasphemous and seditious libel there is a double danger for newspapers. The protection of privilege afforded in ordinary libel does not apply. So a newspaper which reported seditious remarks made at a trial, for example, could be in deep trouble. The standard textbook on newspaper law warns:

> It must be stressed that there are no circumstances in which publication of such matter can be justified in law. There is no defence available of either absolute or qualified privilege; nor can it be pleaded that the matter consisted of a fair and accurate report of what was said at a public meeting or court hearing . . . The reporting, as much as the utterance of the words complained of constitutes an offence — *and a greater offence,* since the newspaper reaches a much larger audience. All this is quite clear and definite.[4]

Nowadays, radical or even revolutionary opinions can usually be expressed in print with complete safety. They are tolerated, probably not so much out of a belief in free expression as out of a realisation that they pose no threat. They may even act as a safety valve, allowing a few people to let off steam in a harmless way. They can be tolerated because there is no risk of them reaching — or influencing — a substantial section of the community. However, in extreme situations (in wartime, for example) that tolerance can wear thin. But for the most part Governments' main concern is with what people *know* rather than what they *think.* How much shall the public be told? — that is the main issue now. And it arises time and again as we see how the modern British state restricts its Press.

The period of censorship during the Second World War provides a revealing insight into Government attitudes towards the Press. It shows what sort of material Governments feel justified in censoring and what methods they would probably use in the future, if the need arose. Worldwide, censorship takes a variety of forms. It can, for instance, involve limiting supplies of newsprint or restricting access to printing facilities. There is also pre-censorship (submission of articles for approval before publication) and post-censorship (sanctions applied after publication — ranging from seizure of offending material to prosecution of publishers). Post-censorship may sound like slamming the door when it is too late — but that is deceptive. Of the two systems, post-censorship is probably the more efficient. It requires less bureaucracy to operate and, because editors are kept in fear and doubt about what is or is not permissible, they are likely to err on the side of safety. It can also be made to appear less dictatorial and may provoke less resistance.

In Britain the traditional weapon is a form of post-censorship — prosecution after publication. During the war this was backed up by pre-censorship which (for British newspapers) was voluntary and relied on editors' goodwill and co-operation; after all, the war was supposed to be about freedom. As an added safeguard, there were ways of making reluctant editors co-operate. In short, a minimum of force and a maximum of subtlety worked wonders.

Newspapers, like the public, were subject to Defence Regulation No. 3 which forbade them "obtaining, recording, communicating to any other person or publishing information which might be useful to an enemy". The meaning of this broad but vague prohibition was clarified by the wartime D-Notices which had been drawn up by Government departments without consultation with the Press and which — in the words of the Chief Press Censor — "covered nearly every conceivable human activity". The D-Notices listed matters which should not be mentioned without first seeking the advice of the censors. Whether to seek or heed that advice was left to the discretion of editors, but there was one great advantage in doing so: Approval by the censors guaranteed immunity from prosection under Defence Regulation No. 3 (though not, incidentally, from prosecution under other Defence Regulations or Acts of Parliament). In addition, memos and instructions were sent to the Press as the need arose. The simplest way was to send notes on the Press Association wire service, usually beginning: "Please make no mention of . . ." etc. However, these could not be protected from prying eyes so notes on more sensitive topics were sent by post, direct to editors, in envelopes marked "Private and Confidential". There were also "guidance" letters which were said to help newspapers avoid "misleading" their readers and sometimes suggested ways of handling the news. One reason for this guidance was that news which had already been published overseas could be published by the British Press without censorship. The problem was that stories from these sources did not always reflect the

British view. During preparations for the D-Day landings, Britain made a series of commando raids on installations on the French coast. The Germans gave the raids great publicity. A guidance letter was sent to editors explaining that small raids would take place from time to time and it was "not desirable to give the reports prominence".

The atmosphere of co-operation was enhanced by the working arrangements for journalists and censors. The Ministry of Information, which was responsible for censorship, had requisitioned one of the London University buildings in Bloomsbury. Journalists were provided with desks and telephones on the same floor as the censors. The major newspapers and agencies had a member of staff there permanently to submit stories and queries and to telephone amendments back to the office. The chief censor, Rear-Admiral George Thomson, in his memoirs stressed the value of this cosy relationship:

> The fact that they worked in adjacent rooms did a great deal to foster goodwill, co-operation and friendly relations between them, which developed to an ever increasing extent as the war went on. They got to know one another as friends . . .[5]

This "nice guys" approach was so effective that unpleasantness was generally avoided. But just to make sure, in 1940 a Scrutiny Section was set up to check every newspaper for breaches of the regulations. If any were found, editors received a warning letter — and normally wrote back apologising and promising not to let it happen again. Throughout the war, only four cases were tried in the courts at the instigation of the censors. Another sanction was to refuse export permits for papers going abroad. It was not effective for stopping particular offending issues, but it could be used afterwards to stop export of a paper permanently or for a period, as a punishment. It was used occasionally, on newspapers which "consistently misrepresented our war effort".[7] It was also used to help get a conviction where prosecution was intended, for — as Chief Censor Thomson explained — "no judge or magistrate would have been convinced of the seriousness of the offence had not all possible steps been taken to prevent the news getting to the knowledge of the enemy."

During the war, some 450,000 issues of newspapers and magazines were published and 600,000 articles submitted for censorship — an average of 1½ articles per issue. The real figure was higher, however, as censored agency copy was used by many newspapers. At first the censors were not sure what they were supposed to do and some erratic decisions were made that could only be reversed by reference to a very high authority. So in 1940 guidelines were laid down. The first was that censors could ban only information that would aid the enemy in its military effort ("military" being interpreted in its broadest sense). The second was that only facts could be censored — not opinions, comments or speculation.

Among information useful to the enemy was the weather. Headlines like: PHEW WHAT A SCORCHER! were definitely out. Forecasts were banned and actual weather could not be reported until ten days had elapsed. Cancellation of sports fixtures could be reported, but not the reason — though the Germans must have guessed the reason was usually bad weather. When the Germans occupied France, it was pointed out that they could see the English weather across the Channel. The rule was relaxed and the weather in the Straits of Dover could be reported — hence the line in the wartime song about "blues skies over the white cliffs of Dover".

In the case of "undesirable" articles which the censors had no power to change, editors were supplied with a comment from the Foreign Office which they could either heed or ignore.

In keeping with their liberal image, the censors usually kept their hands clean when dirty work was done. The Daily Worker was suppressed in 1941 by Home Secretary Herbert Morrison — though Chief Censor Thomson had found the paper entirely co-operative. Morrison said the Daily Worker had not actually undermined morale, but he feared that it might. A year later, the Daily Mirror was threatened with suspension. The official reason was a cartoon showing a seaman clinging to a raft after his ship had been torpedoed — there were heavy losses at the time — and a bitter caption saying: "The price of petrol has been increased by a penny". There is little doubt this was just an excuse. The real reason was that the Mirror had been attacking the Army administration as out of date.

Most of the resistance to censorship came from overseas journalists based in Britain. Because the Government had no jurisdiction over their papers, all copy leaving this country was vetted. Americans particularly resented this because their own censorship rules were more lax. One American journalist ended a report on the bombing of Birmingham (which he was not allowed to name) with this clue: "I know what the citizens of my home town, way back in Alabama's greatest city, would say about it". That ruse was spotted. But the censors were shocked to find a banned report published in the New York Times saying the cruiser Belfast had been attacked in the Firth of Forth. A check on the reporter's telegrams revealed seven short notes to his office. Taking the last word of each, the message read: "Submarines entered Forth. Attacked. Damaged Belfast. Escaped."

The Official Secrets Acts

The Official Secrets Acts are, on the face of it, concerned with spies. And yet they are a real menace to Press freedom, for their scope is far wider than many people imagine. Their awesome threat is largely responsible for the aura of secrecy that surrounds most government activity, even in matters not remotely connected with national defence; for the widespread reluctance of officials to provide information the public might reasonably want; and for the extreme wariness of the Press in tackling subjects that might otherwise be news.

The first Official Secrets Act in 1889 dealt with people who passed on state secrets. Unaccountably, it imposed no penalties on anyone who received them — which made it very difficult to deal with foreign spies. The 1911 Act, rushed through Parliament during a bout of spy fever in the run-up to the First World War, blocked that loophole and did more besides.

An official secret need have no military connection, need be of no interest to a foreign power, need have no importance, need not even be particularly secret — just as long as it is official information. Anyone holding an office under the Crown, whether a soldier, sailor, Cabinet Minister, Social Security official, policeman or postman, could be prosecuted for telling anyone else anything they have found out in the course of their work, unless they have been specifically authorised to talk about it. (This also applies to former office-holders, no matter how long ago they left, and to employees of any company that has a contract with any Government department.) Equally, it could be an offence for a journalist to get — or try to get — information about river pollution, safety checks, equipment costs, prison conditions or the amount of tea drunk at the Foreign Office. In an actual case in 1937 the Official Secret involved was the fact that Southport police had issued a warrant for the arrest of Mr Tansley Munnings, whom they suspected of swindling someone out of £5.

In 1958, two Oxford students were jailed for an article in Isis based on their National Service experiences. They wrote that in order to get information about Russian military activities, the British forces often behaved in a way that was dangerous to peace and sometimes contrary to international law. It was clearly in the public interest that this should be known — but public interest is no defence in Official Secrets cases. It might appear that since the 1911 Act prohibits activities damaging to the "safety or interests of the state", actions which are in the public interest cannot be against the law. But "interests of the state" means government policies rather than the general well-being of the public. This was made clear by the Law Lords in 1962 when they dismissed the appeals of members of the anti-nuclear Committee of 100 who had been jailed under the Act. The group had planned a sit-in at an RAF base that would have prevented the landing and take-off of planes for several hours. In court, they attempted to call expert witnesses to show that their ultimate aim — nuclear disarmament — was a good idea and therefore could not be against the interests of the state. The judge ruled this evidence inadmissible and they were convicted. They appealed and the Lords ruled that the "state" meant "the organised community" or "the organs of government" and that "interests" mean interests according to the policies of the state as they actually were, and not as people might think they should be.[6]

In another case, Mr Edgar Lansbury was fined £20 for publishing two secret documents in a book about his father, George Lansbury, the Labour politician. One document was a speech his father had made to the Cabinet while First Commissioner of Works. The other was a memo he had written about unemployment.

In 1956, a newspaper began to serialise the memoirs of Albert Pierrepoint, the former public hangman. The series stopped after the first article when the Home Office warned that if the paper published information Mr Pierrepoint had got in his official capacity, he would be prosecuted under the Official Secrets Act. It was no idle threat: Thirty years earlier, a retired prisoner governor had been fined for writing a newspaper account of the last days of several murderers.

Military information which is so old that it is of no conceivable value to an enemy can still be an official secret, as Sotheby's, the London auctioneers discovered in 1935. They planned to sell letters written by Lord Nelson and the Duke of Wellington to the British Ambassador in Paris between 1800 and 1830. The government said they contained secrets and stopped the sale.

The danger for journalists lies not only in publishing "secrets" but also in obtaining, or trying to obtain, information. Even a highly "responsible" newspaper which decides against publishing commits an offence unless it can show it was given unauthorised information against its will. A reporter was once prosecuted for making inquiries about a notorious prisoner due for release. He went to a club and got into conversation with a prison officer. Fortunately the reporter had identified himself as a journalist and did not persist when the prison officer said he could not help. The case was dismissed because there was not sufficient evidence of an attempt to persuade the officer to pass on state secrets. But if the reporter had failed to identify himself or had persisted in his questioning, he would probably have been convicted.[7]

The 1911 Official Secrets Act may not have been intended to hamper the Press. But once its usefulness in this area was discovered, governments were reluctant to abandon it. And when it was amended in 1920, its scope was widened still further. In May 1919, the Daily Herald published a secret War Office document ordering commanding officers to find out whether their men would help to break strikes, whether they would volunteer to fight in Russia, and whether trade unionism was growing among the ranks. The Government threatened to prosecute the Herald and the paper replied by publishing another War Office order, this time instructing army officers to intercept copies of the Herald at railway stations and burn them "with as little publicity as possible" so that they would not reach the troops. The Herald got away with it because this sort of action was not covered by the 1911 Act. Significantly, when the Act was amended the following year, a section dealing with the unauthorised *retention* of official documents was included.

The two most recent non-spy prosecutions seem to have arisen from a belief that official blundering and even wrongdoing should be kept secret. In 1970, the Sunday Telegraph published extracts from a British diplomat's appraisal of the Nigerian civil war (which, by coincidence, ended the next day). Britain had supported the federal side during the war. The document revealed incompetence in the federal forces and said that the British government had supplied more arms than had been disclosed. The Sunday Telegraph's editor, the journalist who got the story and a link man were all prosecuted — and acquitted. The reasons for the prosecution were never made clear. Some suspected that the Government was embarrassed because the report cast doubt on the truthfulness of ministerial statements. Others hinted at a political motive — a Labour Government seeking revenge on a Tory newspaper.[8]

In 1978 two journalists, Duncan Campbell and Crispin Aubrey, and an ex-soldier, John Berry, faced a host of official secrets charges. The journalists had been compiling and publishing information on Signals Intelligence, which monitors foreign communications including commercial, private and diplomatic messages, contrary to international agreements. Hardly any of the information involved in the case could be construed as a secret in the ordinary sense; much of it was available from published sources. At one point in the trial the prosecution argued that the crime lay in assembling these pieces of information to obtain an overall picture. The journalists had been arrested after interviewing John Berry, who once served in a signals regiment. Berry apparently told them little that they did not already know. Nor, apparently, did he pass on any information likely to be useful to an enemy. On leaving the army, Berry had been told he must not visit a Communist country for five years; after that he was free to do so because anything he knew would by then be out of date. When the two journalists interviewed Berry, he had been out of the army for seven years.[9]

The trial ended with conditional discharges for the journalists and a suspended prison sentence for the ex-soldier, and renewed pressure for reform of the Official Secrets Acts. That has not come about, although in view of the outcry that the Aubrey/Berry/Campbell case provoked, the Director of Public Prosecutions will probably think twice before embarking on any similar case in future. Even so, what mainly concerns journalists is not the likelihood or otherwise of prosecution but the atmosphere of secrecy engendered by the Acts. Since the ABC case, several MPs have tried to introduce a freedom of information law similar to that in the United States. So far they have not succeeded; open government is something politicians can believe in while the opposition and ignore when in power.

D-Notices

D-Notices sound mysterious and awesome. Even the name reveals nothing about them. And the fact that editors keep them filed away, unseen by ordinary journalists, adds to this aura. So it is hardly surprising that when almost any story touching on the activities of the state fails to get into print, people conclude: "They must have got a D-Notice."

In fact D-Notices are a lot less impressive than they sound. The "D" simply stands for "Defence". They carry no legal force whatever and have safely been ignored on several occasions. The system was established in 1912 to guide the Press away from the pitfalls of the new Official Secrets Act. It is run by a committee comprising newspaper editors and civil servants from ministries connected with defence. Before 1971 notices had been issued as and when necessary, but then they were consolidated into 12 general notices covering the main areas of defence concern. Thus it is no longer correct to speak of newspapers "getting a D-Notice"; there is a permanent set of notices, and editors who want more detailed guidance consult the committee's secretary.[10]

The titles of the notices give a fair indication of what they are about:

No 1: Defence Plans, Operational Capability and State of Readiness.
No 2: Classified Military Weapons, Weapons Systems and Equipment.
No 3: Royal Navy Warship Construction and Naval Equipment.
No 4: Aircraft and Aero Engines.
No 5: Nuclear Weapons and Equipment.
No 6: Photography.
No 7: Prisoners of War and Evaders.
No 8: National Defence — War Precautions and Civil Defence.
No 9: Radio and Radar Transmissions.
No 10: British Intelligence Services.
No 11: Cyphers and Communications.
No 12: Whereabouts of Mr and Mrs Vladimir Petrov.

(For anyone wondering why Mr and Mrs Petrov should merit their own personal D-Notice, the couple defected from the Soviet Union more than 20 years ago and settled in Australia. D-Notice 12 was issued at the request of the Australians and no other defectors have this privilege.)

As an example of what the notices say, D-Notice 10 begins by explaining the distinction between the Security Service (M15), which deals with threats to Britain from espionage, subversion and sabotage, and the Secret Service (MI6) which carries out espionage, subversion, etc, in foreign countries on Britain's behalf. The notice continues:

Attempts are made by foreign powers to plant stories in the British Press. A variation of this technique, which must be taken into account where the activities of foreign intelligence services are concerned, is the planting in an overseas newspaper or other publication of a piece of information about British Intelligence matters with an eye to stimulating the British Press not only to republish the story but also to expand on it. You are requested not to publish anything about:
(a) secret activities of the British intelligence or counter-intelligence ser-

vices undertaken inside or outside the UK for the purposes of national security;

(b) identities, whereabouts and tasks of persons of whatever status or rank who are or have been employed by either Service;

(c) addresses and telephone numbers used by either Service;

(d) organisational structures, communications networks, numerical strength, secret methods and training techniques of either Service;

(e) details of assistance given by the police forces in Security Service operations;

(f) details of the manner in which well-known intelligence methods (eg telephone tapping) are actually applied or of their targets and purposes where these concern national security. Reference in general terms to well-known intelligence methods is not precluded by this sub-paragraph;

(g) technical advances by the British Services in relation to their intelligence and counter-intelligence methods whether the basic methods are well-known or not.

You are also requested to use extreme discretion in reporting any apparent disclosures of information puublished abroad purporting to come from members or former employees of either Service. If you are in any doubt please consult the Secretary.

You are also requested not to elaborate on any information which may be published abroad about British intelligence. On all these limitations some relaxation may be possible: please consult the Secretary.

Although the system is voluntary, the pressure to comply can sometimes be overwhelming. When Granada Television made a documentary about the Official Secrets Acts, the D-Notice committee asked for the address and function of the Government Communications Headquarters at Cheltenham to be cut out because it was a breach of D-Notice 11, Granada refused, pointing out that the address was in Whitaker's Almanac and the GCHQ's function had been described in a book by a former employee of MI6. But then the Independent Broadcasting Authority, which monitors all TV and radio programmes and allocates ITV franchises heard about the row. It *ordered* Granada to cut the reference out. Newspapers, thankfully, do not have the IBA breathing down their necks. But there are pressures, all the same. Andrew Wilson, when he was defence correspondent of The Times, explained:

As a defence correspondent you could be denied all Ministry of Defence facilities, such as visits to military establishments, transport in service aircraft, and most important of all, off-the-record talks in Whitehall. Without these facilities most correspondents would find it extremely hard to do their job . . .

From time to time a correspondent must ask whether the system is being used to cover up facts which in his opinion the public should know. Examples could be a particular practice by a security organisation, or performance deficiencies in a weapon system for which Parliament is voting large sums of money. When that happens a good newspaperman will obey his conscience. He may then get away with it by a skilful use of words,

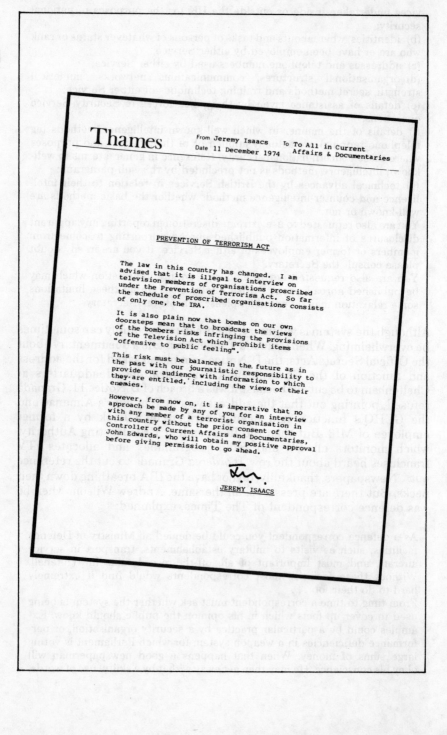

Thames

From Jeremy Isaacs   To To All in Current
Date 11 December 1974   Affairs & Documentaries

PREVENTION OF TERRORISM ACT

The law in this country has changed. I am
advised that it is illegal to interview on
television members of organisations proscribed
under the Prevention of Terrorism Act. So far
the schedule of proscribed organisations consists
of only one, the IRA.

It is also plain now that bombs on our own
doorsteps mean that to broadcast the views
of the bombers risks infringing the provisions
of the Television Act which prohibit items
"offensive to public feeling".

This risk must be balanced in the future as in
the past with our journalistic responsibility to
provide our audience with information to which
they are entitled, including the views of their
enemies.

However, from now on, it is imperative that no
approach be made by any of you for an interview
with any member of a terrorist organisation in
this country without the prior consent of the
Controller of Current Affairs and Documentaries,
John Edwards, who will obtain my positive approval
before giving permission to go ahead.

JEREMY ISAACS

or conceivably by passing the information to an overseas colleague not subject to D-Notices and reprinting the overseas man's story.

It is generally very difficult to know with complete certainty what constitutes a genuine security consideration . . . in these circumstances the D-Notice system has served authority fairly well.[11]

Whether abolition of the D-Notice system would make much difference is debateable. Probably an even more secretive, informal system would grow up in its place. D-Notices are controversial *because* they are formalised — there is something there that people can discuss. But informal pressures are applied continually, in all sorts of ways. Former Daily Herald editor Francis Williams recalled that shortly before the last war, several ministers "made contacts with newspaper proprietors at various times to persuade them that outspoken criticism of Hitler's policy or of the Nazi atrocities against the Jews would be against the national interest. Many of these approaches were, unfortunately, successful." Editors were apt "to find themselves involved in long arguments with their proprietors, who had just received the most confidential information from an important member of the Cabinet that such words just at this moment would do the gravest harm to negotiations then proceeding, as a result of which things would shortly take a turn for the better".[12]

Libel

The idea that the law of libel protects innocent individuals from an all-powerful Press is a myth. Libel operates to the advantage of a privileged elite more blatantly than some other branches of the law. It protects *only* the rich; you cannot get legal aid either to initiate or defend a libel action. For all practical purposes, ordinary people are outside the protection of the law. Newspaper editors are well aware of this. Hence, small-time villainy and the sexual antics of Joe Bloggs are the subject of "investigations" by the popular Sunday papers, rather than more socially-significant, and wealthy, targets.[13]

The law was framed to protect the Establishment from the pamphleteers and authors of broadsheets. It was intended to stop journalists getting out of hand — and it still does that today. It is probably the most important single obstacle to free expression in Britain. In the words of Cecil King, former chairman of the International Publishing Corporation, the law makes it difficult for any author or journalist to tell the truth.

Libel applies to defamatory words published or broadcast about a person (or certain corporate bodies like companies and local authorities). Judges have laid down various tests for defamation: Do the words expose the person to "hatred, ridicule or contempt"? Would they cause people to "shun or avoid" the person or lower the person "in the estimation of right-thinking members of society generally"? Statements of both fact and opinion can be defamatory.

Sometimes, however, such statements can legally be published. Court proceedings carry "absolute privilege" — that is, any fair and accurate report of the proceedings is absolutely immune from any libel action. This is why the Press waited for ex-model Norman Scott to blurt out his allegations of a relationship with Liberal leader Jeremy Thorpe in an unrelated court case before reporting him. (The allegations had, in fact, been the talk of Fleet Street for some time.) Lesser protection — "qualified privilege" — is available for reports of proceedings in Parliament, or other bodies listed in the Defamation Act 1952, eg local councils, tribunals of inquiry and professional associations. In these circumstances, newspapers have to show that publication was for the public benefit.

In other cases, there are two main defences to a libel action: Fair comment and justification. Fair comment can only be used to defend expressions of opinion. The defendant (publisher) must show that the matter is of public concern, that the facts on which the comment is based are true, and that the comment is an honest one. In justification the plaintiff (complainant) does not have to show that what was written was untrue. But if the defendant can prove that it was true, he has a complete defence. If the plaintiff complains about innuendo, the defendant must also prove the truth of the innuendo. An honest belief that what was published was true is not a good defence.

It is in providing this proof that problems arise, Cecil King wrote: "I would be inclined to say, in the course of my 45 years in Fleet Street, that most libels are true".[14] This was certainly the case in 1963, when John Profumo, the War Minister, received out-of-court damages from a British company for distributing copies of an Italian magazine which alleged he had an improper relationship with Miss Christine Keeler. Profumo later admitted the story was true and resigned from Parliament in what became the major political scandal of the 1960s.

In 1964, a report in the Daily Telegraph that the City of London police were investigating a company was found to be defamatory. One of the judges, Lord Reid, said: "The sting is in inferences drawn from the fact that it is the Fraud Squad which is making the inquiry". It made no difference that the story was true — there was such an investigation — or that the investigation was not inconsistent with the company's innocence. Apparently it was enough that the article implied there was a suspicion of guilt.

Some types of statement are notoriously difficult to prove. Generalisations like "pompous", "bigoted", "imcompetent", "bent" are especially dangerous. And it may be obvious that a person is drunk, but try proving it to a sober judge. In 1957, Morgan Phillips, Aneurin Bevan and Richard Crossman won damages from the Spectator for suggesting they had been drunk at a socialist conference in Venice (later referred to by their friends as "the Venetian blind"). This is why Private Eye now describes drunks as simply "tired and emotional" and newspapers call drunken driving cases "drinks-driving" cases. A person may have "more than the permitted level of alcohol" in their blood and — as far as libel is concerned — still be perfectly sober. For similar reasons the papers use the euphemism that a man is "helping the police with their inquiries" when he's probably doing the opposite. Statements that a company is badly managed, that a school has poor teachers, that a football team is inadequately trained or that an architect is responsible for a building falling down are also difficult to prove in court. For every witness called to support the story, the other side will find at least one to deny it.

An added difficulty is that the complainant gets the benefit of any doubt. Journalists are thus expected to be able to prove their stories in court while being denied any constitutional right to obtain the necessary information beforehand. For this reason, newspapers may choose to kill a story which they know to be true but which they cannot substantiate if challenged. Suppose, for example, information comes from an impeccable, highly trustworthy source, but the informant is worried that if he is identified he will lose his job and perhaps even be prosecuted. If it comes to a court case, he warns, "I shall have to deny it". To publish the story in a situation like that would — in Britain at least — be an enormous risk. And yet that was exactly how much of the American Watergate scandal became public — by the Washington Post taking the word of a senior official (nicknamed Deep Throat) whose identity could never be revealed.

It might be argued that if a newspaper made honest and reasonably exhaustive enquiries but then got a story wrong, a prominent apology and correction would be fair redress*. But the law would not agree. Libel is about money. In most civil cases the victim has to prove that he has suffered some damage or loss and compensation is assessed accordingly. Not so with libel. In the famous case of Youssoupoff v MGM (1934), the elderly Princess Irene Youssoupoff sued over a film called "Rasputin the Mad Monk", in which she was misrepresented as Rasputin's mistress during the final period of the Tsarist monarchy in Russia. She was awarded the then astronomical sum of £25,000. Upholding the decision, an Appeal Court judge observed: "No doubt the damages are very large for a lady who lives in Paris and who has not lost, so far as we know,. a single friend, and who has not been able to show that her reputation has in any way suffered . . ."

But the feelings of such "good and delicate" persons don't come cheap! So Randolph Churchill was entitled to £5,000 damages from the People, which had, rightly or wrongly, called him "a hack". There was no reason to suppose Churchill had suffered in any way. And, indeed, the

---

*Many states in the US allow papers to publish a retraction. A complainant may still go ahead and sue but he then has to prove that the paper behaved recklessly in publishing the libellous story.

defence was able to show that he himself had used the same expression referring to the editor of the Sunday Mirror.

In some cases, the courts openly *punish* the author of a libel — as well as compensating the victim. In Broome v Cassell and Co and Irving (1971) Captain Broome was blamed, in a book by David Irving, for the loss of the wartime convoy PQ17. Punitive damages of £25,000 for the outrageous and shocking behaviour of the author and publishers, in addition to £15,000 general damages, were awarded to Captain Broome.

It is the fantastic cost of the law, as much as its nature, which poses the real threat to small newspapers, and which makes libel such an intolerable restriction on free expression. The situation is so crazy it has even been recognised by elderly judges. In 1966, a case described by a judge as "an ordinary simple case of libel", took 15 days to try. "The costs must be enormous," said the judge. "Lawyers should be ashamed that they have allowed the law of defamation to have become bogged down in such a mass of technicalities that this should be possible."

When Clive Jenkins, General Secretary of ASTMS successfully sued Socialist Worker in 1977, the paper's bill for legal costs was more than double the damages. Jenkins and the union were awarded £3,100 damages. But the paper also had to find £2,400 for their own costs and £4,200 to meet the costs of the union. In 1981, when the "Moonie" sect lost a libel action against the Daily Mail, costs were estimated at £750,000.

The cost of the law alone is a powerful deterrent to unfettered journalism. In 1975, Charles Raw, a respected financial journalist, moved from the Observer to The Sunday Times. Soon after, The Sunday Times published several of his articles about the unsavoury activities of City whizz-kid Jim Slater and his colleagues. The allegations resulted in Slater being removed as head of the Slater Walker finance group and an attempt by the Singapore authorities to extradite him on criminal charges. Several years' research had gone into the articles — research done while Raw was working on the Observer. The reason The Sunday Times got the story was that the Observer were unwilling to publish the story — not because they doubted the truth of it, but because they could not afford the inevitable battle in the courts.

To make matters worse, powerful and unscrupulous people can use a libel writ specifically to prevent open discussion. Another of Charles Raw's articles in The Sunday Times appeared in November 1975, headed: "What Slater-Walker did with Mr Heath's money". It suggested that the former Tory Prime Minister had benefited, perhaps unknowingly, from the wheeling and dealing. Mr Heath had failed to get an injunction to prevent publication, but immediately afterwards he issued a writ for libel. This had two consequences. Most important, it stopped the story being taken up by others, including the popular Press and television. And, secondly, it implied that the article had done Edward Heath an injustice. This was not, apparently, the case. Heath never pursued his writ. A year later, when the story was cold, he quietly dropped the action.

Private Eye editor Richard Ingrams has shown how libel writs are used to blackmail his magazine. One complainant told the Eye that he would drop his action if the confidential source of their information was revealed. The proprietor of the Spectator agreed to withdraw his writ on condition that Private Eye published no more about the Spectator without the written approval of the editor. The New Statesman made a similar demand.

One of the consequences of all this is plain to see: An enfeebled established Press. "The attitude of most newspapers," writes Cecil King, "is that muck-raking is not worthwhile and that if the great British public do not want a watchdog they needn't have one."

Contempt

The law of contempt is designed to ensure that people show due respect for the courts and judiciary, even when they don't deserve it. Insulting a judge is as bad as insulting the monarch. Thus, when a man raised two fingers at a bewigged judge in the street a few years ago, he was put on trial for contempt. The man explained that he had mistaken the judge for the mayor, and was acquitted.

Contempt cases are tried by judges alone, without juries, and there are no fixed penalties. Fines sometimes run to four or even five figures and offenders can be imprisoned indefinitely, to be released only when they have "purged" their contempt (for example, by apologising and giving very firm assurances that it will not happen again).

The law covers any interference with the administration of justice, from disobeying a court order to attempting to influence a jury. As far as newspapers are concerned, it includes publishing anything which might prejudice a fair trial. One obvious instance would be a report saying that someone standing trial was a well-known criminal, since an accused person is presumed innocent until found guilty. At that level there is little to quibble about. Newspapers are well aware of the rules and usually do their best to avoid prejudicing trials. There are exceptions, especially when a crime attracts massive publicity before an arrest is made. (The Press treatment in 1981 of Peter Sutcliffe, arrested initially on a charge of stealing a car number plate, is a case in point.)

There are, therefore, good reasons why the Press should exercise some (temporary) restraint in the interests of justice. But there are also occasions when the law imposes unreasonable or unnecessary restrictions on press freedom. There are other times, too, when conflicting interests of justice and free expression are difficult to resolve. A few examples illustrate the problems that can arise:

1. One of the first things journalists learn is to protect their sources of information. Without that confidentiality many important stories would never come to light. Occasionally such stories result in a court case or a tribunal hearing and journalists may be summoned to give evidence.

They may be asked to disclose their sources and if they refuse — like any witness who refuses to testify — they may be jailed for contempt. It happened to two journalists in 1963 when they refused to name their sources to a tribunal investigating the background to the Vassall spy case. It almost happened again in 1980 when an embarrassed British Steel Corporation tried to force Granada Television to reveal the source of leaked documents quoted in a World in Action programme.

2. Once legal proceedings have started, a case is *sub judice* — which means public discussion relating to the case is forbidden. In civil cases, proceedings can drag on for years, especially where big companies are involved. Sometimes an individual court case may be merely incidental to a much wider issue, and yet Press comment is stifled. This is what happened with The Sunday Times' campaign over the drug Thalidomide (which caused horrible deformities in babies). Years after the drug had been withdrawn from use and when its victims were well into their teens, many claims for damages were still being pursued against the company which made the drug. The House of Lords upheld an injunction banning a Sunday Times article on Thalidomide on the grounds that it judged issues before they had been heard by a court. In 1978 The Sunday Times took the case to the European Court, claiming that the ban infringed its right to freedom of expression under the European Convention of Human Rights. It argued that the right to a fair trial (also guaranteed by the European Convention) would not be infringed because the article would not undermine the authority and impartiality of the judiciary. The Sunday Times won, but only after a long and very expensive battle that many smaller papers would not have been able to afford.[15]

3. The *sub judice* rule is open to abuse in that people sometimes start court proceedings simply to delay or prevent Press comment. Contempt also applies to Tribunals of Inquiry set up by Parliament — like the inquiry into the Aberfan disaster. This leaves open the temptation for governments to de-fuse a public outcry by appointing a tribunal which will deliberate for months and restrict discussion until after the initial fuss has died down. It is one of the reasons why people have suggested that if Richard Nixon had been president of Britain instead of the United States he could have kept the Watergate scandal hushed up for years by "inquiries" and minor court cases.

4. Witnesses sometimes give evidence anonymously and the court orders the Press not to identify them. This is necessary in blackmail cases, for example, otherwise witnesses would be reluctant to come forward. In the Aubrey/Berry/Campbell secrets case described earlier, the procedure was used for a different purpose. One witness was referred to as "Colonel B", although his job appointment had been published in the Royal Signals Association's magazine, The Wire, which was available in public libraries. He was also listed in the London telephone directory under his real name, H A Johnstone. There had clearly been no attempt to keep his identity secret for security reasons before the trial, and the

efforts to do so in court looked like a deliberate attempt to create a sinister atmosphere that would influence the outcome of the case.

Johnstone's name was published in the Leveller and Peace News and later in the National Union of Journalists' newspaper, The Journalist. All three papers were warned that they would be prosecuted for contempt. This provoked an angry reaction and soon Colonel H A Johnstone was cropping up everywhere. He was paged in London hotels and his name was slipped into a discussion on Capital Radio and into several motions for the NUJ's conference at Whitley Bay (where it also appeared scrawled in six-foot letters in the sand). Then four MPs named Johnstone in the Commons, where parliamentary privilege gave them immunity from prosecution. The Director of Public Prosecutions warned the Press not to report what had been said — and that dragged almost the whole of Fleet Street into the act. Most papers resented what they saw as the DPP's interference in their right to report parliamentary business and they decided to publish. One paper did so with a massive headline: "JOHNSTONE — THE NAME ONLY MPs MAY SAY".

The prosecution of the original three papers to name Johnstone went ahead, however. In their defence, they argued that the court had never made a specific order banning publication — a fact confirmed by the clerk of the court. All three were found guilty of contempt and were fined a total of £1,200. Many months later, the House of Lords overturned the decision and the fines were refunded, together with the legal costs.

5. When a court case ends, discussion becomes permissible. But criticism of the judge may nevertheless be contempt. In 1928, following an unsuccessful libel action by Dr Marie Stopes, the New Statesman said: "An individual owning such views as those of Dr Stopes [on birth control] cannot apparently hope for a fair hearing in a court presided over by Mr Justice Avory". The Statesman was found guilty of contempt and the fact that its comment was almost certainly true was considered irrelevant. In 1967, after demonstrators at the Greek Embassy were given unusually heavy sentences, the Guardian wrote: "If the sentences are not reduced on appeal . . . there ought to be more demonstrations." No action was taken against the Guardian but the Lord Chief Justice, Lord Parker, said the paper's comment went "well beyond the limit of responsible comment". This leaves editors with the tricky task of deciding what is "responsible" and what is "irresponsible" without any further guidance from the law.

6. There is also contempt of Parliament. The offence is exceptionally vague; it means virtually anything Parliament wants it to mean. Truth is no defence and there is no right of appeal, but the range of punishments is most interesting. For an actual case, see Chapter Nine.

NOTES

1. For discussion of advertising pressures, see James Curran (ed): The British Press — A Manifesto. Macmillan, 1978.
2. Stanley Harrison: Poor Men's Guardians. Lawrence & Wishart, 1974.
3. Paul O'Higgins: Censorship in Britain. Nelson, 1972.
4. L C J McNae/R M Taylor: Essential Law for Journalists (5th edition). Staples Press, 1972.
5. G P Thomson: Blue Pencil Admiral. Sampson, Low, Marston, 1947.
6. For other examples see O'Higgins: *op. cit.*
7. McNae/Taylor: *op. cit.*
8. O'Higgins: *op. cit.*
9. For the background to the trial, see Crispin Aubrey: Who's Watching You? Penguin, 1981.
10. Peace News, 16 June, 1978. Also David Leigh: The Frontiers of Secrecy. Junction Books, 1980.
11. O'Higgins: *op. cit.*
12. Quoted in Stanley Harrison: *op. cit.*
13. Libel — the Paper Tiger. Liverpool Free Press pamphlet, 1978.
14. M Rubinstein (ed): Wicked, Wicked Libels. 1972.
15. For Lord Hailsham's views on contempt and the Thalidomide case, see The Sunday Times, 1 February, 1981.

Note: As this book went to press, a Contempt Bill was passing through Parliament, partly as a result of The Sunday Times' Thalidomide case. Amendments to the Bill were still being discussed so it is too early to say what the effect will be — though it is unlikely that there will be any far-reaching relaxation of the law.

5. Read all about it — if you can

IN BRITAIN, except in wartime, formal state control of the Press is no longer necessary. There is, however, another form of censorship which is less obtrusive, more readily accepted and just as effective — economic control. This gives the appearance of freedom by allowing "undesirable" material to be published, whilst ensuring that it reaches only a small section of the public. And unlike blanket censorship, it is no threat to the established Press (indeed, they benefit from it). So it remains uncontroversial. Most discussion of Press freedom is about the *existing* Press: Constraints on existing newspapers, pressures on journalists, access by the public, and so on. But the issue stretches far beyond this. If there were a truly free Press it would be possible for anyone with the inclination and a modest amount of money to set up a newspaper or even a radio station and be heard by any fellow-citizens who cared to listen. In practice that does not happen, and this chapter explains why.

The 19th century saw the development of a Press which was capitalist, not only in its political stance, but also in its own structure. And with this came a dramatic change in the economics of publishing.

In the early years of the century, the capital needed to start a newspaper was comparatively small. The Northern Star, for example, began in 1837 with just £90.[1] In addition, the limitations of printing presses held down circulations and prevented a single paper, or a handful of papers, dominating the market. These two factors ensured the birth and (for a time) the survival of multitudes of small papers and allowed greater access for would-be publishers and greater diversity in the opinions that were heard. Of course, small circulations did make the price of papers relatively high. But readers could overcome that difficulty by buying copies jointly. According to one estimate at the time, each copy of the London papers was read by 30 people on average, and provincial papers by between eight and 30.[2] Also, as we saw in Chapter Four, radical papers often had the advantage of being cheaper than others because they broke the law and refused to pay the "tax on knowledge". In 1835 — a year before the first big reduction in stamp duty —The Times was selling 7,353 copies and the Morning Chronicle 5,490.[3] At the time, the economics of publishing were such that circulations as small as that could be profitable. The publishers of the radical Charter, for instance, calculated their profit on 6,000 copies at

£20 a week (though in the event they made a loss, mainly because of excessive payments for poor articles, and the paper closed after 18 months in 1840). But even then, changes were beginning. Improved machinery brought some of the biggest rises in costs since printing began. In 1834, Henry Hetherington, a radical publisher, bought a new press capable of 2,500 sides an hour. It cost him 350 guineas. Previously he had used two £30 presses. Improved machinery made huge circulations not only possible, but also necessary in order to cover costs. And to achieve the rises in sales needed, newspapers cut their selling prices — which increased the need for higher circulations still further.

The first big spurt in the growth of national dailies followed the abolition of stamp duty. The Daily Telegraph, born in 1853, cost two pence — half the price which had prevailed since 1836. Two years later its price went down to a penny and circulation rose rapidly to 27,000, half that of The Times. By 1870, the Telegraph's circulation had reached 200,000 — the biggest in the world. Such an enormous daily sale would have been unthinkable only 20 years earlier. How had it been achieved? Undoubtedly the abolition of stamp duty was important, as was the development of railways, which made distribution swifter and easier. But there was also a crucial innovation in printing: Stereotyping. Developments in printing before the 1850s had increased the speed of presses. Despite this, daily print runs of hundreds of thousands or even millions were still out of the question. Circulation was limited by the speed of a single press. The logical answer was to use more than one press, but that meant having more than one set of type for each page — and the only way to do that would have been to set type for each article several times and laboriously make up several identical pages (which would have increased overheads so enormously that the advantages of printing more copies were almost wiped out). These technical limitations help explain the early success of Sunday papers and other weeklies. The Weekly Dispatch, for example, was selling 30,000 copies at 8½d as early as 1836, and 66,000 at 6d by 1842 — far more than any daily paper. Certainly lurid reporting helped sell the weeklies, but they were also fortunate in being able to meet the demand; weekly schedules allowed more time for printing and meant they were less hampered by slow presses than were daily papers.

In the 1850s, stereotyping neatly overcame the problem pf slow presses. Its importance in the history of newspapers is often overlooked, possibly because its advent coincided with the lifting of the "tax on knowledge". And yet the boost to sales of pro-establishment papers provided by the abolition of stamp duty could never have been fully exploited without stereotyping. In essence, the process is very simple. Once a page of type is complete, a mould is made, from which any number of identical pages of type can be cast. The result was that for the first time newspapers could print as many copies as they wished, as quickly as they wished. They were no longer restricted by the speed of a single press; they could run any number of presses simultaneously, all printing the same newspaper. The system proved so successful that it is still used by all the national papers today.

Stereotyping also made edition changes easier. Without stereotyping, it was necessary to stop the press and take out a page of type to make the change. With stereotyping, because the original type is used only for moulding, not for printing, presses can be kept running while alterations are prepared. Then new moulds are made and only a brief stop is needed for the new casts to be fitted to the presses. This enabled national papers to gain sales at the expense of provincial papers by printing editions of particular interest to specific regions. In the same way, advertisements were also editionised. By 1867, the Daily Telegraph was casting up to 96 stereo plates a night.

The development of the popular dailies came at the turn of the century with the so-called Northcliffe revolution. It is often said that the 1870 Education Act prepared the way for this by increasing literacy. But Raymond Williams, a leading Press historian, says this is an error, the result of people looking at the daily papers alone rather than at the Press as a whole — particularly the popular Sunday papers which arrived much earlier. Williams maintains:

> At any time in the 19th century there were more than enough people able to read, to sustain the modern circulation of the Daily Mirror. It was never a case of waiting for literacy.[4]

During the 19th century, newspaper advertising had almost always been of the small, classified kind — though by the later years of the century it was making an important contribution to newspapers' income. More than half the revenue of many papers came from advertising. In 1886, 60 per cent of the Daily Telegraph's space was devoted to advertising, and 49 per cent of that in The Times.[5] Northcliffe pioneered the use of large display advertisements. His Daily Mail, founded in 1896, reached a circulation of a million during the Boer War. It was sold for a halfpenny — well below cost price — with the deliberate aim of building up a market for advertising. An ex-editor of the Daily Herald later recalled:

> The Daily Mail looked for profits even more from advertising than from sales. The slogan "A Penny Newspaper For One Half-Penny" was not just a slogan, it was a statement of economic intent. A method of selling advertising space was employed that has since come to dominate the industry. This was the net sales certificates, the regular issue of a chartered accountant's certificate of circulation on which advertising rates were based at a charge of so much per column inch per thousand readers.[5]

Northcliffe transformed newspaper economics and set the pattern which has continued ever since. A typical national newspaper today depends on advertisers for at least half its income. In some cases, the dependence is much greater. The Financial Times, for example, calculated in 1977 that the real cost of the paper — then selling for 12p — was more than 50p.[6]

Northcliffe's papers were a perfect vehicle for advertisers at the time. Aimed at the lower-middle class, they encouraged readers to sample the delights of new consumer goods and to improve their social standing by buying the things advertisers wanted to sell. In contrast, newspapers which urged readers to improve their lot through trade unions and collective struggle ran into difficulties. Their readers lacked either the money or the inclination to rush out and spend — a fact advertisers were quick to recognise. The left-wing Daily Herald highlighted the problem of trying to compete with the Press barons when, in 1920, scarcity of advertising forced its price up to twopence — twice the price of other similar-sized dailies. In an article headed: SLAUGHTER-HOUSE JOURNALISM, it said the Herald could "dare" to charge more because it had reader's support. It said other papers could afford heavy losses because

> they knew that they would be the residuary legatees. What is a drain on them is, they hope, death to others. They can look forward to the time when they will have something like a monopoly of the market. Then they will be able to take it out of the advertisers and of the readers.[7]

The misfortune of the Herald was that the readers who vaued the paper most, and who were being asked to help pay for its independence, were the very people who could least afford to pay.

Heavy dependence on advertising means, in effect, that the success or failure of newspapers is no longer a matter of reader's choice. The national papers that have been forced to close — the Daily Herald, News Chronicle, Daily Sketch and the radical Sunday, Reynold's News — all had substantial circulations, typically between one and two millions, when they closed. So nobody can say they were not wanted by readers.[8] And yet the notion that readers are the main arbiters of a newspaper's fate persists, even in respected text-books on journalism. One says:

> The policy of the Daily Telegraph, its selection and opinion of the news it reports is decided by the editor and his senior colleagues. But there is a regulatory force which keeps the paper's policy from straying too widely or suddenly from pre-ordained paths; and that force is not the proprietor but the readers. They chose the paper for qualities they expect to see continued. The Press is thus predominantly conservative in tone because its readers are. If any substantial number of people seriously wanted the structure of society rebuilt from the bottom, the Morning Star would sell more copies than it does.[9]

The small circulation of the Morning Star (about 40,000, according to the publishers) is very convenient to this sort of argument, and is often cited as proof that readers can be relied upon to make a sensible choice. On closer scrutiny, however, it is less convincing. Politics apart, the readers' choice is largely made for them. The Daily Telegraph can be found on any newsagent's counter; the Morning Star cannot. A few do display it but more often, if you want the Morning Star you have to order it. And for the average reader, the Morning Star is a highly inadequate newspaper. It costs more than most papers and has far fewer pages. Its staff is minute by Fleet Street standards, which inevitably means a poorer service to readers. Of necessity it relies heavily on the agencies which supply the other papers, and because of shortage of space often has to compress their reports more than the other papers. It can do little more than offer a slightly different perspective on the world and different political comment. With a few exceptions — such as its industrial reporting, it is in no position to offer a different type of *news.* It struggles on, kept alive by donations from the faithful. But it has never had the money to play the capitalists at their own game. The capital needed to join that game with a sporting chance now runs into many millions. Food tycoon Sir James Goldsmith was reportedly willing to spend up to £7 million in establishing his new magazine, Now! So if you want to break into publishing in a *big* way, it is not enough to be any ordinary millionaire — you have to be a multi-millionaire.

Fortunately, not everyone has been deterred by this. In the late 1960s, groups of non-millionaires began exploring an alternative way of publishing — by starting on a *small* scale. And their efforts brought a marked revival in radical journalism. It began with the psychedelic papers spawned by the hippie culture — Oz, International Times, and so on. The striking feature of these papers — apart from the unconventional design and content — was that most of the publishers had very little money, initially at least. One paper started at this time, the London magazine, Time Out, began with just £70. It still flourishes and its annual turnover today is around £2 million. Most of the other papers were not so lucky. They flowered briefly, then withered. But they did show that it was possible to get into print with only limited resources. The new papers that followed their example were often locally based, concerned with community politics and tending to focus on issues rather than promoting a specific party's cause. Others were circulated nationally, catering for particular interests or minorities — papers like Undercurrents (dealing with alternative technology), the feminist Spare Rib, Gay News, etc. Although the circulation of the papers that sprang up was small, the number of individual titles on sale by the mid-1970s was greater than for many years.

Ironically, starting radical papers had become easier for the same reason it had become difficult a century earlier: Because of changes in technology. Traditional (letterpress) printing uses metal type with the surface of letters raised above the non-printing areas. A roller coats the raised surfaces with ink, while the lower areas do not come into contact with the ink or the paper. This system, introduced by Gutenberg about 1440, was the basis of almost all newspaper printing in Britain until the 1960s. About that time a different process — litho — began to be widely used by newspapers, and the radical papers were among the first to take advantage of it. Litho printing removes the need for raised type. Instead, it uses flat plates of thin metal or plastic which have been chemically treated so that ink adheres only where it is needed. The principle was discovered by Alois Senefelder of Munich, about 1798, and the name litho comes from the Greek word *lithos,* meaning stone. Senefelder drew designs in wax crayon on flat, porous stones. The stones were then soaked in water. Because oil and water do not mix, oil-based ink simply ran off the areas that had absorbed moisture and stuck to the waxed areas. Except for certain specialised uses, the technique remained undeveloped until well into the present century when metal plates replaced stones and instead of using crayons, a way was found to transfer the image to be printed on to the plate photographically.

Litho has two big advantages for small papers: It can save money and it can be simple. The most labour-intensive part of newspaper printing is composing the type and making up the pages. In letterpress printing, this is skilled work and correspondingly expensive. But because litho printing does not use metal type, publishers can cut costs by doing some or all of the composing and make-up themselves. Any flat, black and white design that will photograph can be reproduced by litho, including drawings, handwriting and typewriting. Of course, there are more sophisticated methods. For a real "printed" appearance, there are special typewriters like Varitypers and IBM Composers which type on ordinary paper and produce results almost indistinguishable from letterpress type. More advanced still are photocomposers — machines which flash the images of letters on to photographic paper when the keys are pressed. The beauty of litho is the wide range of methods available, from the very simple to the complex, which means publishers can choose the level of technology most appropriate to themselves. Many small papers start life by using text typed in columns on an ordinary typewriter then pasted in position on the page. And the smallest papers are not alone in this. For years, the highly successful satirical magazine, Private Eye, used nothing more elaborate than an electric typewriter. Those papers which prefer "proper" type do not necessarily have to buy a machine. There are plenty of firms who do typesetting for publishers to make up their own pages. Machines can also be hired. Papers with their own machines do not need special premises as they would for the bulky linotype machines used for letterpress work. A Varityper or IBM Composer is portable and no bigger than an office typewriter. And, moreover, it is easy to operate. Unlike linotype machines, it has a standard typewriter keyboard, so with a little practice any typist can operate it. With printing presses the position is much the same — few small papers own them or even want to. Instead, they send their made-up pages to a commercial printer who photographs them, makes the plates and runs off the copies. The smaller papers are not printed on newspaper presses, but on machines designed for the needs of commerce and bureaucracy — for forms, stationery, advertising leaflets and so on. Although this often necessitates a smaller page size than most newspapers, the great benefit is that the machines are specifically intended to print small numbers of copies (from about 500 to a few thousand) very cheaply.

At that level, then, the capital needed to start publishing is minimal. All it takes is a little know-how and the money to pay the printer's first bill. After that, income from selling the papers will, with luck, pay for the printing of subsequent issues. For radical papers, lack of money can be a distinct advantage, certainly in the early stages. It means they need not worry unduly about libel; nobody bothers to sue a paper run by people who are broke because there is no money to be paid in damages. Printers, however, are held equally responsible for any libel that is published — and this can cause difficulties, though it is not an insuperable problem. Firms accustomed to printing office stationery are not familiar with the law of libel, and many of them do not even bother to read what they print. In any case, there are usually plenty of printers to choose from if one is reluctant to do the job. Some radical papers take steps to protect their printers from would-be litigants.[10] And there are even a few firms set up specially to print papers that are likely to be sued. These companies have no assets to be seized; the presses and other valuable machines that they use are owned by a separate company.

Getting a paper printed is one thing; getting it to the readers is quite another. It is at the distribution stage that the gap between freedom to publish in principle and in practice really opens wide. Anyone can publish whatever they like, but there is no certainty that large numbers of people will have the opportunity to read it.

Most newspapers and magazines are not delivered direct to the shops. They go first to wholesalers.[11] The purpose is to cut distribution costs by supplying a variety of titles to each newsagent at the same time. The disadvantage for radical papers is that they have no right of access to this distribution network. Wholesalers can — and often do — refuse to handle them. This would not be so bad if one refusal simply meant approaching a different wholesaler. But it does not work like that. Newspaper wholesaling in many areas is a monopoly. The two biggest firms, W H Smith and John Menzies, together with the smaller Surridge Dawson, control 57 per cent of newspaper distribution in England and Wales. In Scotland, Menzies alone controls 79 per cent of newspaper and 93 per cent of magazine distribution. Such is the power of these firms that in many towns they control the entire supply of newspaper and magazine reading. W H Smith has the monopoly in 43 towns, Menzies 21 and Surridge Dawson 20. Several other towns are controlled by smaller firms. In recent years, wholesalers have begun "rationalising" their trade. In the interests of efficiency, they divide up areas amongst themselves. Each withdraws behind an agreed boundary line while the others give him their trade within that territory. One area where this has been done is the West Midlands, which has been carved up by W H Smith and two local firms. So far, it has happened in only a few places but the practice seems likely to spread in the future. Thus rejection of a paper by wholesalers means, at best, that many shops will not stock it and, at worst, that copies will not be available at all in large parts of the country.

In contrast, some other European countries recognise the importance of effective distribution. In France, for example, any publication has the legal right to distribution under a state-sponsored scheme. And in Sweden publishers receive state subsidies to help their distribution.[12]

The reluctance of wholesalers to handle radical papers is due mainly to the law of libel. Wholesalers, like publishers and printers, can be sued. In the case of big papers there is no problem; they have the money if necessary to make up any loss suffered by wholesalers as the result of a libel action. Small papers can give no such guarantee and in their case a litigant may make a point of suing wholesalers if he knows he is unlikely to get much money from the paper itself. Nevertheless, a few "alternative" and Left papers are accepted by wholesalers. But they find there is a price for admission to the club — and the price usually is to have all their content approved by a lawyer. Whether the price is worth paying is a matter for argument.

Lawyers are, after all, concerned primarily with the law, not with publishing information. They are well aware that if they approve an article which later results in an action, their reputation will suffer and they may even be sued for giving wrong advice. So they err on the side of caution and are likely to block or change articles where there is a possibility of action, no matter how remote.

Wholesalers are not only concerned with libel. Sometimes they seem to regard themselves as arbiters of taste. W H Smith stopped handling Gay News after it published an article on paedophilia. In another incident, Surridge Dawson had made an agreement to handle three radical papers, The Leveller, Undercurrents and Camerawork. After two months Undercurrents ran an article on growing cannabis. Although growing cannabis is illegal, articles on the subject are not, and they have been published several times before without legal problems. Surridge Dawson did not like the article and refused to take any more of the magazines, including the two which had done nothing to offend. Presumably the logic behind actions like these is that if some customers are upset by what they read, it gives the wholesalers a bad name. And as radical papers are not a very lucrative part of their business, wholesalers can afford to be discriminating. On the other hand, there is little doubt that Britain's top-selling dailies also offend some people. But wholesalers do not cancel their orders for the Sun for fear of complaints about revealing pictures. It is probably a case of small papers being more trouble than they are worth and the big papers being well worth the trouble.

Papers which are unwilling to compromise must look for ways around the wholesalers' monopoly. For those published by political groups the task is relatively easy; their members sell papers at meetings and factory gates, and demonstrations and in the streets. And in the tradition of the Salvation Army and its War Cry, they hawk them around pubs. But most of the papers started in recent years are independent of such organisations and lacking a plentiful supply of free labour, must find other methods. During the flower-power boom of the late 1960s, a network of firms called distributors developed. Sometimes the distributors acted as go-betweens, delivering papers to any local wholesalers who were co-operative. Sometimes they delivered direct to shops — often to book, record and other shops outside the traditional newspaper and magazine business. This could be fairly effective. The satirical magazine Private Eye, for instance — which W H Smith still refuses to touch — achieved sales around 150,000 with the aid of a distribution company. The age of flower-power lasted only a few years, however. As the number of titles on sale declined, many of the distributors went bust or moved into porn. More recently, the Publications Distribution Co-operative[13] began to rebuild the distribution network. It has a similar role to the distributors of the 1960s, though with a more political commitment: It specialises in left publications. By 1979 it was distributing some 100 different periodicals and 500 books. As far as books, pamphlets and nationally-circulated papers are concerned, the service is invaluable. But the shops it supplies (bookshops rather than newsagents) are widely scattered throughout the country — so unfortunately it cannot benefit the many locally-based radical papers.

These papers usually have no alternative but to organise their own distribution — and that means supplying individual newsagents. Delivering 15 or 20 copies of a single paper to each shop is the most inefficient and time-consuming distribution method imaginable. It is not simply a matter of dumping papers on the counter. Unsold copies have to be collected, together with money for those that have been sold. If sales have been bad, newsagents have to be persuaded not to reduce their order or cancel it altogether. If sales have been good, they have to be encouraged to take more copies. In some shops, the proprietor forbids assistants to accept deliveries or pay out money. Because proprietors themselves usually take a long break in the middle of the day (they start work early and finish late) deliveries often have to be made at a particular time. The time when the proprietor is most likely to be in is when the shop is busiest — in early morning or late afternoon. There can be a long wait while customers are served. Outside, the roads are busy with people travelling to and from work and it takes ages to get from one shop to the next. Sometimes, in the suburbs, where shops tend to be further apart and sales of papers lower, it is scarcely worth the time and petrol needed to make the deliveries.

Newsagents insist that they do their best to provide what the public wants. In January 1979, after a year marked by industrial trouble in Fleet Street, the National Federation of Retail Newsagents placed this advertisement in national newspapers:

Okay. So you get mad when you can't get your favourite newspaper or magazine. But then — so do we! If your paper or magazine isn't available to us, *we* can't give you the kind of service you want. The kind of service that we're in business to provide. Last year, many newspapers simply didn't appear. Others were late into the shops. Some newsagents got supplied, while others — only a few hundred yards away — didn't receive any. This chaos really is not our fault. And we're tired of being blamed for other people's failings. Because if we want one thing, it's to see *all* our customers get the papers they want, on time, every day. This was impossible in 1978. Hopefully 1979 will be better. And if it isn't — please don't blame the newsagents. We're doing the best we can.[14]

The advertisement was referring, of course, to the big dailies and weeklies which are the mainstay of the business. Some newsagents had become so worried by their loss of income that they threatened to sue wholesalers for failing to supply their papers. But who ever heard of newsagents suing Smiths, for example, for refusing to supply Private Eye? When it comes to small or radical papers, the eagerness of newsagents suddenly evaporates. Only three months after the newsagents had been boasting of their willingness to meet readers' needs, the federation's general secretary wrote an article in Retail Newsagent warning his members that if they sold radical local papers like Nottingham Voice they risked being sued for libel.[15]

The experience of Liverpool Free Press, which for several years was the biggest-selling local alternative paper in Britain, highlights the problems. Out of several hundred newsagents in the city and surrounding areas, only about 80 regularly sold the Free Press. Of those who did, no more than two or three had actually asked for copies. Of the others who accepted it, most needed some persuasion, and only about one in ten showed real enthusiasm for selling it. Almost every newsagent in the city was at some stage invited to take copies. Some agreed to try it, but later gave up. The many who refused to take it at all gave a variety of reasons — some plausible, some patently absurd. A few claimed they could not sell it without the permission of the Newsagents' Federation. The commonest reason given was lack of space, coupled with the length of time it would take to sell the paper. The Free Press was published monthly (sometimes less often) and they felt counter space would be better used for fast-selling dailies and weeklies. Some clearly did not want the bother of selling a paper which would earn them only a few extra pence a month. Some refused because they disliked the politics of the paper — a reasonable excuse, though they seemed not to apply the same criterion to their regular "bread and butter" papers. Occasionally shops stopped selling the Free Press because of pressure from those who had been attacked in the paper.

A growing obstacle to direct distribution is the decline of independent newsagents. In cities, particularly, the traditional husband-and-wife businesses are fast disappearing. Many of them have been driven out — along with their customers — by slum clearance. On the new estates, newsagents' shops are often owned by large chains and run by managers who have little say in what they stock. When Liverpool Free Press wrote to one of these chains, offering to supply papers, this was the reply:

> Thank you for your letter. We have looked into the matter of retailing your paper through our outlets in the Liverpool and Kirkby area but regret that we are still unable to handle your publication. We circulated our managers requesting their views, but the unanimous opinion was that your publication could not add to the service they are already offering the local community.[16]

An added complication in Liverpool is that the largest chain of newsagents — Ricafeg — is owned by the Liverpool Daily Post and Echo, publishers of the city's two daily papers and a host of local weeklies. The Free Press regularly attacked the Post and Echo — and not surprisingly, Ricafeg shops were forbidden to sell it. One enterprising manageress did sell the paper secretly and got into trouble when her boss spotted copies in the shop. Other towns with similar publisher-owned chains include Birmingham, Wolverhampton, Bristol, Portsmouth, Peterborough and Bournemouth. Newspapers naturally regard them as a means of protecting their circulation against closures of independent newsagents. The danger is that they can equally be used to protect the same papers from attacks on their reputation by "alternative" papers or from attacks on their sales by well-heeled competitors.

The distribution barrier is probably the most important single reason why radical papers in Britain do not have the readership many of them deserve and which — in some countries — they would certainly get. However there is one very simple way the barrier might be overcome: By broadcasting. With radio and television there are no distribution problems. Anyone with a receiver can tune in. The scope is enormous. Unfortunately, the government realises that, too. Unlicensed broadcasters have the same rights that unlicensed printers had in the sixteenth century: None at all.

NOTES

1. John Williams: The Role of the Mass Media — A Discussion. Wedge No. 1. Summer 1977.
2. Stanley Harrison: *op. cit.*
3. *Ibid.*
4. Raymond Williams: Wedge No. 1. Summer, 1977.
5. Stanley Harrison: *op. cit.*
6. Advertisement in Liverpool Daily Post, 27 April, 1977.
7. Stanley Harrison: *op. cit.*
8. Raymond Williams: Wedge No. 1. Summer, 1977.
9. John Whale: *op. cit.*
10. Libel — the Paper Tiger. Liverpool Free Press, 1978. See also Night Lawyer: UK Press Gazette, 11 June, 1979.
11. Where Is the Other News? Minority Press Group, 1980.
12. The Other Secret Service. Minority Press Group, 1980.
13. In 1979, mainly for geographical reasons, PDC split into two separate co-operatives: Scottish & Northern Distribution based in Manchester and Edinburgh (for books and pamphlets) and PDC London (operating as Southern Distribution for books and pamphlets in the south and as Full Time Distribution for periodicals over the whole country).
14. Advertisement in News of the World, 28 January, 1979.
15. Retail Newsagent, 28 March, 1979.
16. Letter published in Liverpool Free Press, November, 1975.

6. News you're not supposed to know

LIVERPOOL, 1968. I started work at the Daily Post and Echo as a trainee reporter, checking on fires and traffic jams, getting rid of people with problems and phoning the airport every hour to find out the temperature.

It took only a few days to discover that stories, once written, were used again and again. The first job at the start of a shift was "conforms". The company's morning paper, the Daily Post, and the evening paper, the Echo, had separate editors but a shared reporting staff. A conform involved cutting out a story from one paper and re-wording the first paragraph for use in the other paper. This meant that a lot of the type — except the first paragraphs — could be used twice, once in each paper. Rewriting the first paragraph made the re-use of type less obvious to readers.

Reporters had to leave a carbon copy of everything they wrote in a special box. The box was emptied several times a day by a messenger from Radio Merseyside, the local BBC station. The copies were then read over the air in news bulletins. That was not the end of it: Radio Merseyside in turn passed some of them on to Manchester where they joined the rest of the BBC's news from the north of England. For this service, Post and Echo journalists got a couple of pounds bonus every month.

My first big assignment was the Great Billy Bottle Crusade. Billy Bottle was the creation of the Echo in collaboration with the boss of a local diary. Billy was personified in a drawing of a milk bottle with a smiling face. The dairy was hit by a shortage of bottles which was costing a lot in replacements. Judging by the files in the cuttings library, this bottle crisis — and the Echo's campaign that accompanied it — was a regular event. The aim was to persuade people to return milk bottles promptly and not to throw them away. I had to produce daily reports on the numbers of bottles returned, with human interest touches about schoolboys finding long-lost bottles, and so on. Naturally, the dairy placed plenty of large advertisements to go with the stories.

After a year moving around various departments, I settled down to complete my training, as a sub-editor. At first the work was new and I was learning a lot — which made it interesting. But gradually the way the news was managed became more apparent. Stories were altered or kept out for mysterious reasons.

For a start there was Sir Alick Jeans, who relished the triple title of Joint Chairman, Managing Director and Editor-in-Chief. Sir Alick was a minor Beaverbrook, a knight among the great Press barons, and one of a species that still survives in provincial newspapers. His family had been running newspapers in Liverpool for several generations. He did not only manage the company. As Editor-in-Chief he directed policy and regularly attended editorial conferences. He was aloof from party politics, but deeply conservative. He had only recently relented on a long-standing instruction forbidding all mention of planned strikes — for fear his papers would be thought to encourage them. He spent his holidays in Portugal — then run by the fascists. When the Portuguese leader, Dr Salazar died, the Daily Post attempted to describe him as a dictator. On the orders of Sir Alick, the word "benevolent" was inserted before "dictator". Obscure business friends of Sir Alick received long, glowing obituaries and weddings of their sons and daughters were celebrated with enormous photographs.

It was not always clear whether these things were done at Sir Alick's command or on the initiative of subordinates who aimed to please him. Once, in conversation, he told a senior member of staff he had seen a beautiful sunrise near his home. At dawn the next day a photographer waited in the rain for a sunrise that never came.

Liverpool, at this time, was gripped by the boomtown mentality that was the hallmark of the 1960s. And the Post and Echo revelled in it, expounding enthusiastically on plans for new office blocks, shopping centres and motorways. Even the most improbable ideas got an airing on the front page — like a scheme to hold the Olympic Games on a giant raft anchored in the Mersey. Every hint of a brighter tomorrow, no matter how slight, was dutifully recorded. Liverpool's International Airport ("international" because of the service to Dublin and a few package holiday flights) was a regular favourite. The airport was costing the council millions and it had been a dead duck from the start because of its proximity to the much larger airport at Manchester. But the arrival of any plane diverted to Liverpool from Manchester by bad weather was sure to make the news, usually with a headline like BOOST FOR AIRPORT.

In reality, the city was declining. The Beatles had gone and the heyday of Liverpool poets and artists was past, though a vague air of trendiness lingered on in some of the streets for a few years yet. The last of the great liners, the Empress of Canada and the Empress of England, sailed from the Pier Head, never to return. One by one the South Docks, with names out of history books — Canning, Albert, Salthouse, Wapping, Kings, Queens, Coburg, Brunswick, Toxteth and Herculaneum — once the livelihood of thousands, were falling into disrepair. The new Seaforth Container Terminal could do all their work. Huge cranes, controlled by one man, unloaded cargoes tons at a time. A brief stop on the quayside, then the sealed containers sped away by road and rail, their contents unseen, untouched by dockers' hands. New industries came and went almost as quickly. As a declining area, Merseyside was officially known as a Development Area. That meant there were generous government grants for firms setting up new factories. But there was nothing to ensure that the firms would stay after getting the grants. It was an opportunity any sharp businessman could spot a mile off: take the money and (after a decent interval) run.

And the people? Well, they were a problem. It was their fault, of course, for being where they weren't needed and for living in damp houses with rats and bad plumbing. The stubborn ones stayed but the council did help thousands, transporting them by corporation bus to the colonies of Netherley, Halewood, Kirkby, Runcorn or Skelmersdale. To nice new houses with garages to keep their bicycles in, to wide streets where they would not be obliged to speak to the neighbours or be visited by unwelcome relatives quite so often, where mothers could get plenty of healthy exercise going to the shops or develop a suntan waiting for a bus. Back in the City of Change and Challenge the old houses were knocked down. Acre upon acre stood empty, waiting for the second coming of the Industrial Revolution. Eventually grass grew and the council dug it up to plant official council grass.

A wise man at the university told viewers on BBC-2: "The person in Liverpool who has been defined as a problem might well look upon the planners as a problem. To him the planner is a problem, the police are a problem, the local politicians are a problem." But such thoughts were not the daily diet of Post and Echo readers. Jollity and cheerfulness radiated from their vallium-impregnated paper. One regular page in the Echo aimed at women actually carried the slogan: "The page that lifts you out of yourself". Feeling down in the dumps? Cheer yourself up with a new dress. Or how about this: a musical box disguised as a thatched cottage — just the thing to brighten a bare windowsill. Night after night, women were told how much easier their housework would be if only they bought this or that gadget; how enjoyable it is to go shopping. The message was simple: forget your problems, spending money will make you happy. It certainly made the advertisers happy and at Christmas the Echo merrily reported hearing "the jingle of cash registers" in the shops. But I wondered who really wanted to read the Echo's brand of candy-floss journalism and concluded that most people probably bought the paper for the racing results or place-the-ball contests.

One day all the Post and Echo journalists received an anonymous letter, duplicated in red ink, which urged us to do something about the quality of the papers. I agreed with the letter and wanted to know who had written it. Obviously it was someone at the Post and Echo, but who? The timing of the letter was odd, because no particular incident seemed to have sparked it off. I guessed this might give a clue to the writer's identity. All copies of the letter had been posted in Liverpool, which gave one person a perfect alibi. This was Rob Rohrer, another trainee, who was working in the London office at the time they were posted. He had prepared the letters before he went and got his wife in Liverpool to post them. My suspicions were confirmed later when I found something Rob had typed at home. It matched the typing on the letters.

During the next few weeks I got to know Rob better. He and another trainee, Chris Oxley, were working in their spare time for the Mersey People, a small paper published locally by the Labour Party and circulated in the Labour Clubs. There were predictable articles praising Labour councillors and MPs. But there was also some good hard reporting on local employers, notably the Dock Board, and on harassment by landlords. I was not very enthusiastic about the Labour Party side of the paper, but I helped with several issues.

We were discussing how to waken up the Post and Echo staff when we hit on the idea of a guerrilla newspaper, designed to embarrass the company whenever the need arose. It would chronicle acts of news suppression and manipulation, poke fun at the editors and management and introduce ideas on workers' control. We called it Pak-o-Lies. On the Dock Road was a co-operative workshop where a friend of ours, Derek Massey had a small litho press. He agreed to print it. The cost was not very great, so copies were given away free outside the Post and Echo building by friends who did not work there and who had been briefed to act dumb if anyone asked questions.

The first Pak-o-Lies, a single sheet of nasty yellow paper (yellow journalism, get it?), dealt mainly with the Post and Echo's undeclared financial interest behind its campaign to save the Inner Motorway project (see page 59). The second issue, two sheets of nasty yellow paper told how the Echo had given the Post Office a free advert in an effort to get striking postmen back to work early, and how a story exposing phoney money-off offers on Ajax cleaning powder had been "Ajaxed". There were also snippets showing the absurdity of what passed for news:

> Not long ago the Echo had its 91st birthday. With such great age, senility is not unexpected. And the latest act of buffoonery quite clearly demonstrated this. On Wednesday March 17 an immense area of the front page was devoted to a reverse block that trumpeted the anagram: "RIROLELNEVO-VOPET". Readers were invited yo turn to page 21 and told: "It's the Merseyside mixture for March 27 with Wembley as the prize." Turning inside, readers were told that the anagram stood for Liverpool and Everton. And that was that. No rhyme, no reason. Just 32 column inches of gibberish — where the news used to go.

The effect of Pak-o-Lies was astonishing. For days it was the main topic of conversation in the office. Printers worked with copies sticking out of their apron pockets and waved them cheekily at the Echo editor. There were also a few small changes in the paper. The Echo was obsessed with happy news and invited readers to send in stories about nice things that happened to them. These were used as fillers with a drawing of the sun and the heading BRIGHT SPOT. After Pak-o-Lies poked fun at them, everyone ridiculed them and they were quickly dropped. But an unfortunate effect of Pak-o-Lies was that people no longer talked freely about the idiocies of their bosses and the supply of stories for future issues dried up.

In the meantime, Rob's work for the Echo had brought him into contact with the Marine Ladies' Club, a keep-fit class based at a church hall in Tuebrook, a working class part of the city. It was the sort of keep-fit class that can only be found in a place like Liverpool: the members' exercises included frequent marches to the Town Hall to keep an eye on their local councillors. They told Rob they wanted to start a newspaper. They had plenty of ideas for the paper but little know-how, so Rob and I decided to help get it off the ground.

Meetings were held in the church hall on Tuesdays after the keep-fit sessions ended. There were about a dozen women at first and several men joined later. The vicar came along too and offered his services as editor. On being told that there was no need for an editor, he shook his head in disbelief and went away.

The paper, the Tuebrook Bugle, attracted national publicity on television when it first appeared. In those days the idea that anyone could start up a newspaper without a great deal of money and machinery was still new to a lot of people. One man asked: "Don't you have to get permission?" Rob and I knew that publishing was basically a very simple business and wanted to knock away the mystique. We organised lessons in writing and preparing copy for the printers, sizing up pictures and laying out pages, and bought in several other journalists to help with the teaching.

Judging by the Bugle's sales, copies were going to almost every household in the district. And there was plenty of advertising from the local shops. It was an excellent paper of its kind, full of reports and pictures of activities around Tuebrook and lots of outspoken comment. But it had limitations. It dealt mainly with life away from work — a paper for residents rather than workers. And its scope was restricted to a small part of the city.

In the wake of Pak-o-Lies, and while we were still helping with the Bugle, the idea for the Free Press arose. In a way it was a natural development. Pak-o-Lies had been entirely about the Post and Echo and was intended for employees there. But we were surprised at the response from outside. For instance, the issue describing how the Post and Echo had tried to get the postal strikers back to work early was circulated in the sorting offices. Altogether, 2,000 copies of the second issue were distributed — about ten times more than the number of Post and Echo staff. If there was such a demand for Pak-o-Lies, we reasoned the demand for a paper publishing more general stories of the sort other papers would not print must be far greater.

Our own aim at the Bugle had — from the start — been to pull out as soon as possible. The Bugle's front page always carried the slogan:

"Written by the people for the people", though in the beginning this was more a declaration of intent than a statement of fact. Rob and I had done a lot of the work at first, but we believed it should eventually be produced entirely by residents of Tuebrook — and neither Rob nor I lived there. We saw our role as demystifying journalism and teaching people how to do it themselves. At the time, the Bugle committee seemed unhappy about us leaving, thinking we were trying to abandon them and start a rival paper. We told them there was no need for us to stay. We argued that the Free Press was not a rival, but a complement to community papers. Community papers' advantage was being able to cover very local issues in detail; the Free Press would cover issues affecting the city generally.

The main influence at the start of the Free Press came — not from Moscow or Peking as a few people suspected — but from the United States. Rob's wife was American and had a huge stack of papers which we studied avidly. Two that impressed us particularly were the Los Angeles Free Press and the San Francisco Bay Guardian. They were unlike anything I had seen before. In Britain, the "underground" papers — Oz, IT, etc — born in the Flower Power era, with their heavy emphasis on music and drugs were still thriving. The United States, of course, had this type of paper too. But there were others with a style and content that appealed to the man or woman in the street — and yet made them different from the established Press. This was what we had in mind when we talked about starting "a free press" in Liverpool. As we talked about it more, the "a" became "the" and we were talking about the Liverpool Free Press. The name was hardly discussed. Certainly no alternatives were proposed. We might, perhaps, have plumped for an anti-name, like Pak-o-Lies, or copied the Gutter Press in Islington. But we wanted something that sounded acceptable. "Free Press" was equivocal — it could apply to an "alternative" paper or an ordinary one, and yet it had a meaning and made a comment on the other papers in Liverpool that were not "free". Later, when we began selling papers in pubs, people would say: "How come you have to pay for it when it's free?" We thought they were trying to be funny until several newsagents complained that people were helping themselves to copies, thinking they were free. It was too late to change the name but after that we printed the price in larger type. It seemed a pity that the only meaning of "free" for a lot of people was "something you don't have to pay for".

There was a nucleus of three — me, Rob and Chris. Derek, who had printed Pak-o-Lies, was also interested in writing. But we needed more hands. Holding an open meeting was out of the question because three of us would have to work for the Free Press secretly if we were to keep our jobs at the Post and Echo. In any case, a large group could be unwieldy and might get so bogged down in discussion that the paper would never come out (as it was, planning took six months). So we just invited a few friends. There was Vincent Johnson, a nurse who had been active in the

Campaign for Nuclear Disarmament; John Garrett, a computer programmer who had been involved in an anarchist paper in Swansea; and Barbara Gould, a friend of mine who had helped distribute Pak-o-Lies. The first few meetings were taken up discussing a lot of hypothetical questions — for example, what we should do with letters from the National Front. Some people thought we should refuse to print them, others that we should print them with a reply. After a while, we realised the discussion was leading nowhere. And anyway, such questions could be put aside for the time being and resolved if and when they arose. After that we got down to practicalities. Each member was asked to look into an aspect of production and report back.

We wanted the pages in the Free Press to be roughly the size of those in the Daily Mirror. That was too big for Derek's press, so we had to find another printer. We decided to use the litho process because it is cheaper than traditional printing processes, especially for illustrations. Litho is a photographic method which does not use metal type. This meant we could also save money by making up the pages ourselves. Type for litho printing is set on strips of paper, using a machine like a complicated typewriter. The machines cost several thousand pounds to buy, and paying a firm to do the typesetting for us would have been expensive, too. But we found someone who had a machine and asked if we could use it ourselves. He said we could use it in the evenings for £1.50 an hour. Later, we rented a machine and shared it with Big Flame and the Merseyside Women's Paper — as well as doing a few commercial jobs to raise extra cash.

The Tuebrook Bugle was selling 2,000 copies without difficulty in a small area, so we decided to start by aiming to sell twice as many of the Free Press over the whole city. Several newsagents said they would take copies on sale or return for the standard discount of 25 per cent. We could also get people to sell to their friends and neighbours or at work, and sell copies ourselves in pubs and on the street. The first issue cost £105 to print, plus £20 for use of the typesetting machine — £125 in all. Five of us donated £25 to pay the first bill. The Free Press would sell at 4p, the usual price of newspapers at the time. If we sold all the copies we would get back £120, allowing for the 25 per cent discount. We decided to supplement this with advertising, but did not want to become dependent on advertisers. On average, about 10 per cent of the paper's income came from adverts — an unusually low proportion.

For a long time we had no office. The first issue was produced in Chris's flat. Vincent Johnson's home was used as the address for mail and phone calls — until his wife got fed up answering the phone when he was out. After several changes of address we eventually got a room — rent-free — above News From Nowhere, a radical bookshop.

Our motives in starting the Free Press were primarily journalistic. We saw journalism as a political activity but we did not see the Free Press as a means to a political end. For us, the Free Press *was* the political end.

LIVERPOOL Free Press

News you're not
supposed to kno

No 1   July 1971

The people won't decide after all

IT'S THE M62 STEAMROLLER

BBC bans
Scaffold
film
–page ten

A man helping the police with their enquiries.

Police raid on children's party

Don't talk to the people of Kirkby about the police force being short of men.

For on Sunday, May 3, police in five panda cars and a Black Maria gate-crashed a children's street party in Lindby Road, Kirkby, broke it up and arrested three men for obstruction.

British justice had swung into action ten days before the Cup Final, when local police told Mrs Esther Crosby, of Lindby Road, that street parties were not their concern.

Mrs Crosby had visited Kirkby police station to ask permission to hold the street party. Twice she was told it was up to Kirkby Urban District Council, not the police.

Thinking no more about the matter, the residents went ahead organising the party. In the street lives the father of John McLaughlin, the Liverpool player, and even though most of the men are

Evertonians they thought a party, win or lose, would be a good idea for the kids.

As they were setting up the tables in the street on the Sunday, a panda car drove up and police told the mothers they couldn't hold the party in the street.

When the women protested, reinforcements were called. Police doubtless feared a riot by the 40 young children, and soon four more panda cars converged on the road from every direction and a Black Maria drew up.

Mrs Ann Cahill, of Lindby Road, said: "All they were short of was the Alsatians. You'd have thought a murder had been committed."

Mr John Killen, one of the men arrested, said: "The sergeant told us 'I'm in charge, and there'll be no party in this street today.'

"In my opinion he came up

(Continued on page 2)

When the M62 ploughs through Liverpool thousands of people will be affected – houses will be demolished, communities will be broken up, lives will be disrupted.

And the people won't be allowed to decide for themselves.

The planning of the M62 has been advertised as an exercise in 'public participation'. But MacDonald Steward, Conservative leader of the city council, has shown that up to be a fraud, and demonstrated his scorn for public participation.

"Help to plan Liverpool's road network," said the M62 brochure.

"I don't like mischief makers," said Alderman MacDonald Steward, when he met the Picton Residents Association on Friday June 4.

To their face he told them it was not an exercise in public participation, it was an exercise in public relations.

The residents went for information. They came away feeling angry and astonished after listening to MacDonald Steward's comments.

The residents want to know Why the motorway is being built. But after two public meetings with Corporation officials, and interviews with the leaders of the two major parties they are still none the wiser.

They have found the politicians and planners to be confused, muddled and contradictory about the purpose of the M62.

Back in 1934 Brodie, the city engineer, drew an arbitrary line across a map and said Liverpool needed a road there. Ever since,

it appears to have been accepted as gospel, with no questions asked.

The Picton Residents presented MacDonald Steward with a list of detailed and reasonable questions. He said he would give replies within days. By the end of June he still hadn't replied.

In six months' time the city council will choose the definite route for the £14 million stretch of motorway, and give the go-ahead for construction.

And unless the people fight for their rights to participate, the decision will be taken over their heads.

HER IS T NEV

News is what other p want you to read.

The Liverpool Fr started by a group want to print that n

On Merseyside th of stories that are n For there is a newsp – the Post and Echo happy to ignore it.

Take this issue. T about the police were mentioned in the Ec

Persistently the after story to discre the Docks, Fords, t ers and Cammell La

The Free Press w viding a radical alte paper.

But we aren't af political party. We political line that w subscribe to.

As well as repor planning fiddles, Co petence and the sup news, we will be gi those who are deni for their views... co groups, trade union children, gipsies, th community.

In a phrase – th pool.

We need to kno and what you are and need your support Liverpool Free Pre out each month.

Contact us at 1 Road, Liverpool 1 0264. Evenings: 7.

Drawn from

During an action judge asked the wit her husband back to replied: 'Last year I if I had anything to the football season

Long way to spend a pen

Liverpool's central library in William Brown Street must have one of the finest obstacle courses in the country.

It's at its best when you're trying to find out about planning matters in the city.

City council minutes are kept in a muddled heap on the first floor. A lot of them are missing.

Planning documents are kept on the fifth floor. You're not allowed to use the lifts to get there. Hard luck if you're old or crippled.

You're not allowed to browse through the planning records. They're kept on restricted access.

It's said that when they're left on open shelves they get pinched, which just might have something to do with the fact that they are so expensive and you can't borrow them from the library.

If you want to see them you've got to fill in a form giving your name, address, the title of the report report and its reference number. If you don't know the number you've got to look through the cat alogue and get it.

You're not allowed to borrow the planning reports. But you could have them photo-copied. That is, if you can afford the exorbitant

2s 6d per sheet th

And if you've go think twice about fifth floor. Toilet floor, if you're ca have to leg it dow stairs, race to the over your rally, a name, address an before they'll giv the toilets which side of the buildi national Library.

Who needs to c fee to stop peopl Just call in Liver library as adviser

This was perhaps unusual for a radical paper: Many are started by political organisations as a party mouthpiece, and community papers are often born out of a particular issue in the community. We recognised that newspapers have a political function and did not like the function of the papers we worked for. Also, we believed that newspapers should be controlled by the people producing them.

Faced with that, there were two choices: Either to try and change the papers we worked for, or start a new one. It is an old dilemma, of course. Either choice has drawbacks. Seeking change within the system is slow and may lead nowhere; the system may in the end change the people who want to change it. Change outside the system starts from a position of weakness. In the late 1960s and early 1970s many people were experimenting with "alternatives" — communes that aimed to be self-sufficient, small co-operative workshops, alternative ways of distributing food, and so on. The attraction of alternatives was that there was no need to wait years before the big change that might never come. It was possible to get a taste of the New World immediately, even if it was only short-lived and happened on a small scale. To some extent, we also saw the Free Press as propaganda of the deed, highlighting the faults of the established Press and showing other journalists how newspapers could be different and what was possible, given the right conditions. The Free Press, then, was an experiment in journalism — which was probably the reason why we had difficulty getting non-journalists deeply involved in producing it. Vincent, John and Barbara drifted away fairly quickly, though Derek, the printer, stayed and later took up journalism for a living. Rob left the production group after a couple of years because of domestic problems, but continued writing stories. So, for most of the paper's life it was produced mainly by three people, though many more contributed by writing occasionally, providing information or selling.

We had intended to publish the Free Press monthly, but once the first issue came out we realised this was impossible. Distribution at first took about three weeks — and by that time the second issue should have been ready for the printer. Still, we decided to press ahead and publish as soon as we could. That set the pattern for future issues. On average, the Free Press was published every two months, though the gaps varied a lot. Once there was a gap of six months between two issues and no-one knew when to expect the paper. That was probably not a bad thing (though we did have second thoughts later). Rumours spread from time to time that the paper had been closed down by the authorities, that we had all been arrested, or that it was delayed because we were working on a very big story. And readers continually pestered newsagents — which was good because it made the newsagents more eager to get their papers. But perhaps the most important effect of irregular publication was on the content of the Free Press. Most newspapers appear on schedule, even if meeting the deadline means filling them with rubbish. Radio and television news programmes are always the same length, even if very little has happened. At the Free Press, we waited until we had enough good material to fill the paper. And for the first time in our lives, we had the time to think carefully about what we were writing.

7. Something completely different

IN THE DESIGN and writing of the Free Press we strove to make it acceptable to a wide audience. We did not want people reading it on the bus to be stared at as if they belonged to some lunatic fringe. But we did want them to recognise how it was different. We decorated lamp-posts and bus shelters with stickers saying: "If you read the Echo you'll need the Liverpool Free Press". And a leaflet explained:

> The Free Press is a different kind of newspaper. For a start, it's not part of a big newspaper chain and it isn't trying to make money. The Free Press believes that as long as newspapers are run by businessmen for profit, there will be news that is not reported. The Free Press aims to report this news. In addition, it tries to provide information which community groups, factory workers, tenants and others will find not only interesting — but useful. The Free Press does not represent the views of any political party or organisation. The paper has no editor or owner — it is controlled by the people who work for it (a group of unpaid volunteers). The Free Press really is a different kind of newspaper . . .

The way the paper was run was important to us as producers, and naturally it influenced the content. As there was no editor and no hierarchy, we had to work out an alternative way of making decisions. The first issue caused no problems; everyone simply wrote what they wanted and it went into the paper. The first difficult decision came with the second issue. There were arguments about whether to include a record shop's advert which contained a suggestive drawing. We voted — and the result was very close. Then more people arrived and demanded a second vote, which reversed the previous decision. Nobody was really happy with the way the decision had been made and in the end we compromised. We returned the copy to the advertiser, explained that some members of the group had objections, and suggested changes. That lost us the advert, but we were not unduly worried. The incident made us realise that if we tried to vote our way out of every impasse factions would develop within the group — and that would probably be disastrous for the paper. In fact the more crucial the decision, the less satisfactory voting seemed. For instance, if we were discussing whether to take the risk of a libel action it was vital to consider all points of view. After all, if we made a mistake everyone in the group could be sued. So we adopted a policy of collective responsibility: There were to be no more votes; all decisions had to be unanimous.

In practice this was far less cumbersome than it sounds. It did not mean people working on a story for days only to have it rejected because one person disliked it. After working together for a short time, we knew each other's attitudes. We knew what was likely to be accepted by the others and what needed discussion before going ahead. Disagreements were resolved by argument; either one side recognised it was on weak ground, or changes were made to satisfy the objections. We tried to settle arguments at the earliest possible stage, otherwise they could delay production. But some hold-ups were inevitable. One issue was almost ready for the printers when work stopped for about two hours while we argued about a headline. Although we were under great pressure at the time to get the paper out quickly, that did not interfere with the discussion. On another occasion an entire finished page was scrapped when a friend — who had been asked to check it for misprints — pointed out some serious flaws in the main story which we had not spotted. But despite incidents like these, the system generally worked well — and with the added benefit that there was far more thought and consideration behind articles in the Free Press than in most newspapers.

When we talked of workers' control, by "workers" we meant the people who produced the paper, those who made it their main spare time occupation. But there were others who were more loosely connected: Those who sold it, helped with distribution, wrote occasional articles, gave us regular information, and so on. To take their views into account, we eventually began holding meetings for readers and active supporters. The meetings were advertised in the paper and open to anyone. They were for discussions rather than decisions and gave us an opportunity to listen to criticism, to test opinion on possible changes in the paper and sometimes to get ideas for stories.

The first few issues of the Free Press were really a collection of individual efforts. Many of the stories carried by-lines, either genuine or (in the case of those with jobs to protect) fictitious names. But as the group became more cohesive we began to write stories collectively. It became common for several people to work on different aspects of a story. As research progressed, we discussed how the story should be presented. And with this sort of team-work, by-lines were abandoned, except for specially contributed articles.

With everyone taking a greater interest in what other members of the group were doing, the reasons for writing stories began to be questioned. At first it was a good enough explanation to say: "I'm writing this because I want to and nobody else will publish it". We were, after all, broadly agreed on what the paper should be about: Subjects that were not covered "properly" by the local Press. Often a story would end with an outraged footnote complaining at the local Press' lack of guts in not having published the story themselves. This sense of outrage was tempered gradually as we came to realise that the local Press, far from failing to do its job properly, was merely carrying out its intended function.

A better understanding of the function of the Press led to thoughts about the function of the Free Press. Readers sometimes described it as "libertarian", "broad left" or simply "left-wing", though we resisted attempts to label it. Once, when we were drafting a statement of the paper's aims, Chris wanted to call it "socialist". The rest of us objected, and a long argument ensued. The objection was not to socialism in principle, but to the word. "Socialist" had so many different meanings that it was likely to confuse more people than it enlightened. Also, there was criticism of the way other journalists used descriptive labels to categorise people and signify approval or disapproval. Labels made it easy for readers to accept or reject what people said without having to listen to what they were actually saying. Our resistance to labelling probably paid off. Some time later, when we printed an article arguing against the sale of council houses, a member of the Communist Party told us people where he worked had read the article and discussed it. He noted with a touch of envy that similar articles in the Morning Star had gone unread.

Eventually we did agree on a description of the politics of the Free Press which said:

> The Free Press is not connected with any political party or group. But we do not pretend, like the established Press, to be "neutral" or "objective". The politics of the Free Press are contained, largely, in what we choose to report.

As individuals, we had political differences. We agreed in general on what was wrong with society, but we did not agree on what should be done about it. As far as the paper was concerned, though, that was no problem. The Free Press did not presume to tell people what to do — it posed the questions for readers to work out their own solutions. As the paper developed, we became dissatisfied with the Free Press merely as an outlet for the stories we personally wanted to write and gave more thought to our relationship with our readers. We said: "We want the Free Press to be useful to people struggling for control over their own lives — as well as providing information about the sort of people who actually do have control over them".

In this way we arrived at a new and simple definition of news: Useful information. Our test, then, for measuring newsworthiness was to ask: "In what ways is this story useful?" Useful stories took several forms. The type the Free Press became most noted for was muckraking. Free Press muckraking had similarities in its methods and presentation with the exposés found in sections of the popular Press. The difference was one of purpose. The targets of exposés in the popular Press are usually too small or weak to hit back: "Scroungers", "agitators", small-time swindlers, people with odd sexual habits, prostitutes, even latter-day witches. *Our* targets were those with power, wealth or influence: Public figures who used power for their own ends, who preached one thing and did another, who made people suffer and profited by it. We took on local MPs and councillors, bureaucrats, the police, big business and the Press. There was no doubt this was very popular with readers — though more politically-minded readers tended to regard it as circulation-boosting or as sugar on the pill. But that was not our intention. We did not do exposés in order to clean up public life; our aim was to show that it does not pay to trust those in authority.

Muckraking was the destructive side of the Free Press — though it was *usefully* destructive. But useful information also had a more positive side. A good example was the sit-in at the Fisher-Bendix factory in Kirkby, near Liverpool, in 1972. It was the first factory occupation in England and we decided to produce a special edition. On the first night of the sit-in we went to the factory and interviewed workers. The factory was losing money and its owners, the Thorn electrical group (who had made £37 million profit the previous year) planned to close it, putting 600 people out of work. The workers gave us some background to the factory's problems (mainly mismanagement) and let us look at documents they had found in the management offices. From the documents it was clear that Thorn, despite denials, had for some time been arranging to transfer the work to Spain. With our own experience of researching companies, we produced a list of all Thorn products, which the workers wanted other unions to boycott. The next day Rob and Chris wrote up the background to the sit-in. I did the typesetting and layout when I got home from work and Derek got up at 5 o'clock the following morning and printed 5,000 copies. It was only a single sheet, selling for 1p, but it proved so popular that the Fisher-Bendix workers asked us to do another 5,000 for distribution around the country. Also, our list of Thorn's products was reprinted on 100,000 leaflets sent out to trade unions.

Later in the same year, five London dockers were jailed for defying the Tory government's new Industrial Relations Court and the nationwide protests brought Britain closer to a general strike than at any time since 1926. Fleet Street was closed down, and the local papers too. We produced another special edition which was given away in the streets and carried latest news of the strikes. It explained:

Now, more than ever it is essential that groups of workers in different parts of Merseyside know what others are doing. The Echo and Daily Post have been silenced as part of a wave of protest at the jailing of five dockers. But even if those papers were on the street today they would be presenting their usual coverage of industrial action. Their editors virtually ignored the Liverpool dock strike last week before the dockers were jailed. The Post and Echo represent the port employers, the big shipping lines, the very men behind the unregistered container depots that are taking jobs away from the dockers. When the "responsible" Echo covers the news it has the interests of the ship-owners at heart. The news in this Free Press has been provided with the co-operation of workers throughout Merseyside, and represents their interests.

Often it was difficult to gauge what effect this sort of information had. If a councillor resigned after an exposé the effect was obvious. But it was less obvious when readers were expected to make active use of information. One instance where this did happen concerned plans for Liverpool's Civic Centre (the posh name for a proposed new block of council offices). The Free Press ran a long campaign against the scheme and provided a lot of information leaked by officials. The public inquiry into the Civic Centre was one of the best-attended planning inquiries the city had seen. Many of the objectors used information from the Free Press, and the government refused permission for the building.

The Free Press style of journalism was a far cry from the "objectivity" of the established Press. We did not pretend to be neutral or objective. The paper aimed to be involved in issues and struggles and it readily took sides. But there was nothing dishonest about that; we did not twist the facts — we interpreted them. What we presented was the truth as we saw it, after examining the available facts. We tried, as Americans would say, to "tell it like it is". We never wrote leaders or separate editorial comments. From the beginning we reported the story and explained, interpreted or commented as we went along. Nor did we automatically seek to balance opposing views. Usually our attitude was that those in command had enough ways of making their views known without our helping them. Also, if we were sure of our facts there was no point in weakening a story by inviting denials. For example, in 1976, we reported that 300 workers at the Bear Brand hosiery factory could lose their jobs because the firm had been refused a £500,000 Government loan. The information came from an impeccable source, so we did not ask the company to comment. The managing director was furious and spent more than 20 minutes shouting at us over the phone, denying that they had been refused the loan. We told him he was wrong, but said we would print a letter if he wrote one. The letter arrived:

I note with a great deal of dissatisfaction your article concerning this company in the recent issue of your paper. My dissatisfaction is very fairly founded in that there is not one paragraph in your article that is accurate and that by publishing errors and misleading information, it can do nothing but make matters much more difficult for management to manage. From the structure of the latter part of the article it is apparent that you have no understanding of business and might I therefore suggest that you appreciate the circumstances in running a business before endeavouring to comment on it. I am pleased to say that our employees here are aware of the extension in trade which has taken place and the situation that surrounds this company now is the build-up into a viable entity which is the totally opposite extreme of the company which required money to meet the losses that you refer to last year. — Mervyn E Smith, Managing Director, Bear Brand Ltd.

Two weeks later the firm went bust and the workers lost their jobs.

Surprisingly, considering how ingrained belief in the need for "objectivity" is, our attitude was rarely questioned by readers. Some described the Free Press as "speaking up for working people" or even as "the paper that tells the truth". We had only two letters accusing us of "bias". This was one of them:

I have just read the Liverpool Free Press with great interest. I was impressed with contents of your newspaper particularly with regard to the exposure of council's corruption. However I do think your views are one-sided. I did not read anything about work people who don't play fair. A recent example of corporation workers playing golf during working hours. I am sure there are many such other examples. I would certainly read your paper if you played for to both sides. — A Matthews and E S Cross, Ward G12, Whiston General Hospital.

And we replied:

If readers want information about "work people" who don't "play fair" they will have to get it elsewhere. They shouldn't find it difficult. Newspapers are willing enough to carry stories about idle workers, social security fiddlers, shoplifters, etc. The Free Press does not regard this sort of behaviour as particularly newsworthy. In a society of winners and losers, it's not at all surprising that some of the losers hit back now and again. It may not be playing the game, but who said the rules were fair to start with? The Free Press takes an interest in a different group of people: The people at the top, the winners, those who want us to carry on playing their game, while often breaking the rules themselves. We do this because when politicians, businessmen or policemen break the rules, a lot of us are affected. Yet, strangely, our marvellous "free press" don't seem so interested. The public will probably never know the truth about the Northern Ireland government minister who was a gun-runner, or about alleged torture by police in Runcorn, or about the Cabinet Minister with odd business connections in the Midlands. All these stories have been researched by national newspapers — and then dropped. So, in a sense, our coverage has to be one-sided. We have chosen our side. And that's what it comes down to in the end.

This was not to say that we always took sides. Sometimes, in inter-union disputes, for example, we took a more neutral line. Ironically, it was one attempt to sit on the fence that provoked the strongest reaction we ever had from readers. We had done a series of stories on a private clinic which was charging extortionate sums for abortions. Both pro- and anti-abortion lobbies approved of our campaign. The anti-abortionists, naturally, because they opposed abortion in general. And the pro-abortionists because the clinic put abortions beyond the pocket of many women. Shortly after we did these stories, the anti-abortion Society for the Protection of Unborn Children wanted to advertise a rally they were holding in Liverpool. They put us in a dilemma. We had a clear policy on the private abortion clinic, but not on abortion itself. We should have had a thorough discussion, but we kept putting it off. The day of the paper's deadline arrived and we were still uncertain, so we compromised. We included the advert and placed a news item next to it, announcing two pro-abortion meetings. An important factor in deciding to include the advert was that the pro-abortion lobby, especially the local Women's Liberation group, were also publicising the rally because they planned a counter-demonstration. So there seemed no harm in the Free Press letting people know when and where the rally was happening.

Towards midnight a few days after the paper was printed, there was an anonymous phone call at the house where Chris, Derek and I were living. The caller said the Women's Liberation group were on their way to seize the papers, most of which were still in the front room of the house, waiting to be distributed. We hurriedly hid bundles in cupboards, under beds and under the stairs. But about half the papers were still in the front room when the door bell rang. I stayed in the front room, took out the light bulb and pushed a table against the door. There were about a dozen women outside. They asked to come in and discuss the advert. Derek let them in. Then the knob of the front room door turned. When they found the door did not open easily, about six of them heaved and burst in. There was no light but they drew back the curtains and a street lamp shone in. Then they opened the window and threw the papers out while someone loaded them into a car.

They had taken about £80-worth of papers and we were alarmed the next day when we heard that they planned to destroy them. But there was nothing we could do except wait. They held a meeting and obliterated the offending advert with potato slices dipped in ink, and inserted leaflets about abortion. Then they returned the papers. Although the incident was very unpleasant at the time, it made us realise the importance of avoiding ill-considered decisions and made us think more about our own attitude towards abortion. And eventually we ended up on amicable terms with the Women's Liberation Group.

Producing a paper that was different meant using different sources, or at least using conventional sources differently. We were not interested in reporting formal events as such. We probed behind the events. Council meetings, courts and the like provided a starting point for a story rather than the story itself. In local government, for example, we soon discovered that the usual sources — councillors — really knew very little of what was going on. So instead we made use of officials. They were usually quite junior officials, people of our own age who we met at parties or through friends. They were often disillusioned, critical of their bosses and council policies — and only too willing to give us information and documents privately. After a couple of years we knew so many of them that we could get virtually any Liverpool council document that we asked for, whether or not it had been seen by councillors. Getting the information was easy because officials constantly sent each other memos which were filed, and notes were kept of all formal meetings between officials. Important discussions often involved several departments, so if one source failed to deliver the goods we could try sources in other departments. Of course there was still the problem of knowing what to ask for, because council officials did not always recognise an important story when they saw one. So we kept a close watch on the published council minutes for likely topics.

Other stories came from systematic checks. One was keeping an eye on the business activities of local worthies. Councillors were a prime target because of possible conflicts of interest. The council yearbook helpfully included their business addresses — so we could check their involvement in companies and whether they were directors. Later, the council established its own list of councillors' interests which was open to public inspection.

Complaints about landlords usually came from individual tenants and often we needed to trace other tenants to find out if they shared the same problems. Once we had the name of the landlord's company we checked the records at Companies House. The records there included a list of all property the company had mortgaged (and mortgaging was the way most landlords bought their property). This sort of checking was time-consuming and not always fruitful. But it was worth the effort for the good stories it did produce. One example of the usefulness of routine checks was the story of Gerald Zisman. Zisman announced plans for a £500 million "Trade, Industry and Export Centre" in Liverpool. It would, he said, cover 36 acres and include 2,250,000 square feet of office and exhibition space — more than the total built in the city in the previous ten years. The Liberal leader of the City Council was delighted and said that as far as he was concerned, they could "start laying the first brick tomorrow". The Labour leader of the County Council said: "We will do everything we can to assist". And the Daily Post and Echo, welcoming the scheme, called it "imaginative". None of them had checked up on Gerald Zisman. If they had, they would have found that imagination played a greater part in the project than they realised. Our investigations showed Zisman worked from his home, a smallish semi in Kingston, Surrey. We asked him what he had built before. "Many major projects," he said. Such as? "Office blocks, city office blocks." Where? "I'd rather not say." Could you name just one? "No, I'd rather not".

That story was just the result of curiosity. Sometimes we already had suspicions when we began inquiries. In 1976, a British National; Party candidate stood for the first time in a council election in the city's Fairfield Ward. We knew that a candidate's nomination papers had to be signed by ten "assentors" living in the ward. We thought the party might have had difficulty getting ten people to sign. So we got the names of the assentors and went to see them. We found they had one thing in common. No, they were not all National Party supporters. They all filled in Littlewoods pools coupons. The woman who collected the coupons was a Mrs Matchett, the wife of the candidate . . .

While she was collecting the pools, Mrs Matchett also collected the signatures, but seems to have forgotten to tell most people what party her

husband represented. An old gentleman thought he'd signed a form for Littlewoods, and another couple received an irate call from the Liberal Party, who thought they had lost two supporters. They had been told they were signing for an independent and have since cancelled their pools. In four cases, Mrs Matchett asked the wife of the household to sign on her husband's behalf, which is illegal, and has annoyed some husbands. One angry husband declared he would "bone that old faggot next time she calls."

Ordinary people had a much greater part in the Free Press than in most newspapers — both as sources of stories and suppliers of information. Sometimes we sought them out; sometimes they came to us. For example, we had no routine coverage of the courts, so virtually all our court and police stories were the result of someone involved in a case contacting us. Occasionally we received information anonymously. The real spur to the Kirkby investigation (see Chapter 8) was a brief, anonymous letter from someone working in the council architect's department. We would have dearly loved to make contact with the person who sent it, and even appealed in the paper for him or her to come forward, but without success. Fortunately we were able to check the information in other ways. Sometimes, however, this was impossible. We once had a very long, detailed letter — apparently from someone high up in the police force. The letter made very serious allegations, but the writer seemed to assume we had some magical powers to get information. Hard as we tried, there was just no way of checking it. Another story, about a private intelligence network set up by General Sir Walter Walker to spy on industrial militants, came from someone who walked into the office, handed over a bundle of documents and left without giving his name. He explained that he had opened a letter which arrived where he worked. It was addressed to a colleague who had recently left, and invited him to join the network. The man wrote back, using his colleague's name. Then he received the documents.

In 1971, the Heath government published a White Paper, "Fair Deal For Housing", which later formed the basis of the Housing Finance Act (nicknamed the "Fair Rents" Act). When it became law there were demonstrations and rent strikes all over the country and Labour councillors at Clay Cross in Derbyshire were penalised for refusing to implement the Act. But when the proposals were announced, the Press gave them a warm welcome. The Daily Express spoke of "the wisest reform of housing this century" and the Daily Mail said: "It's fair and bold". The left-wing New Statesman — then edited by former Labour Housing Minister Richard Crossman — called it "the first entirely logical approach to housing finance" and the Observer said: "The basic principle . . . deserves a warm welcome". The basic principle was to put up rents. None of the papers bothered to ask tenants what they thought about it. (Probably it did not occur to them. Some years later an associate editor of the Observer, a man with a high reputation as an award-winning journalist, came to Liverpool to investigate the problems on a new housing estate. We saw him afterwards and he seemed excited. Had he found a great story? No, he was excited because it was the first time in his life he had been inside a council house.) Together with a group of council tenants, we studied the White Paper and produced what — as far as we could discover — was the first detailed criticism of the proposals published anywhere.

8. Where there's brass there's muck

KIRKBY is a New Town on the edge of Liverpool, built mainly in the 1960s and early 1970s to rehouse people from the city's slums. But the move brought only a brief respite. Within ten years hundreds of the jerry-built houses and flats were themselves slums and many stood empty, ready for demolition. Unemployment in Kirkby is massive and permanent. Thousands of youngsters there have never worked — and are never likely to work. About one-third of all families live on the dole. It is little wonder that a lot of them supplement their incomes in the only way possible — by crime. Kirkby police station prcvided the setting for the famous television series, Z-Cars.

In the healthiest part of Kirkby is a cluster of better, privately-owned houses. Among the more splendid of these was the home of the town's boss, Dave Tempest, OBE, JP. Tempest was the veteran Labour leader and a friend of the local MP, Prime Minister Harold Wilson. Apart from one year of Liberal rule, Tempest had dominated the town since its birth. In the absence of any serious opposition, he did what he liked. And he shrugged off the town's problems by accusing the Press and television of "giving Kirkby a bad name".

Anyone passing Tempest's house shortly after dawn one summer morning in 1977 would have been struck by an ironic sight. A scene unlike any shown in Z-Cars. For detectives were arresting the great socialist for his part in a conspiracy which had systematically cheated the people of the town. The bad name of Kirkby had gone back where it belonged.

It might never had happened but for the Free Press — and one disastrous blunder. In the 1974 re-organisation of local government, Kirkby was due to merge into a larger unit called Knowsley. Any of Kirkby council's money left unspent at the time of the merger would automatically go to Knowsley. Tempest did not want this to happen and decided to have a final fling. But the money had to be spent quickly; there was no time for a bricks-and-mortar building project. Then someone had the idea of a ski slope. It would be both quick and simple. All it needed was a gigantic heap of earth, topped off with a special surface for ski-ing.

The ski slope first attracted the attention of the Free Press when a contributor from Kirkby told us that the council, in their haste to finish it, had used volunteer children to lay the ski surface during school hours.

When they could not get enough volunteers, they paid children 25p an hour to work at the weekend. Then a journalist on the Kirkby reporter told us that the slope had been built without planning permission, on land which Kirkby council did not own (they later had to buy it from Liverpool). Worse still, the slope was built on top of the pipe carrying the town's water supply and it faced on to a main road, which could cause a hazard to any skiers who failed to stop at the bottom (though that was perhaps an academic point as the slope could not be opened because the council's insurance company refused to let anyone ski on it).

Responsibility for the project — and the mistakes — lay with the council architect's department, headed by Eric Spencer Stevenson. The decision to build it was taken by council leader Dave Tempest, using his delegated powers and was never approved by the full council. And the main contract for the work was awarded to local builder George Leatherbarrow without inviting formal, competitive tenders.

Shortly after our first story on the ski slope was published, we were joined by Steve Scott, a reporter who had just left a job at the Cambridge Evening News. Steve had been a student at the Centre for Journalism Studies in Cardiff, where he had read the Free Press and become interested in it. Before going to Cambridge, he worked on Merseyside for the Bootle Times and had written several stories for the Free Press. Derek, meanwhile, had gone off travelling round Europe, so there were still only three of us doing most of the work. We divided Merseyside into three geographical areas, with the idea that each of us would specialise in stories from one area. Steve grumbled at being given Kirkby because it was further away than the others. But he quickly became enthusiastic when he saw a letter which arrived in response to the ski slope story.

The letter, which was unsigned, purported to come from someone working in the architect's department. It alleged that Leatherbarrow, while charging the council for the earth used to build the ski slope, had not paid for it himself. He had advertised the site in the Liverpool Echo as a "free tip" for builders. But more significantly, the letter gave us the first inkling of the relationship between Leatherbarrow and Stevenson and Tempest. It said they were on very friendly terms and named a pub where they often had lunch together.

Steve began his inquiries by approaching councillors. He talked to several opposition Liberal councillors and one or two on the Labour side who had the reputation of being honest. But they knew nothing and suspected nothing. He spent the next two weeks in Kirkby library, going through old council minutes. From his notes, we compiled a list of contractors who had worked for Kirkby council and we ran company checks. Two things in particular stood out. One was that most of the building contracts — about £10 million-worth — had gone to George Leatherbarrow, while the big national firms which usually won contracts from neighbouring councils, scarcely got a look in. The other was that whenever anything odd happened, the council's architect, Eric Spencer

Stevenson was in the thick of it.

The council minutes also gave the names of people who might be willing to talk: The Personnel Committee minutes included names of officials who had left the council. Steve tried to track them down and eventually found one who was co-operative, but warned that he would never get another job in local government if it became known that he had talked. Steve went to see him. Actually he knew very little about Leatherbarrow, but suggested several other lines of inquiry. But more important, he confirmed our suspicions that something was wrong in Kirkby. After that we had no doubt there was a story, if only we could get it. One piece of information the ex-official gave us was about the first private office block to be built in Kirkby. He remembered that the developer was Philip Moore-Clague, who had been middle-man in the slag heaps affair. (The slag heaps affair had been a national scandal some months earlier, and involved Tony Field, the brother of Marcia Williams, Harold Wilson's secretary.) Moore-Clague's arrival in Kirkby was all the more interesting because Kirkby was Wilson's constituency. We got what extra information we could and splashed the story in our next issue. But it was a tantalising story, and we never really got to the bottom of it. Several questions could not be answered; in particular, how Moore-Clague, who lived in the Isle of Man, heard about the building land in Kirkby. We had expected the national Press to take it up, but they did not, and after this diversion we turned out attention back to Leatherbarrow and friends.

There were rumours that Leatherbarrow had done building work for several prominent people connected with Kirkby council. Through a tenants' organisation we found someone who had been a shop steward at Leatherbarrow's. He gave us the names of other workers, and they told us there had been something called the Star Gang — a group of privileged workers who went round doing "special" jobs. We got their names and Steve and Chris went to see them. By that time Leatherbarrow knew we were asking questions and the Star Gang were reluctant to talk. Steve recalls the visits to one of them: "We must have been there five times. We just kept turning up on his doorstep and each time he kept adding a bit more. He was the driver who had delivered some of the materials and he kept denying it."

Eventually the Star Gang revealed that Leatherbarrow had built a kitchen extension for Stevenson and a much larger extension to Tempest's house. Materials for both these jobs had been taken from the site in Kirkby where Leatherbarrow was building council houses.

Meanwhile, Chris had traced a former manager of Kirkby Stadium, the council-run sports centre. The manager had lost his job when he was jailed for obtaining £2,000 by deception. In court he had explained that high living while he worked for Kirkby council had.led him to crime. He had told the court of lavish entertainment and trips to Europe paid for by contractors. He gave us details of these trips and mentioned one to

London paid for by George Leatherbarrow. Among the party had been Tempest and Stevenson. Then he dropped a bombshell: He said Stevenson had a car that was known as "Leatherbarrow's car".

More details of the car came from another source. George Leatherbarrow had been divorced and re-married. His first wife told us the car was a maroon Alfa Romeo, and gave the rough date when Leatherbarrow bought it. And she put the friendship between Leatherbarrow and Stevenson in a new light. She said the best man at Leatherbarrow's second wedding had been Stevenson.

At this exciting news, Chris and Steve rushed to Birkenhead Register Office and bought a copy of Leatherbarrow's marriage certificate. And there, on the certificate, were the signatures of the two witnesses — Eric Spencer Stevenson and Elizabeth M Stevenson.

By that stage we had the basic outline of the Leatherbarrow story. The rest was a matter of getting the proof and tying up loose ends. There were several weak points. One was the trip to London — how to prove that Leatherbarrow paid for it. First we tried the hotel where they were supposed to have stayed, without any luck. Then we got the name of the travel agent where Leatherbarrow had booked the train tickets. Chris decided to try subterfuge. He phoned the travel agent, posing as Leatherbarrow's accountant. He said he needed to know the cost of the tickets and would hang on while they checked. Certainly, they said. They would have a look. There was a long, tense pause. Then the answer came. £114.90 — and the bill had been sent to Mr Leatherbarrow, marked "Personal". Fortunately, the party had travelled in style, by Pullman. And Pullman tickets carry the names of passengers. Among the seven names were Leatherbarrow, Tempest and Stevenson.

Another problem was the building work done for Stevenson and Tempest. Was this legitimate work which had been paid for, or not? The work at Stevenson's was especially suspect because he lived in Heswall, some 20 miles from Kirkby. If he had been paying it would have made sense to call in a local firm. While Tempest's extension was being built he had shown no concern about the cost. He had made several changes of plan after work had been done — which would have made the job very expensive. In any case, Leatherbarrow was no jobbing builder; he specialised in big contracts.

Steve decided to confront Tempest about the extension. He phoned him and asked first about the trip to London:

Hello. Mr Tempest? My name is Stephen Scott from the Liverpool Free Press.
. . How've you got my number? Well, I got it from somebody. I've got a couple of questions I'd like to ask you about your work in Kirkby if I could, if you have a minute. One of them is about a trip to London in July 1972 which was to see the White City, the sports stadium down there. Did you authorise that trip? Did I authorise it? Yes. What do you mean, did I authorise it? *Well, did you say it could happen?* I don't know anything about a trip to White City. *Well, perhaps it was the Crystal Palace.* I, I've never been on a trip

anywhere. *You've never made a trip anywhere?* On a trip, no. *Not a two-day trip to London to see . .* I've never been on a trip anywhere. *Yes, well the trip was on July 18, 1972.* Was it? You see, it all depends on what you mean by a trip. *Well I mean it was a trip to London staying overnight in a hotel, the fares being paid by George Leatherbarrow.* I don't know anything about that. *You were on it.* Nobody's paid my fare or anything else other than official . . . er . . . meetings I've gone on by the council. *So you absolutely deny that you were on that trip?* I don't deny anything. I'm saying nobody's paid my expenses anywhere other than when I've gone officially by the council or I've paid for myself. *So if George Leatherbarrow bought, say, the tickets — first class Pullman tickets to London for £114 — Then you would have paid him for your ticket?* He certainly wouldn't have bought mine. *He wouldn't have bought yours?* No. *Yes but you . . . you did go on that trip to London.* I don't know what you mean by a trip to London, you see. I . . . I made arrangements myself to go, to go to the White City, er Crystal Palace rather, and I paid my own expenses. What George Leatherbarrow did, I wouldn't know . . .

OK. I'd like to ask you, on a slightly different note, about the extension on your house. Yes. *Can you tell me who built it?* Why? *Well, because I'm interested.* Well, what's it got to do with you? *Er, it may or may not have anything to do with me. I mean I'm just asking you the question.* If you say . . . I had . . . I had my extension built . . . with a, er, a further mortgage from my building society and it's my business and it's not your business. *Did . . .?* I pay my building society every month on my house. *Yes, er, was it George Leatherbarrow who built your extension?* Are you asking me or telling me? *Well I'm asking you. Was it George Leatherbarrow?* Well then, I,'m saying whoever built my extension it's none of your business. I don't . . . You see I don't see why you should be able to pry into my private affairs like this. *Well, that depends on whose private affairs they are.* Yes, it, it depends on what you want to do really, doesn't it? *Well, well it does. I mean Eric Spencer Stevenson could say the same thing to me: Why do I want to pry into his private affairs?* Well, there's a very good reason why. Well I don't know. But there's no reason why you should pry into my private affairs and if you want to take any steps then it's a matter for yourself . . . *Sure, OK.* But er, I don't see in these particular circumstances and that the sort of rag you represent that I should talk to you like this. *Well, that's up to you. I'm simply asking you the questions. If you say it's none of my business that's fair enough.* Well, it isn't any of your business. *Well, let me just say on the extension, this might be of concern to you.* Yes? *The materials, or some of the materials for that extension. If I said to you they came from the Tower Hill site where George Leatherbarrow was working, what would your reaction be to that?* I would say that, er, that somebody's trying to put ideas into your mind probably with a view to trying to get me into some sort of trouble. *Well if I say to you that I've checked this out and I'm convinced that some of the materials, not all of them . . .* Well, I wouldn't know anything about that. *Yes. Would it be a matter of concern to you, say, if they had come from the Tower Hill site, because of course the council . . .* All I can say is this. That I've paid for my extension quite legitimately and above board. Now if somebody builds an extension for me I don't go following them round where they get their materials from. *It was in fact a very expensive job, wasn't it, because . . .* No. well it doesn't matter what sort of an expensive job it was. All I'm saying is

LIVERPOOL Free Press

Homeless:
Who's
to blame?
Page 4

Action
save
Speke job
Back

MAY—JUNE 1975

CORRUPTION IN KIRKBY

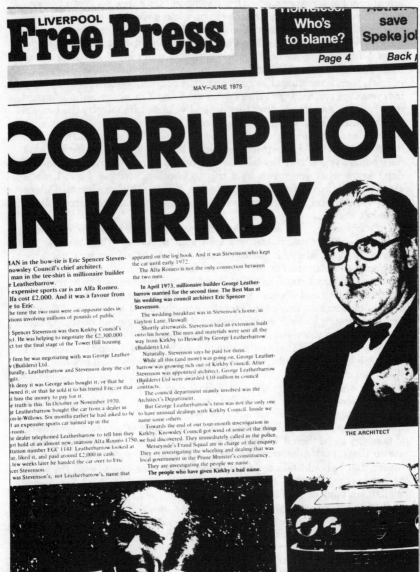

[M]AN in the bow-tie is Eric Spencer Steven[son] [K]nowsley Council's chief architect.

[The] man in the tee-shirt is millionaire builder [Georg]e Leatherbarrow.

[The] expensive sports car is an Alfa Romeo. [The A]lfa cost £2,000. And it was a favour from [Georg]e to Eric.

[At t]he time the two men were on opposite sides in [nego]tiations involving millions of pounds of public [money.]

[Eric] Spencer Stevenson was then Kirkby Council's [archite]ct. He was helping to negotiate the £2,300,000 [contra]ct for the final stage of the Tower Hill housing [estate.]

[The] firm he was negotiating with was George Leather[barro]w (Builders) Ltd.

[Natu]rally, Leatherbarrow and Stevenson deny the car [was a] gift.

[Both] deny it was George who bought it; or that he [ow]ned it; or that he sold it to his friend Eric; or that [he lent] him the money to pay for it.

[The] truth is this: In October or November 1970, [Georg]e Leatherbarrow bought the car from a dealer in [Newto]n-le-Willows. Six months earlier he had asked to be [told i]f an expensive sports car turned up in the [show]room.

[The] dealer telephoned Leatherbarrow to tell him they [had] got hold of an almost new, maroon Alfa Romeo 1750, [regist]ration number EGC 114J. Leatherbarrow looked at [the c]ar, liked it, and paid around £2,000 in cash.

[A f]ew weeks later he handed the car over to Eric [Spe]ncer Stevenson.

[It] was Stevenson's, not Leatherbarrow's, name that

appeared on the log book. And it was Stevenson who kept the car until early 1972.

The Alfa Romeo is not the only connection between the two men.

In April 1973, millionaire builder George Leatherbarrow married for the second time. The Best Man at his wedding was council architect Eric Spencer Stevenson.

The wedding breakfast was in Stevenson's home, in Gayton Lane, Heswall.

Shortly afterwards, Stevenson had an extension built onto his house. The men and materials were sent all the way from Kirkby to Heswall by George Leatherbarrow (Builders) Ltd.

Naturally, Stevenson says he paid for them.

While all this (and more) was going on, George Leatherbarrow was growing rich out of Kirkby Council. After Stevenson was appointed architect, George Leatherbarrow (Builders) Ltd were awarded £10 million in council contracts.

The council department mainly involved was the Architect's Department.

But George Leatherbarrow's firm was not the only one to have unusual dealings with Kirkby Council. Inside we name some others.

Towards the end of our four-month investigation in Kirkby, Knowsley Council got wind of some of the things we had discovered. They immediately called in the police.

Merseyside's Fraud Squad are in charge of the enquiry. They are investigating the wheeling and dealing that was local government in the Prime Minister's constituency.

They are investigating the people we name.

The people who have given Kirkby a bad name.

THE ARCHITECT

THE £2,000 CAR

INSIDE: Men
who gave
Kirkby a

Free
up to

WE REGRET the
price of the Fre[e]
Whatever the
due to unreason[
Because there a[
Our workers [

that I've paid for my job to be done and I got a further mortgage from my building society to do it.

Tempest was clearly lying about his trip to London and, we suspected, about the "further mortgage". (In fact later, during ther police investigation he denied the mortgage story and offered a different account of how he paid for the extension.) But at that time, despite our suspicions, there was no way we could prove Leatherbarrow had done the work for nothing. So we changed tack and looked at the source of the materials. As they had come from the site of Leatherbarrow's council contract, did they actually belong to the council? At first this seemed equally difficult to prove. We thought we would need evidence that the council had paid for specific bricks, doors and so on that had gone to the Stevenson and Tempest homes. But then we had a stroke of luck. A surveyor with a firm in Liverpool told us we had all the evidence we needed. Councils advanced money to contractors to buy materials. This meant that once the materials had been checked on to the building site they belonged, at least in part, to Kirkby council. And even if Stevenson and Tempest had paid Leatherbarrow for the materials in their extensions, Leatherbarrow had no right to sell them.

The last major problem was the Alfa Romeo car. The one Leatherbarrow had bought for Stevenson was described as maroon. At the time of our investigation, the Alfa Stevenson was driving was cream. Had it been re-sprayed? We checked with the licensing office, using the pretext that it might have been involved in an accident. But it was not the car we were looking for. Stevenson had got the cream Alfa some time after the date when he got his car from Leatherbarrow. We checked local dealers who might have records of Stevenson trading in the Leatherbarrow car, but drew a blank. By that time we were very hard up and approached the BBC's Nationwide programme, with a view to selling the story. They liked it and sent a producer, David Geen, who shared Stevenson's taste for fast cars — and knew something we had overlooked: Very few garages service Alfa cars. He checked these and found one where Stevenson's maroon Alfa had been repaired. The garage gave him the registration number. It was then a simple matter of finding the present owner and asking to look at the log book. The log book gave the name of the garage which had sold the car, ostensibly to Stevenson. But the man at the garage told a different story. He remembered that George Leatherbarrow had paid for the car, that he brought a man answering the description of Stevenson to look at it, and had given the impression he was buying it for this man.

The picture was then complete. We published the story and the BBC's film was broadcast a few days later. Tempest had lost his council seat in the elections the previous month and Stevenson was immediately suspended from work. The police began a long investigation. Tempest, Leatherbarrow and Stevenson were arrested on conspiracy charges and later jailed.

The story-behind-the-story was actually far less straightforward than it may sound. In the first place, the Leatherbarrow affair was only part — but the most effective part — of the whole investigation. A complicated business deal involving soil, and the tactics of other firms to win contracts for the sports centre put it in a broader context. Also, a lot of the inquiries proved unfruitful. Rumours were rife and anything that seemed important had to be checked. For example, Stevenson was not the only person said to have got a car from Leatherbarrow. And Tempest was rumoured to own a hotel. Checking these two rumours alone took a great deal of time of led us up blind alleys. More time was taken trying to get a picture of Stevenson at Leatherbarrow's wedding, and we even spent an afternoon at Chester races because Leatherbarrow and Stevenson were thought to be there.

Time (which also means money) is the main reason why such stories are rare in the Press. By the shoe-string standards of the Free Press it was an expensive story. We paid no-one for information, but travelling and phone calls probably left us £100 out of pocket. And the time we spent could have been used more profitably doing something else. The BBC paid £250 for the story and got a bargain. Our return on that worked out at a few pence per man-hour. The BBC were able to do the story because the ground-work had been done and they knew the story would check out. Had they employed a reporter from a cold start, it would have been a very different matter. The cost would have run into thousands — a powerful deterrent. Of course, similar stories do sometimes come to light, usually despite, rather than because of, the Press. The Poulson case in the north-east is the most famous example. The story was taken up because it was handed to the Press on a plate. Poulson went bankrupt and it was the bankruptcy court, not the Press, which began the digging. All the Press had to do was send someone to take notes. Until that happened, as far as the Press were concerned, Poulson's hench-man, T. Dan Smith, was one of the great men of local politics.

It would, however, be wrong to suggest that investigations like ours at Kirkby are beyond the pocket of the national Press. They are not. National newspapers frequently spend thousands of pounds on stories — as the Express did in finding escaped train robber Ronald Biggs. But the difference is this: While there is little value for readers in knowing the whereabouts of Ronald Biggs, there is enormous value for a newspaper in being able to tell them.

9. On the offensive

THE BREAKING of the Kirkby gang brought on a kind of post-natal depression. The problem was knowing that the next issue was likely to be less exciting than the previous one. Kirkby was not only a good tale, but big; as big a scandal as any local paper could hope to get. And its interest for us was not only in the tale itself, but in the investigation. It was the biggest, longest investigation we had done — or could afford to do — and it involved every investigative technique we knew. Where could we go from there? And more relevant: Where *should* we go from there?

In a footnote to the Kirkby corruption story we explained why we had published it:

The Free Press has spent four months looking into the affairs of Kirkby Council. It means other articles — probably more useful articles — have not been written. A "good story" at the end of it is not, on its own, a good enough reason for that. So why do it? The story will be taken up by television and probably the national Press. It's unlikely they would have done it alone. National newspapers can't afford a reporter sitting in the Adelphi Hotel for months with nothing to go on but rumours. More important, why bother? Nothing's gained by upsetting the authorities. Anyway, corruption and odd goings-on in local government are hardly "news" any more. There's so much of it, the Press are looking for a new angle. (There's no need to mention in detail "our" libel laws, the most oppressive in the "free" world.)

Why, some asked, didn't we go to the police? The police were in Kirkby a couple of years ago when £6,000 disappeared from the Labour Club. Nothing happened. A few weeks ago they were called in to investigate the outrageous use of hired vehicles by Knowsley Architect's Department. But they were not concerned with why the architect had spent £56,000 hiring vans. Instead, they wanted to find the man who was spotted moving his furniture in them. It's just like all those men who've been done for pinching a few bricks or a piece of wood from George Leatherbarrow. The Free Press is not interested in doing police work. Locking up bent politicians will change very little. Whether or not our rulers are "good" or "bad" makes very little difference to most of us. They are still there . . . But the real justification for our story is this: It's true, it happened, it affects the people of Kirkby, and they have a right to know about it. Kirkby people will be paying for Tower Hill, the ski slope and all the rest for years. And our story puts the record straight. Kirkby has a "bad name". In lots of ways it's a bloody awful place. But that's not the fault of the people who live there. The people to blame are people like those in our story. The people who built it.

We did not usually find it necessary to justify our stories in print. One reason for doing so then was to try to forestall criticism from some readers. The sort of criticism we expected came mostly in conversation, but this letter, published a few months later, shows the typical lines of argument. It came from Rick Walker, a supporter of the paper who helped with distribution and sometimes wrote articles:

PUBLISH OR BE DAMNED! I don't think it would be unfair to say that there has always been a section of the Free Press's faithful readership which has been concerned that the paper displays some of the tendencies of the gutter Press. For example, the last few issues have had a number of sensational headlines, and the paper has always tended to treat occasional serious issues frivolously.

Many of the stories in the paper rely on corruption, on scandals. In other words they rely on the breaking of rules. Now of course I recognise the value in this, that people who read about Dirty Tricks may come to the general conclusion about things like the distribution of power in society. But in the end it must be made clear that the rules themselves (even if strictly adhered to) are grossly unfair. And sometimes the Freep's coverage of almost incomprehensible fiddles seems self-indulgent. Obviously examples of dark dealings will always go down well with Free Press readers because we can all agree broadly about what is wrong in existing society. The disagreements start when we talk about how we can change it and which direction(s) we want to go in . . .

The letter went on to propose "articles on experiments in self help and mutual aid, in short: Building the community". Most critics were less specific; usually they talked about giving more coverage to "struggles".

Possibly our justification of the Kirkby story was not intended for readers alone, but for ourselves. For there was another, more personal reason for doing it which we did not mention: Job satisfaction. Technically, journalistically, it was very fulfilling. And perhaps at the back of our minds we were wondering whether that had influenced us too much. There were dangers in doing such a satisfying story. After the first good break it became totally engrossing. It had its own momentum which would have been difficult to stop. And at the outset we could not be sure where it would lead. We had tied up virtually the whole of the paper's resources on this one story for four months. When published, it took up five pages — half the paper. Had it been worth it?

My own feeling was yes . . . this time it paid off. But it had been a gamble. All the signs had been that something fishy was going on, but an enormous amount of energy had gone into the project before we were really confident of proving it. Another time we might not be so lucky. An

nt shortly after we did the Kirkby story highlighted the point.
one came to us with a story about fiddles on a council contract in
another part of Merseyside. After some preliminary enquiries there
seemed only one way to check the story. This was to interview all three
directors of the firm separately to see if their answers contradicted one
another. The difficulty was to prevent the directors getting together and
sorting out their story beforehand. To do that we had to surprise them at
their homes and interview them simultaneously before they had a chance
to phone the others. All lived miles apart and we would have to check that
they were all at home before approaching any of them. We arranged extra
transport and extra help. The complicated logistics of the operation were
almost worked out when, abruptly, we stopped.

Suddenly, the whole thing seemed ridiculous. What if the story was
true? Was it significant? Not really. How much space would we give it?
Hardly any. We had made a silly mistake. We had already spent hours
planning an investigation simply because it was a challenge. First we
should have asked: If all the allegations we have heard can be proved, will
we want to print to story — and why?

Discussion about the value of corruption stories led us to re-
examine the role of the paper — or rather, to ask whether the paper was
fulfilling the role we had given it. The purpose of the Free Press, we all
agreed, was to provide useful information. Useful stories could be
destructive or constructive. The destructive side was muckraking,
showing people that it does not pay to trust their superiors. The other
meant providing information that people could use in their arguments
and struggles, and trying to give them confidence by reporting the efforts
others were making. The paper had always been a mixture of both — the
"Kirkby corruption" issue, for example, included a long piece on efforts
to form a union at Marks and Spencer — but the balance was heavily
tilted towards muckraking. Even the production process was geared to
the demands of major investigations; publication was often delayed until
"the big story" was ready. On the other hand, people came to us wanting
advance publicity for events they were organising and we had to say:
"Sorry, the paper may not be out in time."

There were several reasons why "destructive" information pre-
dominated. One was that it had a broad appeal and was read by people
who were not necessarily committed to the paper's politics. It helped us
to avoid the problem of talking to the converted that many Left papers
face, and it could start people thinking about the way society is run. The
muckraking stories were the ones people talked about, and the amount of
detail they remembered showed the stories were read thoroughly.
"Constructive" stories were a minority interest, but the minorities
seemed to value them. Also, the results of "destructive" stories were more
tangible. Sometimes heads rolled or victims fought back; politically it did
not matter which, but it did show that the paper had credibility. Those in
control reacted, apparently because they thought the paper was believed

or in danger of being believed. Lastly, "destructive" stories were much easier to do. In the first place, it was easier for readers — and ourselves — to agree about what was wrong than about what should be done. Also, we felt the number of really significant attempts at change were very limited. There were plenty of examples of people blocking dangerous roads but usually there was little to be said about them. The pitfalls of a paper primarily supporting struggles can be seen in Socialist Worker or Big Flame. In some issues virtually all the pictures show people waving placards or picketing factories. Individually, the stories may be worth doing, but the overall effect is unrealistic. It gives the impression that practically everybody is marching somewhere about something. That may be unintentional, but it must make the casual reader wonder who they are trying to kid.

Still, we did think the balance of the Free Press needed shifting more in the "constructive" direction. The first step was a decision to publish once a month, on the dot. This meant investigations would no longer be allowed to hold up publication to the detriment of everything else. Either we would hold them over until they were completed or we would publish "the story so far". It also meant we would be able to cover — and perhaps help — struggles while they were happening instead of holding an inquest into how they were won or lost.

Speeding up production was not just a matter of working harder or faster — we had to save ourselves work. Setting the type, making up the pages and processing the photographs — all of which we did ourselves — took about a week. When the papers came back from the printer they were in flat sheets. We had to collate and fold them by hand. Then we had to distribute them. Collating and distribution took about two weeks. Sometimes deliveries were held up while we folded more papers. That meant that if we cut down the production cycle to one month we would only have one or two weeks to research and write articles.

One possibility was to get the typesetting and make-up done commercially. This seemed unlikely to save much time. Copy would need extra preparation and we would have to draw up detailed page schemes. We decided that on balance the enormous additional expense would not be justified by any time saved. In any case, using a commercial typesetter would add another area of vulnerability to outside pressures, and we wanted to keep that to a minimum.

A more promising area was distribution. Using a near-monopoly like WH Smith — even if it agreed in principle to handle the paper — would be risky. The London magazine, Time Out, had found themselves with thousands of copies they could not distribute when Smiths refused to handle a particular issue. But we discovered that Sunday newspapers in Liverpool had an entirely different distribution system. Sunday papers were in the hands of five small wholesalers, each covering a section of the city. The owner of one of these firms turned out to be a Free Press reader. He agreed to deliver the Free Press in his area along with the Sunday papers and said he would have a word with the firms covering other areas. Three out of the five eventually agreed to take the paper. A fourth took 500 copies of one issue but later returned them, saying nobody had bought any. The wholesalers would take fifteen per cent of the selling price in addition to the 25 per cent taken by newsagents — but that was probably no more than what we had been spending ourselves on petrol, especially in the suburbs whose shops were often long distances apart. It seemed a good arrangement. There was no need to sign away exclusive distribution rights, so we could continue our own sales through individuals and trade unions and also do the lucrative city centre deliveries ourselves because newsagents there were closed on Sundays. It also offered the possibility of a large increase in the number of outlets for the paper.

The snag was that we had to have large numbers of copies ready folded on the first Saturday of each month. The solution to the problem was obvious — though actually solving it was less easy. We would have to change our printer. Previously all but two issues had been printed on sheet-fed presses which were pretty common — there were several printers in Liverpool who could do the job. What we needed was a web-offset printer. This type of machine uses a reel (or web) of paper and has an attachment at the end to fold the papers and slice off individual copies. The web-offset plants in the area were owned by local newspaper groups. One — owned by the Daily Post and Echo — could hardly be expected to print criticism of its owners. The other quoted a reasonable price. But this firm also published the Liverpool Weekly News. They raised no objection at the time, but we were apprehensive in case they left us in the lurch by suddenly refusing to print.

We also had a chat with the proprietor of the Liverpool-based Catholic Pictorial. We knew he read the Free Press and seemed to like it. He did not have his own press, but offered to arrange the printing for us. However, he wanted a letter of indemnity from us, promising to compensate him for any libel action he suffered as a result. While we were mulling this over, we got a cheaper quote from a printer in the south of England who already handled several "risky" publications. He agreed to print the paper in two days — making the plates on a Thursday, printing on Friday morning and putting the papers on a train to arrive on Saturday, in time for the Sunday wholesalers. We were reluctant to send our original artwork to him by train, in case it got lost. So we decided to have negatives of the pages made in Liverpool and send them instead. The Catholic Pictorial agreed to make the negatives and said they would not need a letter of indemnity for that. They were cheap and took only a few hours to do the job. But it was perhaps lucky we had not got them to arrange printing as well. They did the negatives for two issues and then stopped. They were upset by a story that the local BBC radio station seemed to be favouring anti-abortion campaigners.

Web-offset presses are best suited to print in multiples of four pages. The Free Press was normally ten pages. We decided to increase the number to twelve, which would make space for new features.

To broaden the scope of the paper we introduced a half-page "News from Everywhere" section. This was snippets of news culled from other radical papers. The stories were usually edited or re-written. We explained to readers that we had not the resources to check them, but as a guide to reliability, the sources were included. In line with our normal policy, the items chosen were those which had attracted little attention from the commercial papers. A typical example, from our first "News From Everywhere", was this:

> The British Steel Corporation are proposing to invest £3 million in a plant to produce ferro-chrome in Johannesburg. In doing so, they will be breaking the economic sanctions against Rhodesia, for the chrome will come from Rhodesia. BSC's excuse for this investment is that this is the only way to use assets in South Africa which have been frozen by the government. Since then, however, South Africa has unfrozen the money, leaving BSC free to take it out and use it elsewhere. There are several other countries capable of supplying BSC with the chrome it needs — *Sheffield Free Press.*

The "Informer" section, previously a single page "what's on" guide, was expanded to include contributed columns on rock groups, folk clubs, beer and pubs, etc. The emphasis was on local, people's culture rather than the arty-farty. One unusual — and successful — idea was a series of portraits of local buskers.

The role of the centre pages also changed. In the past they had usually contained long, heavily-researched articles by ourselves. To save time, we encouraged contributors with a special knowledge or interest to write their own material. We realised this would need a lot of advance preparation and we would have to have several articles in the pipeline in case contributors failed to meet the deadlines. To kick off, we fixed up a series on the politics of Soccer. The series ran for three months, which gave us a breathing space to get people working on other articles. The series showed how what had once been banned as a "worthless" and "subversive" mob sport, was institutionalised and given rules by the public schools; how it later became accepted by governments "as a means of recruiting troops, boosting morale at home and national prestige abroad," and how it became commercialised. The motif for the series was a picture of the England team giving Nazi salutes at the start of an international with Germany in the 1930s.

Sport was a new area for the Free Press and we hoped these articles would have a long-term effect on the paper. We regarded most sports reporting as sycophantic. Most writers depend enormously on the co-operation and goodwill of the clubs, with the result that the fans are often maligned and their interests ignored. We wanted to redress the balance, but as we lacked the right contacts, behind-the-scenes sports stories were hard to come by. We had noticed that a lot of our tip-offs came as a result of stories people had read in the Free Press. After the Kirkby story, for example, we had several calls about "corruption" (most of them were actually about nothing of the sort, but people seemed to be using the word to try and arouse our interest). We hoped that by showing an interest in sport, readers might come forward with stories. And in fact they did. A few months later several people phoned to complain about the way Liverpool Football Club were selling tickets for their UEFA Cup Final game in Bruges through a travel agency run by one of the club's directors.

The other two new features were in response to specific requests from readers. One was a selection of short stories under the heading "Local Action". The first one reported a free riding school being set up for children on a council estate, a petition against heavy lorries, and two tenants suing their landlord. We explained:

> A number of readers have said they would like to see more "positive" news — what ordinary people are doing to sort out their problems. As time goes on, we hope this section will expand. If you're doing something interesting, give us a ring.

Well, they did not ring very often, and it did not expand. Later, we changed tack and did some detailed reports on large — and supposedly radical — projects like housing co-ops and the government-backed workers' co-operative at Kirkby Manufacturing and Engineering. These seemed to arouse more interest, some of it critical, though there was a glowing letter from Aberdeen People's Press praising the KME report as "one of the best pieces of journalism in the alternative press for years".

Readers were also urging us to introduce "debate" into the paper. But what sort of debate? We wanted to avoid the usual left v right arguments and did not want to get bogged down in theoretical discussions about Marxism, Leninism and the like. We wanted debates on down-to-earth subjects that questioned traditional left-wing ideas, but from a left-wing standpoint. Our plan was to have a new topic every alternate month and to publish replies in the intervening months. The title of the series was "Offensive" — and the first article offended more people than we had bargained for.

This was about the "Lump" — a system in the building industry where workers are technically self-employed sub-contractors. It has been much criticised as being anti-trade union, and leading to both shoddy building and dangerous working conditions. The article examined arguments used by the Left's anti-lump campaign and raised doubts about whether the campaign was in the best interests of building workers. It included some provocative statements like: "It was the Lump workers as much as the miners who hammered the nails in the last Tory Government's incomes policy". The author was a former building worker who had earlier written a pamphlet, "The Lump: An Heretical Analysis".

ERIC OGDEN M.P.

Who does he serve?

We made it clear we did not necessarily agree with articles in the "Offensive" series (and actually we all disagreed with this article to some extent). But the reaction was startling. We received only two letters — one agreeing, one disagreeing. Several building workers who normally sold the paper at work decided not to sell it. Others told us they would rather ignore the article than reply. Altogether, we lost about 400 sales as a result of the article (though we did regain them a couple of months later, thanks to a lot of diplomatic activity). The discussion articles that followed this one seemed to attract little attention. Whether readers discussed them among themselves I don't know, but none of the articles brought more than a handful of replies. Eventually the series fizzled out.

To publicise the paper's re-appearance as a monthly we decorated the city with posters. These showed the Queen pulling a miserable face, with the slogan: "Liverpool Free Press goes monthly in November — some people won't like it". The council certainly did not like it and threatened to prosecute us if we did not remove the posters. But their own workmen got there first and did the job for us.

Welcome additional publicity was provided by a local Member of Parliament, Eric Ogden. Some of his constituency Labour Party were trying to unseat him. About the same time another Labour MP, Reg Prentice, was under attack from his local party for his "moderate" views (he later joined the Conservatives). Ogden tried to jump on the bandwagon and pose as yet another "moderate" threatened by extremists. Our inquiries showed Ogden's opponents were nothing of the kind — they included a Justice of the Peace and former Lord Mayor of Liverpool. Further inquiries into Ogden's Parliamentary career were very revealing (see page 147). Ogden rose to the occasion and condemned the article in the House of Commons. "I seek not the protection of this House," he moaned, "but its judgment as to the truth or falsehood of this article." He claimed the article was a breach of Parliamentary privilege. The Speaker thought it might be and referred to the Commons Committee of Privileges. We first heard about it on the radio.

No-one can be quite sure what Parliamentary privilege means. It means what Parliament wants it to mean at any particular time — like a game where the winning side can change the rules if they ever look like losing. Generally, a breach of privilege is anything which brings Parliament into disrepute. A common example is where a newspaper suggests that an MP's speeches were not entirely motivated by the deepest love for his constituents. Naturally, the only people fit to judge such cases are MPs themselves, the job is done by the Privileges Committee who act as lawmakers, judges, prosecutors and jury all rolled into one. And they hold the trials in private. The punishment is more clearly defined than the crime. Offenders are usually summoned to grovel at the Bar of the House and be told off by the Speaker. Those who prefer to grovel by letter may be allowed to do so. Anyone who refuses is liable to be marched off to the Clock Tower by the Serjeant-at-Arms, where they may be detained until the next General Election.

A few days after Ogden complained we received a letter from Mr J C Boulton, the clerk of the committee. He thoughtfully enclosed a booklet giving hints on preparing our defence. Truth, it said, was no defence. And it was doubtful if "fair comment" was a defence either; it had never been a successful defence in the past, though there could always be a first time. "However," it added cheerfully, "there has never been any doubt that 'fair comment' can be raised by way of mitigation of the offence."

We told our readers: "In these circumstances, we have decided to let the committee get on with the 'trial' by themselves. We do not propose to waste our time providing evidence in our defence, since this would almost certainly be 'irrelevant'. Nor have we yet been given any good reason why we should apologise for the article."

The Privileges Committee met surprisingly quickly and — equally surprising — refused to consider the complaint. They realised that what Ogden was asking them to do was decide whether the article was libellous or not. They made an important ruling: That members who thought they had been libelled should sue instead of bothering the committee. Ironically, almost all the information in the article had comefrom Hansard, the official Parliamentary record. And of course Ogden did not sue. But there were repercussions at a Labour Club in Ogden's constituency. A member there regularly sold about 70 copies of the Free Press. Suddenly those copies stopped being sold.

10. Under attack

THE FREE PRESS had survived for five years and seemed to be flourishing. Its circulation had climbed to 10,000; at last it was appearing monthly; and there was a lively — and generally enthusiastic — response from readers. We had got by without any serious legal problems and now, suddenly, we had two. The fact that both fizzled out before they got to court did not lessen their effect — it showed the damage even the *threat* of legal action could do.

Solicitors in Liverpool make their money from crime, divorce and property sales. What most of them know about libel is what they have read about it. And their letters threatening libel actions usually followed the formula set down in legal textbooks. They would demand a retraction and an apology within seven days, and say that in the meantime they reserved their client's position. In other words, they would like us to admit we were in the wrong. Even if we did so, they might still go ahead and sue — and then the only thing to be decided would be the amount of compensation. On the other hand, if we stood by what we had said, that could make matters worse. In libel, truth is a dangerous defence; if you insist what you said was true you persist in the alleged libel and if the case goes against you the damages are increased.

Our attitude, therefore, was not to rush off and find ourselves a solicitor, but simply to refuse to write back. That way we neither admitted blame nor re-iterated the alleged libel.

In the case of the Free Press, these attempts to get a written response served an additional purpose. The publishers (and, nominally, the printers) of the paper were "The Free Press Group". And in law they did not exist. They could not be sued as a corporate body, like a company. The only way was to sue the individuals responsible. No doubt some solicitors hoped that by opening up a correspondence at least one person would admit involvement with the offending article.

We spelled out our view of the law in the paper following a complaint from a company director:

The English law of libel has correctly been called a Rogues' Charter. It requires journalists to prove allegations in court, while denying them any right of collecting the necessary information. It is a law for the rich only. A working man cannot sue a newspaper for libel because the law does not allow him legal aid. A wealthy man who is able to sue and win is rewarded

with even more money. This, apparently, is the only way to clear his "good name". And there is some logic in it when newspapers are published for profit.
But this does not apply to the Free Press. Our aim is neither to make money nor to mislead our readers. Not even "justice" can make us pay money we don't have. This does not mean we are "irresponsible". But our responsibility is to ourselves and to our readers. So when we make a mistake v. :'ll put the facts straight and apologise. And that will have to be that.

Probably most of those who complained had no intention of suing but hoped the language of a solicitor's letter would frighten us into an apology. Our reaction was to treat solicitors' letters as if any ordinary person had written them — and publish them. If we thought the client might be serious, we usually printed the letter without comment. When someone seemed to be just trying it on, we felt freer to reply — indeed, one such letter, and our reply, was printed under the heading: TRYING IT ON. Some solictors' letters were riddled with jargon and one or two were ungrammatical and full of spelling mistakes. One solicitor even wrote "liable" when he meant "libel". Publication of badly-written letters did solicitors no good. It was bad for their business and led to ridicule from the rest of their profession. The paper was read eagerly by a lot of lawyers in the city. Some even kept a note of coppers who were named in the Free Press for use in defending future clients who were arrested by them. Our general aim in publishing threatening letters was to show that people who paid solicitors to write on their behalf fared no better than those who wrote their own letters. Probably some would have done a great deal better by giving their own version. The ploy seemed to pay off. Certainly we heard of several solicitors trying to persuade their clients to be sensible.

Much of civil law, and particularly libel, is like the ancient upper-class pastime of duelling; it depends on both sides playing the game. A challenge is made. Both sides appoint seconds to decide what weapons shall or shall not be used. Then they present themselves like gentlemen. But if one side refuses to come into the open and instead takes pot-shots from the bushes, the game has to be abandoned. Usually. But when we crossed swords with E Rex Makin it was different; he fought in the bushes, too. Makin was one of the city's most prosperous crime lawyers and had the habit of replacing his Rolls with a new one about as regularly as most people replace worn-out shoes.

We were running a series called "The Oil Sheikhs of Liverpool", about a period in the 1960s when fortunes were made by getting permission from the council to open petrol stations. Several councillors had been suspected of oiling the works to help would-be owners get permission. A Labour councillor accused a taking a bribe in connection with this had been defended — successfully — by Makin. We noted in passing that a trust fund for Makin's children held shares in another garage, run by another Labour councillor. The reference was incidental and there was no suggestion Makin or his trust fund had been involved in malpractice. Makin was furious and sent a long, blustering letter threatening to sue. It was marked: "Not for publication" and we published it, with a detailed reply, in our next issue. We were not unduly worried at first because we did not believe the article was libellous (and a barrister later confirmed our view). But then we discovered Makin had written to all our wholesalers, threatening to sue them. He had also visited several newsagents, making similar threats and had even written to a doctor who had copies of the Free Prees in his waiting room. The immediate effect was that two of our three wholesalers decided to stop handling the paper — and we could hardly blame them, knowing the cost of fighting libel actions and the fact that they were getting only about £15 a month extra from the deliveries. Several newsagents who received copies direct from us also stopped, though two of them said they would start again when there were no references to Makin in the paper.

We tried to laugh it off by producing badges and T-shirts saying: "Rex Makin is innocent, OK", but the damage was serious. It meant we could no longer publish monthly because of all the extra deliveries we would have to do ourselves, and our hopes of a rapid growth in circulation were dashed. There was no way we would ever get large numbers of copies distributed by wholesalers again. And it was all the more annoying because Makin showed no sign of issuing writs.

At the same time we were threatened with prosecution for contempt. Contempt can be any action likely to interfere with the course of justice. By "justice", what is actually meant is the law — and the words are not necessarily synonymous. Sometimes the law conflicts with true justice or the public interest. For example, it is often said that if Watergate had happened in this country the laws of contempt would have made sure the truth never came out. Contempt cases are tried without a jury and the penalties are unlimited. That may explain why the big newspapers sometimes criticise the law but never challenge it. The dirty work is usually left to small, comparatively weak papers like The Leveller and Peace News (see Chapter 5). The safest course in a contempt case is to apologise and promise not to do it again. Legal defences rarely work because the law is so vague and changeable on the whim of a judge. A political defence that exposes the law at its weakest point does sometimes work. In 1972, five London dockers were jailed for contempt in defying the Industrial Relations Court. Thousands of workers throughout the country displayed their own contempt for the court and went on strike. Very quickly the Government wheeled out an obscure civil servant called the Official Solicitor who had previously-unheard-of powers to get the men released.

The Free Press probably committed contempt several times, though in the uncertain state of the law it is difficult to be sure. But we did not invite trouble indiscriminately; we risked contempt when the public interest seemed to warrant it and when arguments for doing so would

Two regular strip cartoons from the Free Press.

appear reasonable to the ordinary person, even if they failed to impress a judge. Contempt was most often a problem when there were complaints against the police. We heard of numerous stories of people being tried for crimes which they could not have committed without the police being present. In a typical case, the police would stop someone in the street, apparently because they did not like the look of him. They would ask questions and if the person became un-cooperative they would rough him up and arrest him. They would then find something to charge him with. If all else failed he would be charged with assaulting the police. In other cases, people were arrested for a real, but often quite minor crime, then beaten up while in custody. There were two problems in reporting these stories. The first was a legal one: The victims were invariably facing charges and any comment on the police behaviour might be construed as contempt. The second problem was the journalistic one of credibility: There were rarely any witnesses apart from the police — and the police could (and often did) excuse their behaviour on the ground that the accused tried to resist arrest or to escape, and in those circumstances they were permitted to use "reasonable" force.

In the case of John Lannon, a 35-year-old Kirkby man, there was no shortage of witnesses. He had been celebrating his daughter's thirteenth birthday. After the party he stayed at home, drinking. Between three and four in the morning he went out. By all accounts he was very drunk. About 4.30 he was arrested at the back of the Woodpecker pub, a short walk away. The Woodpecker stands in the centre of a square, surrounded by flats and houses on all sides. More than a dozen people saw what happened to Lannon. Two had had difficulty in sleeping. The others were awakened by the noise. One even phoned the police to complain. Following his arrest, Lannon was beaten by two police officers and dragged to the side of the pub. There he was attacked again, with two more officers and the landlady of the pub joining in with what one witness said was a trucheon. The officers then ran, bouncing and dragging him along the ground. He was screaming, his clothes were ripped and covered with blood. Skin and flesh was scraped off his back and backside. At the police station he asked to see a doctor but his requests were refused. Eleven hours later, while still in custody, he began coughing blood and was rushed to hospital. There he had an emergency operation for a punctured lung and was treated for a broken rib, facial injuries and severe bruising. He faced ten charges: Attempted burglary, stealing dog food, damaging a car, damaging police uniforms, three charges of assaulting police officers and a further three of common assault on the same police officers.

The story, complete with a sketch map and statements from witnesses, took up more than half a page. Most papers would have refused to touch it for fear of contempt, though journalistically, it was entirely sound. We waited . . . but nothing happened. Not a murmur from the police. Had someone decided that in view of the evidence it would be prudent to take no action against us?

When Lannon's trial began, the prosecution approached his defence lawyer. They would forget about the five most serious charges if he pleaded guilty to the minor ones. Lannon agreed. The judge sentenced him to 200 hours community service and ordered him to pay £18.90 towards the damage. It was a neat solution: An unusually light sentence but — most important — there was no need to call any embarrassing witnesses. John Lannon had a long record, and if we had not published the story it is very likely he would have gone to jail again. He was planning to sue or prosecute the police when, little more than a year later, he died of a heart attack.

Trouble over contempt did come a few months later. We did a story about a police inquiry into a detective in the Serious Crimes Squad. The detective had helped arrest a well-known criminal on 16 charges of burglary, theft and handling stolen goods. After a four-week trial the man was acquitted on all charges. Interestingly, the man had repeatedly claimed that a safe containing stolen property could be found at the detective's home. While in custody awaiting trial the man had escaped. He maintained that while on the run he had a meeting with a police superintendent, discussed the allegations about the safe — then went back on the run. The safe was eventually found, allegedly by accident, by the detective's wife. It was cemented into the garage wall behind a freezer. It contained stolen jewellery and pass keys and a pistol which the police described as a replica. At the man's trial, the prosecution claimed the safe had been 'planted' to discredit the detective. Someone, presumably, had sneaked in, undetected by two burglar alarms at the house, removed several bricks, installed the safe, cleaned up the mess and got away without anyone noticing. The problem in reporting this was that the detective under investigation was an important prosecution witness in another major trial. The story of the safe could be contempt because it was likely to affect the detective's credibility in this later trial. We went ahead with the story because it seemed unlikely there would ever be a time when the detective would not be a witness, or at least a potential witness, in some case or other.

When the story came out someone — probably a defendant in the later trial — left copies of the Free Press lying around the court building. The judge was furious and reported the incident to the Director of Public Prosecutions. The Chief Constable shrewdly asked his Commercial Branch to investigate. Shrewdly — because they were the department who had handled the Kirkby case and knew most about the Free Press. But although they knew who had worked on the Kirkby story, they had difficulty establishing who was responsible for the story of the safe. We refused to answer questions or say whether we had worked on the offending issue. So the police interviewed advertisers, shopkeepers and anyone they could find who had dealings with us. They were looking for signatures on receipts, cheques, and so on. This naturally added to the harassment caused by Mr Makin's libel threats. But it did not do much damage because most of those likely to be bothered had already been scared off by Makin. It did cause extra cash problems for a time when the last cheque from one of the wholesalers bounced. He said the police had advised him to stop payment — though he paid later when we complained.

The detective 'planted' with the safe was suspended from duty shortly after the story appeared. He was reinstated some months later, but the police would not say what action, if any, had been taken. And shortly after that, the Director of Public Prosecutions decided to take no action against the Free Press.

To add to our troubles, we had financial problems. The decision to publish monthly had been an all-or-bust move. When the Free Press began it was a spare time activity. We all had other jobs. The paper's income covered printing costs, but no-one was paid for their labour. In the years that followed, Chris and I left the Post and Echo to become freelances. We earned less money but had more time to work for the Free Press. Later, when Steve joined, we formed a news agency, supplying stories to radio, television and other papers. Some extra money came from doing commercial typesetting on the machine we used for the Free Press. As we lived in the same house costs were shared and we did not need much to live on. Our income was divided equally, regardless of how much work any individual actually did for the news agency. This meant that anyone who became heavily involved in an unpaid Free Press story would not suffer — he would be subsidised by the earnings of the others. This worked reasonably well while the paper was published every couple of months or so. Once it became a monthly we all had less time to earn our living. Of course we had expected that; we wanted to give the Free Press one big push and hoped that the situation would become easier after a few monthly issues. We hoped that regular publication would increase the flow of stories from readers, and that distribution by wholesalers would bring a rise in sales — perhaps enabling the paper to pay one person to work for it full-time. But it was not to be. The loss of two of the wholesalers put us back where we started.

The Free Press itself ran short of money. Partly it was a cash-flow problem — we were paying for more copies to be printed and waiting longer for the money from newsagents. Also, the paper was having to pay its share of phone bills and transport costs because we could not pay them ourselves as we had done often in the past. We appealed to readers and raised more than £400. It was a magnificent amount, but it did not solve our own problems and did little more than extend the paper's life by a few months.

Chris, particularly, was worried about debts and left the Free Press, first to concentrate on freelance work — and then to work for television in London. Steve stayed with the Free Press but went on the dole — and was better off. Unfortunately the Department of Employment computer found him a job, writing bulletins for the Merseyside Council for Voluntary Service. He found this very boring and went off to London. Derek and I stayed behind. But despite help from several new people, we found the news was getting out of date faster than we could write it. It was impossible to carry on.

Extracts from the Free Press

H ere are some extracts from stories published in the Liverpool Free Press. They are not necessarily the best stories, though they do include some of my own favourites. They are intended mainly to give readers some idea of the range of the paper's coverage and to show the differing styles and reporting techniques used. One or two minor alterations have been made for the benefit of readers unfamiliar with Liverpool and some of the stories have been shortened, but most of them are reprinted unchanged.

£20 — the price of a lost job

A photographer who refused to employ a young black man because of his colour, has had to pay compensation of £20.

Stewart Bale, who's been described as the Lord Snowdon of Liverpool, advertised in the Liverpool Echo for a photographic apprentice.

Anthony Ogunsiji, a British-born black lad, phoned the number given and was put through to a man who, he later discovered, was Bale.

In his statement to the Race Relations Board, Anthony described what happened:

Anthony: I am ringing about the advertisement in last night's Echo.
Voice: What is your name?
Anthony: Anthony Ogunsiji.
Voice: What's your religion?
Anthony: Protestant.
Voice: Are you of foreign descent?
Anthony: Yes I am.
Voice: I don't want any foreigners.

Anthony explained that he was English.

Voice: What colour are you — are you black?
Anthony: Yes.
Voice: We don't want any of them here.

Anthony complained to the Race Relations Board and their conciliation committee decided that unlawful discrimination had taken place.

Bale paid Anthony £20 compensation and promised not to discriminate in future.

Anthony's case was unusual because most employers have more subtle ways of giving black people the brush-off. Often discrimination is extremely difficult to prove.

Where there is proof, compensation is usually so small that many black people don't bother going through the time-consuming process of making an official complaint.

November, 1974

Letters to accused are intercepted

Letters — posted to a Liverpool man accused of conspiracy — are being intercepted and opened.

Frank Keeley is one of fourteen pacifists charged with conspiring to seduce troops from their allegiance to the Queen.

Since the middle of January, at least five letters sent to Frank have failed to arrive. One was from his solicitor, one from the Defence Group in London and another from the Defence Group in Manchester. Two letters from his cousin have also vanished mysteriously in the post.

A tax rebate did arrive, though the envelope had been ripped open. It had been stuck together again with sellotape and a scribbled note said: "Envelope damaged by sorter 6/2/75".

On learning of this, the Free Press sent Frank a specially prepared letter. Inside an ordinary white envelope was a light-proof bag containing undeveloped photographic film.

If the letter arrived unopened, the film could be developed and a picture would appear. If it had been opened, the film would turn out black. If someone realised the trick and substituted fresh film, there would be no picture.

We posted the letter — First Class — at 4.30 pm on February 13.

It did not arrive next day. But on February 15, Frank Keeley got two letters.

One was our own white envelope. Close scrutiny showed it had been slit open at one end and skilfully resealed with an unusual type of glue.

The film was inside, but the light-proof bag had disappeared.

The other letter was a large brown envelope with a smudged postmark. Frank opened this mystery envelope and was astonished.

Inside was the missing light-proof bag! And clipped to the bag were two pieces of paper.

One was a photocopy of what looked like a printed letter-head. It had the Royal Coat of Arms and the words "Ministry of Intelligence Department Six.."

The other piece of paper was a photocopy of a message, very carefully hand written in capitals. It said: "I wonder if you'll get the same as Daly? He was too hot as well. Still, that's your funeral."

On the back it said: "Two of your 'friends' have blood on their hands. Have they told you?"

It is unlikely that the "letter-head" is a genuine Government document. But it is difficult to see who, other than some official intelligence department, would have the opportunity or the desire to interfere with mail in this way.

We suspect that what happened was this: the letter was opened, probably officially, and whoever opened it spotted our trick. They then made up a letter-head, using Letraset to give it a 'printed' apprearance (the lettering is slightly crooked).

This would be a protection against embarrassing questions. They could simply say: "There is no Ministry of Intelligence. The document is a crude forgery."

The other piece of paper is more interesting. "Daly" — we eventually discovered — is probably a reference to Tim Daly, a poet who got a long jail sentence several years ago for a protest in which he tried to burn down the Imperial War Museum.

His case was not widely reported outside the pages of Peace News. The most avid readers of back numbers of Peace News at the moment are the Special Branch.

They are trying to collect evidence for the conspiracy trial. One of the Peace News editors is among the fourteen accused, and several articles from the paper are expected to be used as evidence by the prosecution.

The charges arose after leaflets entitled "Some Information for discontented Soldiers" were distributed at army barracks near Oswestry last August.

The leaflets were produced by the British Withdrawal from Northern Ireland Campaign.

February, 1975
● *Frank and the other 13 accused were later acquitted.*

Claimant plays a trump card

As claimants well know, the Social Security are very fond of quoting boring and incomprehensible bits of Acts of Parliament to justify not giving you any money.

A claimant in Kirkby has just played them at their own game and won.

The Social Security Act of 1966 gives the SS the discretionary power to make cash payments over the counter in cases of "urgent need". Their discretionay power usually decides there is no urgent need and there's very little the claimant can do to change their minds (apart, perhaps, from dying of starvation).

When our Kirkby claimant, Tommy Ewing, called in the local SS office, said he was in urgent need and asked for a cash payment, they followed their usual policy of evasion and down-right lies. Firstly they said he was not in urgent need. When he proved that he was destitute the clerk said: "We can't make cash payments to students." The manager repeated this statement.

Unfortunately for them the claimant was a student of the 1966 Social Security Act, which says in section 29b that if anyone: "for the purpose of avoiding or reducing any liability under this Act: Makes any statement or representation which he knows to be false, he shall be liable on summary conviction to imprisonment for a term not exceeding three months or to a fine not exceeding £100 or to both."

In simple English, if anybody, including clerks and managers, makes an untrue statement which reduces or stops a claimant's benefit he is a criminal and the police have a legal duty to prosecute.

The 1966 Act does not say cash payments cannot be made to students, and the SS officers were consequently lying. It does not matter if the claimant is a student, a single parent or an unemployed lion tamer. The only criterion should be "urgent need".

Tommy Ewing went to Kirkby police station and asked for the strong arm of the law to intervene. The sergeant at the desk was somewhat bemused so he passed the matter to his superior in the CID.

When the law was pointed out to him, the CID man had to agree with the claimant and he phoned the Social Security manager saying the police might have to prosecute. The SS of course denied making the statement but they did send a Giro out immediately by recorded delivery and the claimant got it the next day.

We are not saying the law, the police and the courts will be on the side of claimants — far from it — but if the SS make a fase statement to you such as the common "We don't make cash payments", "We can't give clothing grants" or "We can't pay gas and electricity bills" the method is worth a try.

Ask them to give a refusal in writing (which is your legal right), use this as evidence and ask the police to prosecute, quoting section 29b of the Social Security Act.

February, 1976

A career with good prospects

The death of an unemployed Kirkby boy who joined the army — and became the hundredth British soldier killed in Ireland — has led to protests about recruiting methods.

Kirkby councillor John King commented: "I think it is wrong that the army should move into a town like this. They are taking advantage because they know that young lads here are desperate for money."

On August 5 this distressing story found its way into the Daily Post, where, by some horrible blunder, this announcement appeared just above it: "BOYS! WIN A DAY WITH THE ARMY — NEW CONTEST" On another page were exciting pictures of the army in action and details of the Daily Post's contest:

"Be where the action is! Here is a great opportunity for *ten boys* aged 13-16, to spend a day with the British Army on September 27. Our party of winners will be guests of the Army's School of Infantry, based at Warminster, Wiltshire. A comprehensive programme has been arranged, which includes rides in tanks and personnel carriers and the firing of infantry weapons.

"The party will stay overnight and

every waking minute promises to be *action packed full of excitement.*"

Competitors were asked to place in order eight things which "make the army an interesting and worthwhile career."

The 'correct' order decided by the judges was: 1 good career prospects; 2 the challenge; 3 the comradeship; 4 opportunity for travel; 5 good pay and allowances; 6 ample sports and recreation; 7 generous leave; 8 use of latest equipment.

Not surprisingly, nobody from Kirkby got it right.

September, 1972

Peeping Tom
the schools inspector

Sex makes Tom Clarke mad. And as Liverpool's Chief Inspector of Schools, his pious utterings about morality, along with his attacks on progressive education, attract widespread attention.

In July, for instance, the Liverpool Echo gave plenty of space to his attack on "trendy teachers and educational experts".

"We want no more of their mental aphrodisiacs," Clarke declared at a school prize-giving.

He went on to condemn "pornography" in school books. "Unlike burglary or other crimes, sex — by its hold on the imagination — can reproduce itself even by report.

"We must protect our children against appeals to this instinct . . . whether the smut be in Shakespeare or Chaucer."

Mr Clarke's audience could be forgiven for getting the idea that the Chief Inspector of Schools considers sex a crime and smut intolerable. Yet nothing could be further from the truth.

Shortly before that stirring speech, Clarke was at a gathering of a different kind.

There are no speeches and no prizes given at Gatsby's Club, in the city centre, during Friday lunch-times. Men like Tom Clarke go there to study the young Go-Go dancer and the two (female) striptease acts.

This Friday, Tom Clarke arrived early at Gatsby's and secured a ringside seat. Men at the front obviously get a better view of the girls. And, if they're very lucky, are sometimes invited to play a small part in the act.

This was Tom Clarke's lucky day. One of the strippers danced tantalisingly close. Then, down to her last garments, she indicated that he should remove her bra. Being a gentleman of old-fashioned values, the Chief Inspector of Schools naturally obliged.

Usually this lunchtime titillation of city gents would be of no interest to the Free Press or anyone else. But Tom Clarke's little performance is an interesting contrast to his publicly stated views.

He insists, for example, that corporal punishment "must be retained for all found guilty of personal violence, with a special recommendation against mercy for those who *lay hands on women* and children."

He announces that "There can be no compromise with evil . . . no matter how attractively it is presented."

He is against children being allowed "to develop their personalities in a natural sort of way."

He proclaims that the only alternative to the "standards" he supposedly supports is "chaos, tyranny with all its most frightful consequences — the primacy of the most vile over the most noble."

And so — armed with all these fine phrases — Tom Clarke was able to appeal to the parents of the girls of Notre Dame High School, last autumn, to have the moral courage to antagonise those who would corrupt the young.

These are not, of course, fine, honest men like Tom Clarke. They are "teachers who disrupt and subvert" who must be "rooted out and sacked."

And all this has to be done to preserve an educational system which turns out frustrated, ignorant, bitter, hypocritical individuals like Liverpool's Chief Inspector of Schools, Tom Clarke.

September, 1976

Labour men buy council houses

Three Labour councillors living on council estates have escaped rent increases under the Government's Fair Rents Act.

For a Free Press investigation shows that councillors James Mottram, Tom Bailey and Bill Lafferty have bought their council homes.

A fourth member, Councillor Bill Smyth was in the Labour party when he bought his house but has since joined the Liberals.

Rightly, one of the first actions of the Liverpool Labour Party when they came to power in May was to stop the sale of council houses. And there was very little dissension when this policy was agreed at a Labour group meeting.

Councillor Lafferty only missed rent rises under the Act by a hair's breadth. The sale of his house, 17 Garsfield Road, Anfield, wasn't completed until July this year, whereas the other three councillors bought their homes in 1968.

Three of the councillors — Smyth, Mottram and Lafferty — failed for various reasons to attend the critical council meeting when Liverpool agreed to implement the anti-tenant Act.

The one who did attend, Councillor 'Thrasher' Bailey (he supports corporal punishment in schools) voted with right-wing Labour colleagues for implementation.

Soon after the council decision on 'Fair' Rents, Bill Lafferty joined the 21 Labour members who are continuing the fight against the Act and refusing to attend any meetings called by the official Labour group.

However this flurry of opposition didn't last long. He didn't attend meetings held by the 'rebels' and has now returned to the official Labour group.

December, 1972

Write your own adverts . .

Those people shy enough and lonely enough to answer advertisements in the 'Mersey Magnet' personal column naturally think their replies are confidential.

They supply their name and address, with often very intimate personal details to the equally lonely person who paid for the advertisement.

There are people cruel enough and callous enough to 'advertise' for a joke — somehow finding the replies amusing. But the two advertisements reprinted below (from the Mersey Magnet of January 19) are more than a sick joke.

Attractive tall young lady, 22 years, interests badminton and lively living, parties etc., wishes to meet young man 25-30 years similar interests. Replies Box MM 4009.

Intelligent young lady 24, interests theatre, music, politics, seeks gentleman 26-35, similar interests (car owner preferred) view friendship. Replies box MM 4010.

Both were included at the instigation of Magnet boss Jim Chapman who had problems of his own — too few adverts to fill a gap in his page.

Family-man Chapman soon found the answer. He asked some of the tele-ad girls to make up adverts of their own. The details were accurate enough — only the girls aren't really lonely.

One girl did go out with one of the men who replied. But others who wrote in were not so lucky. Their letters provided entertainment for Magnet staff before being thrown in the waste-paper bin.

As the Magnet itself says: "Our box reply service is strictly confidential."

●The Mersey Magnet, a give-away advertising paper, is published by Mercury Promotions Ltd (part of the Daily Post and Echo combine) — and cashes in on loneliness at a rate of 5p a word, plus 25p for box numbers.

Liberal way to get rid of your father-in-law

You can't beat the Liberals for fairness. Especially if you join them. Take Liverpool Liberal councillor John Wilde, for instance. The Liberals have been very fair to him.

Councillor Wilde had a problem. The sort of problem that can upset even the

Sneak picture taken inside Lewis' with a camera hidden in a Christmas parcel.

nicest family. He got landed with his father-in-law.

And unfortunately, as Mrs Wilde so charmingly puts it, her father is "a very awkward person" and doesn't mix very well. He's only 60 but "he acts a lot older". (The charming Mrs Wilde again.)

So the Wildes decided to get rid of him — during the day, anyway. Last November councillor Wilde's father-in-law became a day patient at Croxteth Lodge, a residential home for the elderly.

He goes seven days a week, gets two square meals, watches television . . . and he's unique. There hasn't been another "day patient" at Croxteth Lodge in the last ten years.

For the princely sum of 15p a day the semi-detatched Wildes seemed to have solved their problem. But they're still not satisfied.

All that driving from Woolton to Croxteth Lodge is getting Mrs Wilde down. It would be far better if her father lived in the home actually.

And, with that nice Councillor Johnston (Liberal chairman of the Libraries and Leisure Committee) taking a personal interest, anything is possible.

Of course, to suggest all this is underhand, that Coucillor Wilde abused his position, or that he is better able than most to look after his relatives, that thousands of old people need the council's help more than his father-in-law . . .

To suggest anything like that would probably be unfair.

May, 1975

'We'd rather close than pay for fire safety'

Lewis's, Liverpool's largest department store have threatened to close down rather than spend £600,000 on fire safety.

When the Corporation asked them to make alterations which would improve fire safety, they said they couldn't afford it.

Lewis's Ltd — who have other interests besides stores — have capital reserves of over £20 million.

Lewis's is a subsidiary of Sir Charles Clore's vast empire, Sears Holdings, which made £38 million profit last year.

The disastrous fire which swept through Henderson's store in 1960, killing eleven people, is remembered only too well by Liverpool fire officers.

But it is something a lot of the stores would rather forget. Despite the Corporation's efforts to tighten up on fire precautions, most stores in the city still have no fire safety certificate.

Businessmen generally are more interested in building fortunes than fire escapes. They tend to make as few safety provisions as they can get away with and then hope the provisions will never be put to the test.

In March last year Mr Denis Greensmith, Lewis's Managing Director, and two senior executives met top Corporation officials for a confidential chat about the situation. Details of their talks were kept so secret that not a word has leaked out until now.

Mr Greensmith said the alterations suggested by the Corporation to improve safety would cost £600,000. Business was not as good as it used to be, and if the Corporation remained adamant the store would have to close.

He pointed out that the Association of Department Stores were objecting to some of the Government's new fire regulations, and these might well be changed as a result. (Naturally they were objecting — to save money).

The threat to close faced the Corporation with an impossible dilemma: Should they be strict and risk seeing Lewis's staff in the dole queue, or should they compromise and risk seeing people killed?

Mr Greensmith asked the Corporation to make "tolerances" over such things as distances from staircases, and floor populations. The result of "tolerances" over fire precautions was shown this summer in the Isle of Man.

Mr Greensmith said Lewis's were in any case thinking of altering the store (for business reasons). The plan at the time of the meeting was to close the

Renshaw Street half, and extend in the other direction onto the Central Station site. This might take five years to complete, providing various negotiations were successful.

He hoped that until this plan was either abandoned or completed the Corporation would put up with "some modified requirements" as far as fire safety was concerned.

In the light of all this the Corporation agreed to reconsider the matter.

That was more than a year ago. Since then there has been silence. It is high time both Lewis's and the Corporation made public statements of their intentions.

October, 1973
● *The Daily Post and Echo hastily assured their readers that all was well in the store. But over the next few months the safety work was carried out under the guise of a "facelift".*

Letter from a Liberal landlord

Liberal councillor and landlord Michael Hefferon is due to receive £250,000 in improvement grants.

His big problem has been how to get rid of existing tenants to that his property can be converted.

In an attempt to persuade a mother of four children to leave her flat, he sent this letter:

"It is proposed within the next six weeks to convert this property into six self contained flats. As we have pointed out to all tenants there will be quite a lot of discomfort while this work is in progress. The estimated time for this conversion is approximately twenty weeks .

"Mrs . . . . . . has four young children and we have advised her in her own interest to seek alternative accommodation as there will be quite a lot of dust and building rubble in the atmosphere due to these operations."

When she has gone and the alterations are complete, new — possibly higher — rents will be fixed for the flat.

Councillor Hefferon will have increased the value of his property and

also his income from rents. And what's more, three-quarters of the cost of the "improvement" work will be paid for by the public.

Councillor Herreron has interests in at least fifty properties in Liverpool, most of them multi-occupied and ripe for the Government's 75% improvement grants, and he is wasting no time in making them even more multi-occupied than before with a grant of £1,800 per flat.

Now this is hardly the sort of Liberal image we have been led to expect — perhaps it's not only the paving stones that are cracking in Liverpool.

At the recent Liberal Party conference, the deputy leader of the party in Liverpool said: "What better way is there for involving people in their community than giving them a real stake in the housing in which they live?"

He also suggested the gradual abolition of the landlord system in privately owned accommodation.

You bet it will be gradual, with the likes of Councillor Hefferon in the party.

On pages six and seven we take a more detailed look at landlord Hefferon, and also at the business interests of the Liverpool Liberal leader, Cyril Carr.

Our investigation has highlighted some striking contradictions between Liberal policies and actions.

Des Wilson, former director of Shelter, and now a Liberal candidate for Parliament, makes a strange bedfellow with the Liberals' men of property.

Thorpe himself has property interests. He's a director of six companies, including London and County Securities. A subsidiary of London and County Overseas Financial Trust was revealed at the beginning of the year to be charging an interest rate of 280% on its second mortgage rackets.

Despite militant noises from the Young Liberals, Cyril Smith, the party's fat fund-raiser make it quite clear where the party really stands. He has no compunction about collecting money from anyone, because, he says, it is 'cleansed' by being devoted to Liberalism.

"I never fail to remind company directors that there are two free enterprise parties in this country, not one. Liberals don't object to profit. What we are concerned about is how it is obtained and what happens to it when it is obtained,"he wrote recently in Liberal News.

The Liberal Party have committed themselves to raising £250,000 to fight the next General Election, but committing themselves to their policies is to be avoided . . .

In a leaflet for party members entitled "How to be Political", the following advice appears:

"Every effort should be made to avoid embarrassments for the speakers. For instance, if one of them is a pacifist, the case for the Liberal defence policy should not be argued on that occasion, unless of course a defence issue is the burning topic of the day."

The Liberals' success in Liverpool is based upon a programme of community politics, a subject they are very sensitive about. The same leaflet advises:

"Avoid being dubbed as an association and/or candidate concerned merely with local issues. At the same time ensure that as many as possible of your national policy issues are related to actual local circumstances."

Contrary to popular thought, the Liberals do have national policies, in fact they have too many of them, and most of them are so contradictory they seem to have been picked out of a hat.

But it is not policies that the public are demanding of the Liberals — just a focus for their discontent, hitched to a feeling that new faces open new doors.

It is purely a matter of time before the public discover that the new faces are no different from the old ones and the door is slammed in their faces.

October, 1973

● *Many of the Liberals themselves were unaware of Councillor Hefferon's activities. In the uproar that followed our story he eventually resigned.*

Eric Ogden MP: Who does he serve?

For over ten years the national press ignored Eric Ogden, the minor backbench Labour MP for West Derby, Liverpool.

But suddenly he shot into the limelight when censured by his local party. Newspapers have pictured him as a heroic, moderate MP. A man challenged by dangerous extremists on the executive of the West Derby Labour Party.

The censure vote was on a minor issue and had nothing to do with a struggle between left and right. One of the movers of the motion was Merseyside councillor Francis Burke, a JP and former Lord Mayor of Liverpool. Hardly a dangerous agitator.

The fact is that local Labour parties and voters have little real control over an MP once he is elected.

Here we look at some of the little-known activities of Eric Ogden, and we ask: "Who exactly does he represent in the Commons?"

A cheap trip to Rhodesia

In the summer of 1972 Eric Ogden, a Methodist and former miner, toured Rhodesia.

Who paid his fare? — That was a question which intrigued a number of MPs in the Commons.

Ogden answered: "I paid my own fare . . . at least from Johannesburg to Salisbury."

Finally he spilled the beans: "I went under the umbrella of a company which happens to be called Ogden's Tobacco Co, with which Mr Speaker knows I have unfortunately no financial relationship. I have no directorship with that company."

After his cheap tour, Mr Ogden returned to Parliament to speak powerfully against economic sanctions.

"Apart from a few dedicated people and organisations there is little support for the continuation of sanctions against Rhodesia."

The way to reach a settlement, he said, lay in "investment and persuasion."

Perhaps Mr Ogden was himself

and Free Press, October 1973

TARNISHED SIDE OF THE LIBERALS' SHINY IMAGE

FOCUS ON A SPECULATOR

MICHAEL HEFFERON is a Liberal councillor and a property speculator. This special Free Press investigation shows some of the things he's been up to...

● He is due to receive about £250,000 in public money to develop his growing empire.

● He has appeared in court for breaking the fire regulations.

● He has received numerous orders from Liverpool Public Health officers to do repairs.

● He has used a loophole in the Rent Act to over-charge his tenants.

Mr Hefferon, who lives in Maghull, specialises in buying large houses which are ideal for converting with the help of grants. In May this year he was elected a District Councillor for Tuebrook.

£250,000

TENANTS WERE OVER-CHARGED

THE LIBERAL FACE OF CAPITALISM

CYRIL CARR and his businesses

THE CARR FAMILY

HENRY CARR.

CYRIL CARR.

MALCOLM CARR.

PAT STONE.

VARIETY OF COMPANIES

CHANGING VALUE

LANDLOR

persuaded by the economic plight of that multi-national firm the Imperial Tobacco Company, who own Ogden's Tobacco.

Later in the debate one MP pointed out that sanctions were seriously damaging the tobacco industry in Rhodesia. (Much of this industry was owned by Imperial.)

If the government had been of the same "persuasion" as Mr Ogden, sanctions would have been lifted. And Imperial could legally have got their hands on that Rhodesian tobacco, picked by cheap black labour.

Mr Ogden probably wouldn't look back on this speech as his only proud moment in Parliament. There have been others.

Helping docks to lose work

One of his achievements was to help the Mersey docks lose work valued at £1,850,000 a year.

Behind this feat lies an interesting tale. In the late sixties and early seventies the giant oil firm Shell were looking for quick and cheap ways of pumping oil from their massive super-tankers to their refineries at Stanlow, Merseyside.

At the time their super-tankers had to anchor in Liverpool Bay and unload into smaller tankers which then sailed up the Mersey to pump the oil ashore at Tranmere terminal.

This wasn't fast enough for Shell. There were too many tidal delays. And time meant money.

Far simpler would be two mooring buoys out at sea, where the super-tankers could tie up and pump their oil directly ashore.

They found the ideal place. But it wasn't on Merseyside. It was off the unspoilt beaches of Anglesey.

Shell first had to persuade Anglesey council that what was good for Shell was good for Anglesey.

Quite a task. But, as the Sunday Times said, "Shell's public relations officers criss-crossed Anglesey meeting people, showing films, explaining, cajoling, dampening talk of pollution."

Anglesey council agreed to promote the necessary Bill in Parliament, and to rebuild Amlwch harbour at a cost between £¾ million and £1½ million.

The council accepted that pollution would be negligible and wouldn't affect tourism. And they agreed to Shell building 15 storage tanks, each twice the size of Conway Castle (though not quite as attractive).

The council's attitude stunned a number of MPs. One said: "The way in which they have approached the Bill has been negligent, cavalier and superficial to a degree which is a betrayal of the people they represent."

Another said more bluntly: "Shell are taking Anglesey for a ride."

There was still a possibility of opposition from Merseyside, where the docks stood to lose over £1m a year in revenue because of the move.

But Shell's public relations officers came across Eric Ogden.

They didn't find the West Derby MP on Merseyside, nor even taking a last dip on Anglesey's unpolluted beaches. They found him in sunny South Africa.

Mr Ogden was there with two other Labour MPs as guests of the South Africa Foundation, a public relations organisation, which publicises the other attractions of South Africa (apart from apartheid).

While he was there Ogden was shown around Shell's oil terminal and single buoy mooring in Durban. This was similar to the one they wanted to impose on Anglesey.

Ogden returned, a firm supporter of the Anglesey plan.

Forget about pollution fears. Tankers didn't discharge into the sea instead of the pipes. He told Parliament he had walked on beaches for whites, for coloureds and for blacks — and they were clean.

Yet in the same debate the local MP for Durban was quoted. He had said oil (from the Shell terminal and other ships) was "making these beaches so unpleasant that people cannot use them."

Ogden himself admitted there were 32 spillages totalling 80 tons of oil from the terminal in Durban.

Parliament was told that the Anglesey terminal would take away work from the Mersey docks worth about £1.3 million a year.

Ogden was quick to reply: "The £1.3 million is a balance, the figures are false."

To be kind, perhaps Mr Ogden forgot who gave Paliament this figure. It was Commander Leonard Hill, port manager of the Mersey docks, in answer to a question . . . from Eric Ogden.

At today's prices that figure is about £500,000 higher.

Ogden's help benefited only Shell. Merseyside will lose about £1.8m a year. Anglesey will end up with just over £1¼m over the next five years (most of it already spent on the new harbour), oily beaches and giant tanks.

Some might think that Mr Ogden has been taken for a ride, just like the Anglesey council.

But Mr Ogden doesn't think so. He said in the Commons: "I have no financial interest . . . in the Bill."

And he added: "I want to put on record my appreciation of the help I have had as a member from Merseyside from the Shell Oil Company with information and statistics."

Paid by the pharmacists

Ogden, once a miner in Bradford Colliery, was the first parliamentary candidate outside a mining area to be sponsored by the National Union of Mineworkers. The union pays the constituency £50 a month.

But Ogden never let this hinder his enthusiasm for the oil terminal plan. Nor did he let his sponsorship hide his distaste for a private member's Bill which was likely to help former miners suffering from pneumoconiosis (a deadly disease caused by coal dust).

The Dangerous Drugs and Children Bill indirectly helped these sufferers to claim badly-needed compensation.

It was also designed to improve standards of safety in the manufacture and sale of drugs, help thalidomide victims, and make it easier to sue drug companies for negligence.

Ogden is the paid parliamentary adviser to the Pharmaceutical Council for Great Britain, the organisation which represents pharmacists. Naturally he declares his interest.

The NUM supported the Bill, and Ogden eventually voted for it. But he spent much of his time attacking it. He said it wouldn't help in pneumoconiosis cases. And he came to the aid of companies who made thalidomide.

"As I may have incurred some unpopularity I might as well go the whole hog and say something good about thalidomide," he said.

"To keep a balanced debate, we should put on record that thalidomide has done many people a great deal of good."

There is one mining interest Ogden has supported ever since he entered Parliament. The Channel Tunnel.

Ogden became chairman of the all-party group for the Channel Tunnel. And then the scheme — which would have cost anything up to £2,000 million — was chopped, by the Labour government.

The West Derby MP was furious.

The promoters of the tunnel included some of the most powerful business interst in the country. There was Rio Tinto Zinc (in which the Queen owns many shares), there were the bankers, Morgan Grenfell, Robert Fleming, Hill Samuel, Kleinwort Benson, S G Warburg, plus three American banks.

It was clear who stood to gain from the tunnel . . . and who was taking all the risks.

Anthony Crosland, the minister, said the promoters were "determined to wrap their project round a considerable government cocoon."

And another MP said: "The real motive of RTZ and S G Warburg and all the other bankers . . . was to make money."

Support for £70 pay rise

Slashing the wasteful Channel Tunnel caused Ogden to link arms with the Tories. But cuts in housing, social services and education have scarcely raised a murmur from the Honourable Member. Certainly not when they were made by a Labour government.

He is presently accepting the cuts meekly. And in 1968 he voted to end free school milk in secondary schools and voted for 20p prescription charges. He did this knowing that the West

Derby Labour Party had a policy against any charges on the National Health.

But then some of Ogden's most passionate speeches are made when he's telling ordinary working people to make sacrifices.

In July this year he voted for the £6 wage limit. The same month he condemned as 'miserable' the £24-a-week pay rise to MPs. Ogden wanted another £70 a week, plus expenses.

"The new salary scale panders only to the prejudices and ignorance of the uninformed inside or outside the House," he said.

Ogden certainly wasn't living in poverty. Just a few months earlier he had moved from his small house in Middleton to an expensive one in Essex.

And when his son had to have his tonsils out, Ogden spurned the National Health. Yes, our Labour man chose to pay for a private consultant.

Perhaps Mr Ogden summed up his own position better than anyone:

"When I came to the House I thought I was a left-winger. I have been pushed by circumstances so far to the right that I have come to think there was only Woodrow Wyatt between me and the extremity of the right."

November 1975

● *Ogden took us to the Committee of Privileges over this story (see Chapter 9). the article is an interesting example of what can be achieved by using published sources — in this case the transcripts of Ogden's own speeches in Hansard — with the addition of some background information.*

Corruption in Kirkby

The name George Leatherbarrow will long be linked with Kirkby. In the last ten years his building firm has been awarded around £10 million worth of business by the local council.

Council contracts changed George Leatherbarrow (builders) Ltd from a modest family concern into an outfit capable of winning business away from construction giants like Wimpey and Cubitts.

It all began in the mid-sixties with the start of the massive Tower Hill estate in Kirkby. Early on, the Unit Construction Company did most of the work. Leatherbarrows had a £390,000 contract for 120 houses.

But the big prize was still to come: the £4½ million contract for 1,100 homes forming Tower Hill Phase 2B. With it went a follow-up contract on the final phase, 2C, worth a further £2½ millions.

Front-runner for the contract was the Reema Construction Company, well-known for their work in Skelmersdale. Chasing Reema were Unit Construction and George Wimpey.

None of them got it. At a special housing committee on March 11, 1968, the Phase 2B contract went to George Leatherbarrow.

At the following council meeting the five Liberal members walked out in protest. Why, they wanted to know, were houses in Kirkby costing far more to build than elsewhere? The chairman of the Finance Committee, Councillor Dave Tempest, explained. Kirkby was getting better houses, he said.

They needed to be. The final bill is not yet settled. But that £4½ million contract is now estimated to be over-spent by no less than £1 million.

It's the same story with Leatherbarrow's two other big jobs in Kirkby. Tower Hill Phase 2C, completed last year. Contract: £2,300,000. Overspent: £135,000. Kirkby Park estate improvements. Contract: £670,000. Overspent: £267,000.

Council tenants in Kirkby will be paying for the houses George Leatherbarrow built for a very long time.

George's Best Man

There are, of course, good reasons for some of the overspending. The collapse of the Ronan Point flats in London, for instance, caused long delays on similarly designed blocks at Tower Hill.

But local councils are supposed to keep a careful check on the quality of work done for them; and also on costs, responsible for those checks was the Architect's Department.

On Phase 2B, for example, Senior Architectural Assistant Peter Roberts would spend half of each day at Tower Hill. (Roberts is now in business with a man he used to see there — Mr Fred Dunbavin, Chief Surveyor for Unit Camus, the main sub-contractors on the site.)

But in overall control was Kirkby Council's Architect, Mr Eric Spencer Stevenson. He is now the Borough Architect for Knowsley Council.

He is the man who authorised payment to Leatherbarrow; the man who reported to councillors on Leatherbarrow's work.

Stevenson is the man who helped negotiate the £2½ million Phase 2C contract with George Leatherbarrow.

And Stevenson is the man who, when he was negotiating that contract, became the proud owner of a maroon Alfa Romeo 1750, registration number EGC 114J. A car bought for around £2,000 in the autumn of 1970. A car paid for in used fivers. *A car paid for by George Leatherbarrow.*

But Eric Spencer Stevenson is the name which appeared in the car's log book. Stevenson, the man who told us he had 'definitely not bought the car from George Leatherbarrow."

And Eric Spencer Stevenson is the man who, in 1973, was Best Man at George Leatherbarrow's second wedding. The wedding breakfast was at Stevenson's home in Gayton Lane, Heswall, on the Wirral.

So the Free Press asked Stevenson just how close he was to George Leatherbarrow. "I have known him for a number of years," he said.

His best friend? *"I shouldn't think so."* But you were his Best Man? *"This is totally irrelevant. It is no concern of yours."*

Special deliveries

Of course, none of this can be directly connected with the work George Leatherbarrow was doing for Kirkby council. But there was a connection. A concrete connection . . .

Building Materials. Building materials delivered to Tower Hill to build council houses. Building materials which later disappeared. Which were loaded onto Leatherbarrow lorries. And which fell off those lorries at a number of private houses.

Private houses like:

● "Sherwood", Gayton Lane, Heswall, home of Architect Eric Spencer Stevenson.

● Number 7 Deerbolt Crescent, Kirkby, home of Councillor Dave Tempest.

● "The Roundhouse", Ince Blundell, home of Mr Eric Hufton, a director of George Leatherbarrow (Builders) Ltd.

The work renovating Hufton's house and extending Tempest's and Stevenson's was carried out by Leatherbarrow.

We asked Stevenson about the building blocks, stone, bricks, timber, sand and cement delivered to his home. He said he paid Leatherbarrow for them.

We asked him whether a set of Lovelady kitchen units, delivered to Tower Hill as a sample, were taken to his home.

"Not that I'm aware of," he replied. To have building materials carted all the way from Kirkby to Heswall must be expensive. But the way Stevenson had a Leatherbarrow lorry make individual trips with a young tree and a concrete block to moor a boat was real extravagance.

We asked Tempest about the materials for the extension Leatherbarrow built on his house. Tempest refused to say who the builder was. And he hadn't a clue where the bricks, timber, flagstones etc came from.

"I wouldn't know anything about it," he said. "I've paid for my extension quite legitimately."

If he paid the full price it was a lot of money. There were difficulties with the foundations: special facing bricks were brought from St Helens: then Tempest changed his mind about a window at the front; and then a door at the back.

The garage door was too narrow for his car and the bricks had to be shaved back. It was an expensive job alright.

All above board?

Well, were all the extensions perfectly legitimate and above board?

Leatherbarrows were working on multi-million pound public contracts. They did not do minor extensions to private houses. So why did they work on these?

And there's another strange thing. A lorry driver who delivered some of these materials was later charged in connection with other materials stolen from Leatherbarrow.

The driver remembered those unusual deliveries he'd made. The times there were no delivery notes. And the times he was slipped a couple of quid.

The driver threatened to cough the lot. Leatherbarrows told him to keep his mouth shut and they'd look after him. So he did.

He appeared in court, was found guilty, fined £200 . . . and then given his job back.

But there's something else. Just who did those building materials on Tower Hill belong to?

On deliver to the site Leatherbarrows would receive an invoice from the manufacturers. On the strength of this Kirkby Council would pay 80% of the price — so Leatherbarrows always had council money to buy more materials as work progressed.

This means that the council had invested in the materials from the moment they appeared on the site. In other words George Leatherbarrow had no business selling them off.

A Leatherbarrow worker we spoke to about this was later called into the office at work and told: "Don't worry, they're just bluffing you. We've got it all covered with bills."

That sounds like a good idea.

Free trip to London

No doubt Leatherbarrows also have a good cover story for a little two-day trip to the Crystal Palace sports stadium in London. At the time they were interested in the council's grandiose plans for sports facilities.

Kirkby councillor Dave Tempest, who awarded many of the sports contracts personally, has his own cover story.

"I made arrangements myself to go to Crystal Palace and I paid my own expenses. What George Leatherbarrow did, I don't know."

The Free Press does know. On July 17, 1972, he booked seven Pullman tickets through M D Travel, in Moorfields, Liverpool. The bill was sent to him marked "Personal". And it was for £114.90.

Pullman tickets have names on them. The names were:

- Mr George Leatherbarrow
- Mr Eric Spencer Stevenson, council architect.
- Mr David Tempest, councillor
- Mr Peter Roberts, architectural assistant.
- Mr Peter Jennings, of E H Williams Ltd, landscape gardeners.
- Mr Peter Hobbs, a quarry merchant.
- Mr Richard Lane, manager of Kirkby stadium.

Strange, Tempest didn't know about that. Stevenson didn't either. So they probably didn't know it was E H Williams Ltd who paid their hotel bill. Or that E H Williams Ltd shared the night-clubbing expenses with Leatherbarrow.

And it can't be that Tempest has forgotten. "No-one has ever paid any expenses for me on any trips," he told us.

George Leatherbarrow was certainly generous. (Generous enough, for instance, to sell a company car to a policeman . . . and lend him the money to pay for it. Inspector Harold Hayhurst must have been very grateful).

Dirt in high places

People may get the idea there was dirt in high places. There was. It was all over Tower Hill and it had to be shifted.

Building sites have to be cleared. And Leatherbarrows got paid for clearing Tower Hill. Paid very well indeed for some of it.

The real expense in moving earth is loading the lorries, not actually carrying it. The handling costs for moving earth 50 yards or 150 yards are very much the same.

So why, on Phase 2C, Leatherbarrow should have been paid according to the distance they moved it (e.g. £1 for 50 yards, £3 for 150 yards) is a mystery.

It was worth thousands. "In my

opinion it should never have happened," said a man qualified to pass an opinion and in a position to know.

But it did happen. And the man who authorised payment to Leatherbarrows was Mr Eric Spencer Stevenson.

Removals by tractor

Leatherbarrows also made a lot of money moving furniture.

Furniture moved out of tenants' houses on the Kirkby Park estate where Leatherbarrows were carrying out improvements.

Tenders were invited for this job. Leatherbarrow's was the most expensive. So of course they got the contract.

The explanation was — a mistake. Leatherbarrow's tender figure of £40 a removal turned out to be £40 each way: total £80.

So we asked Architect Stevenson, who dealt with the tender, how it happened. No, the mistake was not his, he said, rather a "misunderstanding of the committee."

That's another "mistake". Leatherbarrow's tender didn't go before the housing committee. It was accepted, personally, by housing chairman Frank Lawler.

One last thing. Leatherbarrows are not a removals firm. Tenants were furious about removals on an open lorry and in a box-car pulled by an unlicensed tractor.

Ski slope disaster

Then there was the ridiculous, and extremely expensive, Kirkby ski slope.

The more you look at it the more it looks like the only people who will get anything out of it are the builders.

The contract to supply and mound the earth went to George Leatherbarrow. There were no tenders. councillor Dave Tempest, first Pharoah of Kirkby, accepted "the lowest of four quotations". That meant £25,000 for the local lad.

One way George 'earned' his money was by placing an advert in the Liverpool Echo for a free tip in Kirkby.

Strange, with money-saving ideas like that, that the £90,000 project is

currently overspent by about £30,000.

Few people want to be associated with the ski slope.

Eric Spencer Stevenson "doesn't really know" who dreamt it up. But he does remember doing the rough drawings for it.

Assistant Architect Alan Wright said he was definitely not involved. The unfortunate truth is that Wright was in charge of the project.

One of his jobs was to check in all those lorries answering Leatherbarrow's tipping advertisement.

Secret code

So George leatherbarrow did all right out of Kirkby. And he's still doing all right, because what's good for Kirkby Council is good for the new Knowsley Council.

Leader of the new council, until May 1 was Dave Tempest. And the council's Architect is still Mr Eric Spencer Stevenson.

Last December, Architect Stevenson presented a report on overspending on council contracts to the housing committee. It was highly damaging to George Leatherbarrow (Builders) Ltd.

The firm stood out as the overspenders over all others. They compared badly with Holland, Hannen and Cubbits Ltd, who had carried out council contracts worth £3½ millions in Huyton (now joined with Kirkby under Knowsley Council). Total overspending on these . . .NIL.

At the same meeting the committee were to award two new housing contracts. There were a number of tenders for each.

Mr Eric Spencer Stevenson introduced a novel way of presenting these tenders to the committee. Instead of naming each firm, they were identified only as "Firm A", "Firm B" etc.

Stevenson told the Free Press an unidentified group of councillors had persuaded him to do this. "I don't like that way of doing it", he said.

Presumably it was not the same group of unidentified councillors who quickly told him to discontinue the practice.

Anyway, at the December housing committee, Stevenson recommended acceptance of the lowest tender in each case from "Firm A". The committee followed his advice.

You guessed it. "Firm A" turned out to be the one that delivered all that stuff to Stevenson's house, that paid for his trip to London. The firm run by the man who bought the Alfa car, Stevenson's old mate, George Leatherbarrow.

May, 1975

The con-men who hide behind a cheetah

Another nasty little finance operation has surfaced in Liverpool. The companies involved, Ronchil Ltd and Austin Lowe (Travel Division) Ltd use lies and deception to tempt people into joining their racket or taking out loans.

They get their business by placing illegal and phoney adverts in the Liverpool Echo. And the publicity symbol the companies use is a drawing of an animal: a cheetah.

The man putting up the money is that veteran Welsh money lender/grabber, Sir Julian Hodge. Hodge, a close friend of Labour Minister James Callaghan, was exposed on TV a couple of years ago for his vicious interest rates. Ambition and greed have made him a director of over 100 companies.

GENTLEMAN required to earn £2,000 p.a. part time working from warm leads, applicants must be aged 25-45, married with car and telephone. For appointment Phone The Branch Manager, 051-227 3511.

Illegal

This advert, which has appeared several times in the Liverpool Echo, is illegal. Under the 1973 Fair Trading Act the advert should give the company's name, address and details of what's involved. It doesn't.

The advert also promises £2,000 a year for part-time work. This too is illegal. The Act forbids promises of unguaranteed earnings.

The advertisers, Ronchil Ltd, are

looking for area managers. But people who take the jobs are more likely to lose than gain.

Before they start they have to buy £1,200-worth of shares (which is rather strange since the total share capital of the company is only £100). And, of course, those who don't have the money borrow it from Sir Julian Hodge.

Under his contract the area manager must find £20,000-worth of business (loans) every three months. In return, all the company really promises is to pay commissions. As the contract states: "The area manager is an independent contractor and is not . . . a servant, partner or employee of the company."

And if he leaves, he gets the £1,200 back? Probably not. The company only agree to sell the shareholding for what they can get, AND THEN DEDUCT £500 FOR THEMSELVES. That's always assuming they don't go bust in the meantime.

Ronchil and Austin Lowe Travel are really selling second mortgages, though they don't like to call them that.

"People get very frightened of second mortgages," explained their accountant, Tom Proctor. "The only problem with second mortgages is if you don't intend to repay."

People are right to be wary. The small print of the Hodge Loan agreement allows interest rates to be raised, imposes additional costs, and makes the loss of your home a possibility for being just 15 days late with a monthly repayment.

1971 K HUNTER GL, metallic cedar one owner, lovely condition; no deposit, finance available. - 051-639 3158 £745

Phoney

Ronchil find some customers by placing adverts like the one above in the 'Cars For Sale' section of the Liverpool Echo. The company do not own the cars and are not interested in selling them. The cars are simply a ruse to get people interested in their loans.

Proctor explained: "We had a Cortina we advertised for £450. We got 20 enquiries for it. One of the blokes went out and saw 18 of these people, signed up 15 for the same car . . . 11 were passed and actually received cheques.

"Although it seems a little unfair at the outset it's good business and certainly not offending anybody. That's the type of thing we are doing on secondhand vehicles."

Nice people. But fear not. According to Proctor the law are already taking an interest in their unsavoury activities. He said an ex-Chief Inspector from the Liverpool force, who retired early, and a former solicitor are both now working for them.

Map of Wallasey for sale: Only £1,200

A man who gave up his job in Portugal and returned to Wallasey when his wife died was just the person Ronchil were looking for.

Mr W (the Free Press agreed not to print his name) had been a shipyard manager but now, with four young children to look after, he needed a job which allowed him to work from home.

He answered an advert in the Echo and went for an interview in the Adelphi. There was smooth talk and promises of jet-set conferences abroad.

He agreed to join Ronchil as an area manager and parted with £1,200.

His cheque was made out to Mr Robert Dyson, of 1 Wallacre Road, Wallasey, who is secretary of Ronchil and Austin Lowe Travel.

Mr W didn't really have £1,200 to spare, but was persuaded to take out a Ronchil loan for that amount. He is now repaying this at £29.04 a month for the next ten years . . . a total of £3,484.

For this investment he was given Wallasey Or rather a map of Wallasey and the grand title 'area manager'.

Why did he pay the £1,200 to Dyson personally and not to the company? He was told Dyson was the previous area manager for Ronchil and Austin Lowe in Wallasey, and had done well in selling the companies' loans.

But Dyson could only have been area manager for a matter of weeks. Austin Lowe Travel was formed on July 27 this year, and Ronchil on June 7. Mr W

agreed to join the company in the second week of August.

Mr W was told the £1,200 bought him 1% of the company shares. And that every area manager had to own this number.

So Ronchil and Austin Lowe are wealthy companies worth £120,000 each? Actually both have a share capital of only £100. And according to records at Companies House 99 shares have been issued . . . 33 to each of the directors!

Another unusual feature about these unusual companies is that Mr W has never received any share certificates.

Mr W is now selling second mortgages for Ronchil and Austin Lowe. In the first two months he's persuaded two people to take out loans amounting to nearly £2,000.

For this he is due to receive commission of £30 and £20 (£50 altogether)—not much really when you remember he has to pay £29.04 each month for his loan, plus all his telephone bills, all his petrol, his own insurance stamps and his own heating and lighting bills as he works from home.

So Mr W isn't very happy. And he's still not been to any conferences abroad, as he was promised.

He was due to go on a free trip to Monte Carlo but that fell through. The directors blamed it on the Court Line crash.

Not-so-simple Simon

One of the brains behind Ronchil and Austin Lowe Travel is 26-year-old Simon Harris. He became a director of these pyramid-style companies just three months after a similar firm went bust owing thousands of pounds.

He was the largest shareholder-director of Excalibur Finance Brokers, which was compulsorily wound up in March this year (Free Press Nos. 15 & 16).

The assets of his company were described in court as "negligible" but the full amount of money owing is still not known.

The claims against the company are so complex, that the official receiver has had to seek advice from barristers.

The main reason for the confusion is that Harris, with his other directors, Philip Myatt, a male nurse from Lincoln, and Derek Williams, a printer, of 15 Garswood Close, Kenyon Park, Maghull, didn't have just one Excalibur company.

As as spokesman for one of the largest creditors said: "They were trading uner a variety of permutations of Excalibur.

"They had their own printing press, and just seemed to change the name of the company when they wanted."

Harris's old Excalibur company still owes about £500 to Lawtons, the Liverpool stationery firm, and nearly £2,000 to a London company which supplies printing and office equipment.

Perhaps more important, a number of individuals have lost hundreds of pounds which they "invested" to buy their way into the pyramid company, while salesmen are still waiting for their commissions.

Some time ago Mr Harris told the liquidators that there was enough money to meet all the LEGITIMATE claims. But so far he has not handed over one penny. And there's little doubt that he will take a very narrow view of the word 'legitimate' if he ever does.

Not dismayed by collapse, Mr Harris bounced back. Just three months later, on June 7, he helped to found Ronchil Ltd, and then Austin Low (Travel Division) Ltd on July 27.

Both these companies have the same directors, each holding 33 £1 shares. Besides Mr Harris, of 31 Strathmore Grove, Sherdley Park, St Helens, there is Gerrard Jackson of 38 Hampton Crescent, Neston and George Leslie Lowe of Belle Vale Road, Liverpool.

Now what guarantee is there that these companies won't end up in the hands of the official receiver? Precious little. The similarities between Excalibur, Ronchil and the Austin Lowe Travel Organisation are a clear warning to anybody about to part with hard-earned cash.

November 1974

● *Harris, Jackson and Lowe were later jailed for their activities.*

All sewn up at Bear Brand

An amazing tale of underhand dealing lies behind the threatened closure of Bear Brand, the Liverpool hosiery firm.

The factory has been working flat-out, with overtime at weekends. Yet it was losing money. Why?

Behind the scenes another firm had persuaded the directors to keep the price of their tights low. This firm then bought thousands and thousands of tights—to re-sell them.

The collapse of Bear Brand was inevitable, without further finance. And when the Government turned down their plea for a second crisis loan, the board had to call in a receiver.

Bear Brand has made a loss for eleven years, and owes at least £¾m, including £350,000 to the Government for a loan last year.

However the company which has been influencing Bear Brand's policy now hopes to step in and buy the factory, but without having the burden of the firm's heavy overheads and vast debts.

This company is a distribution firm called Benson Hosiery (which merged with another firm, Tranwood, last year). Two of its directors have been involved with a number of interesting firms which have 'lost' their records of their accounts.

Benson/Tranwood have received no publicity during the downfall of Bear Brand.

Yet they are the major power behind the boardroom.

Since October 1974 Benson have owned 27% of the ordinary shares of Bear Brand (nearly £600,000). What's more, they buy—to resell—at least 20% of the tights made by the Woolton firm.

Being the largest shareholder and the largest customer has put them in a very influential position.

There is no doubt that they have been influencing the policies of Bear Brand from a safe distance.

But they could not act openly. If they had been seen to be managing Bear Brand they would have been forced under the Companies Act to take them over completely.

This Benson have tried to avoid at all cost. They wanted a ready supply of Bear Brand tights at a 'competitive' price. They did not want to be lumbered with Bear Brand's heavy debts.

This is why the largest shareholder has not put up one penny to save Bear Brand. "We cannot risk our own shareholders in what has been a bottomless pit," said one director to the Freen Press.

Benson bought their shares for about £40,000. But within months they were written down in their accounts to a value of just £1. So these shares are of 'influence' rather than monetary value. During the last six months this has proved to be very true.

Less than twelve months ago, the Government gave Bear Brand a £350,000 loan. Most of this disappeared within months on debts, and only £30,000—£40,000 was spent on badly-needed nachinery,

Then, last October, there was a boardroom upheaval and the chairman, Mr P. Rougier, left.

He was replaced by two men, Mr Mervyn Smith, a 'professional managing director or company doctor' and Mr Ken Medlock, who had just been pushed out as the leading man at the Birkenhead Co-op. He is also a Radio City director.

Who chose these two men? One Benson/Tranwood director, Mr S Carpenter said his company did not select them, but only approved them.

He wasn't telling the whole truth.

Mervyn Smith is an acquaintance of George Davis, group secretary of the Tranwood Group.

Mr Medlock is known by at least one Benson/Tranwood director. The firm have a company on the Wirral where Medlock worked. And they knew he was about to be pushed out of the Co-op and was 'available'.

A number of meetings were then held between the directors of Benson/Tranwood and the directors of Bear Brand. Bensons spelt out the policy they thought Bear Brand should follow to be successful.

Firstly, Bear Brand would have to keep prices down. Secondly they would have to increase production to spread costs.

This was, Bensons claim, good commercial advice. Certainly the new Bear Brand directors agreed.

Suddenly the 400 workers found they were working overtime as production shot up from about 17,000 dozen tights a week to about 23,000 dozen.

But there was a catch to Benson's advice. Bear Brand have always produced good quality tights at a very competitive price, but the firm has been burdened with massive overheads, due to top-heavy management and a vast, expensive site which was 75% empty.

These overheads meant Bear Brand now had to sell about 32,000 dozen a week to break even. This number is a result of Bear Brand agreeing with Bensons to keep their prices down, at a time when other manufacturers were putting them up.

And here's the rub, Bear Brand could not make this number of tights each week. Already their machines were in use 24 hours a day. And Bensons did not offer to buy Bear Brand more machines.

Meanwhile Benson/Tranwood were, as one senior man said, buying from Bear Brand "all the tights we could lay our hands on. They couldn't produce fast enough to meet our needs."

Benson/Tranwood say they helped by cutting their profit margin in the shops. That may be true. But there's little doubt they benefited by Bear Brand's new policy of keeping prices down.

What sort of men are behind Benson/Tranwood?

● Several top men used to work for Bear Brand, including chairman Harold Bainbridge. He was previously chairman of Bear Brand until it was found he had built up a private 9% stake in their customers, Benson, through a private company. He was then eased out.

● Chairman Bainbridge and managing director Brian Norman have taken over a number of their own companies. They managed both Benson and Tranwood before the companies merged.

● They have fiddled account figures so they seem to be profits when they are really losses, they have shifted around assets and revalued property when convenient.

And it's the same sort of people who are likely to benefit when the Government gives loans to private industry when workers have no control over how that money is spent.

March 1976

Kirkby man kicked by police, say witnesses

Sunday, August 10 was John Lannon's daughter's thirteenth birthday. There was a party and John stayed on drinking at his parents' home at 49 Changford Road, Northwood, Kirkby.

Sometime between three and four in the morning, John left the house with a friend. By all accounts he was extremely drunk.

The Woodpecker pub is a few minutes' walk away.

What happened there before he was arrested is not yet known. Whether or not Lannon committed any offence will be decided in court.

We are not concerned, here, with that. Whether he did wrong or not, John Lannon certainly did not deserve what happened to him at the hands of the police.

The Woodpecker is at a road junction with a forecourt at the front and sides and a car-park at the back.

There are houses and low-rise flats close by on every side.

The pub was being run by Mr and Mrs Conway, with Mrs Gladys Conway taking the more active part in the business. Local people say the police regularly drink after hours at the Woodpecker, often well into the night.

Whether any of the police were drinking there on the night of the arrest is not known. They were certainly on the scene quickly.

The four police mainly involved were in two minis. One of the minis was seen arriving. Another police car appeared later.

John Lannon was arrested by two shirt-sleeved police at the rear of the pub. From that moment he was "safely" in police custody.

He was beaten, dragged to the side of the pub, and attacked again. Here, Mrs Gladys Conway and two more policemen joined in.

The police then ran, bouncing and dragging John Lannon along the ground to one of the minis parked in Brook Hey Drive at the front of the pub.

He was screaming and badly hurt. His clothes were ripped and covered in blood. Skin and flesh was scraped off his backside.

What exactly happened is described below by some of the eye-witnesses. One couple told us they did not want to be mentioned for fear of police reprisals. The others have decided to speak out.

It was about 4.30 am. The street lights were on and the dawn was coming up.

WITNESS ONE: Mr Christopher McKenna, 101a Bigdale Drive (a first floor flat). He is an elderly man who was looking out of the window.

"The first I seen a mini came down and pulled up on Bigdale Drive. Two cops jumped out and ran round the corner. Somebody came over the wall and went on the floor. Two police followed, they all more or less came over together.

"They had him on the floor and were threatening him, punching him an' yelling 'Where's your mate?' I said: 'Knock it off, you're getting seen.' They were really rubbing it in, kicking and punching. I've seen it on the pictures.

WITNESS TWO: Mrs Dorothy Lloyd, 92 Bigdale Drive. She heard the noise and saw four policemen.

"One of them said, 'Where's your mate?' and then one of them kicked him underneath (in his groin) and ground his heel in. All of them had a go at him . . . there was no need for that."

WITNESS THREE: Mr Gerard Ashton, 92 Bigdale Drive. He and his wife, Pat, were woken by the shouting.

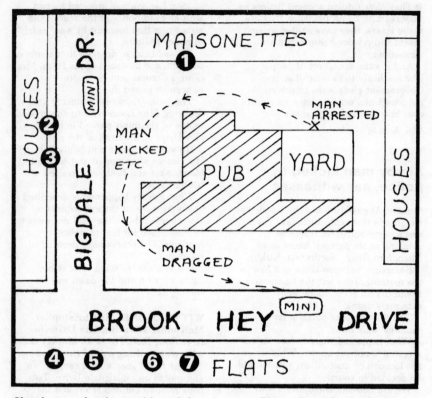

Sketch map showing position of the witnesses. The wall mentioned by the first witness surrounds the yard at the back of the pub. It is about seven feet high.

"There was a woman shouting: 'I've seen what you're doing to that man'. The man was lying on the floor. There were policemen booting him and punching him, and they dragged him, and then she (Gladys Conway) came and hit him with a baton.

"They were kicking that man in the ribs. She was striking him with a pick handle. I said: 'Eh, what's going on there?' and they said: 'Go to bed'.

"They dragged him on his back and he was screaming."

WITNESS FOUR: Mr Jim Power, 70a Brook Hey Drive. An elderly man.

"I could hear him say 'Ah, ah, ah'. When he fell back, two constables got him by the arms and they ran with him."

WITNESS FIVE: Mr Bill Hunt, 72a Brook Hey Drive.

"I was woken by the dog. They were bouncing this guy along, three of them. She (Gladys Conway) was hitting him about the legs."

WITNESS SIX: Kathleen Bentre, 78 Brook Hey Drive. A young woman who is pregnant and has difficulty sleeping.

"I heard someone scream. It was a horrible scream. It seemed like a young lad.

"I saw Mrs Conway hitting him with a stick. I woke my mum and dad and they were still booting him then. It made me sick.

"Two policemen had his arms behind his back and another one was kicking him. She said: 'Let go of his arm. Don't break it, they'll see it in the station.'

"Four of them picked him up and bounced him round to the mini.

"I phoned the police station. I told the desk sergeant that three policemen were virtually killing a young lad. He said 'What do you want us to do? There's nothing we can do unless the young man prefers charges'."

WITNESS SEVEN: Mr Leslie Fowler, 80 Brook Hey Drive.

"They shoved him in the car. I heard Mrs Conway shouting 'Don't hit him there, they'll see it' . . something like that. She was carrying a truncheon.

"She called me over and said: 'Did you see all this? Did you see me hitting this lad?' and I said: 'I'm not saying nothing till I've seen the lad's solicitors.' And she said, 'I'll have you up for slander'."

John Lannon's ordeal was not yet over. Witnesses agree that the two police minis drove up Brook Hey Drive towards Simonswood Lane.

That is not the quickest way to Kirkby police station. They should have turned down Bigdale Drive or gone over the other way along Brook Hey Drive, and down Roughwood Drive.

We have found no witnesses to what happened next. But John Lannon says he was taken to a field off Simonswood Lane and attacked again. The same four police held him, punched him and grabbed his testicles.

When he was eventually taken to Kirkby police station, he was taken in by the back door and put straight into a cell. He says that he was not checked in by the desk sergeant, not searched, and was left alone until late that morning.

His requests to see a doctor were ignored. But eleven hours later he began coughing blood and was taken to Walton Hospital in a police car.

There he underwent an emergency operation for a punctured lung and was treated for his other injuries. He signed himself out of hospital the following Saturday.

●In August last year another Kirkby man, Kenny Williams, died after being arrested in Liverpool city centre for taking a car. The evidence pointed to a vicious assault in the back of a police Land Rover. But an inquest found no connection between his injuries and his death. No action was taken against any of the police involved.
September, 1975

Car workers make time their own

Workers in some sections of Vauxhall's Ellesmere Port plant are free of the burden of 'clocking on' and 'clocking off' because the company's clocks are being continually wrecked.

A recent notice from the Car Assembly Production Manager, Mr R. O'Neill, admitted that "as a result of extensive clock vandalism our time recording procedure is out of control."

Mr O'Neill reminded workers that it was not the job of supervisors to record and sign clock cards. "To do so places a heavy burden on our Foremen," his notice said.

He appealed for help to "overcome our current clocking situation which is of considerable concern to the Company."

Vauxhall's Personnel Manager, Mr D. D. Irons, has also found it necessary to remind workers of the company's rules "due to continuing acts of vandalism with the apparent objective of enabling employees to either clock out early, or to avoid clocking out at all . . ."

So many clocks have been wrecked so often that management no longer bother to have them repaired. A common method of sabotage has been to put glue on clock cards and leave them in the machine.

Some time ago Vauxhall management thought they had discovered a 'vandal-proof' clock. But their plans came to an abrupt end when their special clock shield disappeared before it could be fitted.

July 1976

How Ivor made a million

Few people on Merseyside have heard of Ivor Gershfield, a shy financier who lives in Switzerland. Yet his was the key role in the take-over of the Fisher-Bendix factory at Kirkby—a role which has never, until now, been revealed.

Two years ago Fisher-Bendix was the scene of Merseyside's first—and most effective—sit-in. 600 workers occupied the factory to try and save their jobs when Thorn Electrical Industries, who employed them, tried to close it down.

Thorn sold the factory for £1.2m. The firm who eventually took it over, International Property Development, bought it for £1.8m. And middle-man Ivor Gershfield pocketed the difference.

This was only one in a series of deals connected with Fisher-Bendix from which Gershfield's total profit was a million pounds or more. Once his business was done Mr Gershfield went home to the Alpine health resort of Crans-sur-Sierre, where his condition has been described as "extremely comfortable".

The Fisher-Bendix sit-in began days on January 5, 1972. Four days later Thorn announced they had sold the factory for £1.2m, and Jack Mendoza, a London estate agent, said he had agreed to buy it for a client.

The timing of the announcement was curious, for the sale had actually been agreed the previous autumn and kept quiet. More curious still was the identity of the anonymous client.

The secrecy becomes easier to understand when you know the client was Gershfield. Luckily for Thorn no-one in Kirkby discovered the identity of the buyer during the sit-in. There would have been uproar if they had.

For about the time Gershfield was negotiating with Thorn over Fisher-Bendix several of his companies were under scrutiny in the High court.

Ironically, some of the union officials at Kirkby once met Gershfield, though they had no idea at the time who he was. He visited the factory posing as an economist.

"He was fifty-ish, thin on top, with gold-rimmed glasses and a moustache," they recall . . . "and a manner like an English army officer."

Fortunately for him, Mr Gershfield has not been seen there since.

Gershfield bought the factory in the name of Stanbourne Properties. He didn't much want to run the factory himself and began looking for someone to rent or buy it. One man he thought of was Harold King, whom he had recently met.

King, a Merseyside man in his mid-thirties, had had a chequered career. He worked as a telegram boy, postman, shopkeeper, car hire operator and trainee buyer, His first venture, a newsagent's shop, proved to be too much work on top of his office job.

He gave up the car hire service "because it never made a penny". A baby linen shop did better, but only made enough to pay off the mortgage.

Eventually King looked like making his fortune with a soft drinks firm, K.C.Developments. But this collapsed during the scare over cyclamate, the artificial sweetener.

At the time of the sit-in King was running another fruit juice firm, A.F.Foods (a subsidiary of British Vending Industries) at Morden in Surrey.

A.F. Foods was not doing too well (it had lost £130,000 in 1971) and British Vending Industries wanted to get rid of it. They were willing to let King go as well.

But A.F.Foods could not handle Fisher-Bendix on their own, and it was here that International Property Development (IPD) fitted into Gershfield's scheme.

Newly-formed company

The plan was for Reginald Rowland, who was then chairman of IPD, to step down and for King to take his place. IPD would then buy the factory and take off some of the engineering work previously done by Thorn, as well as King's fruit juice business.

In order to do this, Gershfield bought a newly-formed company, Clohurst, in February 1972. At this stage Clohurst was nothing more than a name and a bundle of documents. But during the next two months, as a result of the Fisher-Bendix negotiations, Clohurst was provided with a factory, machinery, work and money:

1. Gershfield's Clohurst agreed to buy the Fisher-Bendix building and land for £1.8m from his other company, Stanbourne Prosperties.
(Stanbourne, remember, had got it for £1.2m.)
2. Clohurst bought the factory's plant and equipment from Thorn for £405,000.
3. Another agreement allowed Clohurst to make the radiators and night storage heaters which had been made at the factory under Thorn.
4. Clohurst borrowed £600,000 in cash from Thorn.

Clohurst was now ready for King's new company, IPD to take over. But IPD had lost money in six years out of the previous seven and had no cash to spare. So they paid Gershfield in shares . . . 5½ million of them, which was equivalent to £550,000, as the value of the shares then stood at 10p each.

After the takeover the shares rose in price (they have been as high as 41½p). Which was good news for Mr Gershfield. Not long after the deal he sold three million of these shares.

Half of them went to King (it's not known how much he paid, though rumour has it the terms were 'favourable' to King). The other half went to Joe Hammerson, a property consultant, for 35p each.

So on 1½ million shares—just a fraction of his total shareholding—Gershfield made 25p per share . . . which means his profit of this part of the deal was at least £375,000.

Waiting to be paid

Gershfield also had a profit of £600,000 on the sale of the factory, but as yet this was only a paper profit—Clohurst had agreed to buy the factory but had not actually paid for it.

It was not up to King to find the money, and Gershfield had to wait until July to get it. King's only hope was to borrow and the big banks were not eager to help, especially in view of the factory's history.

So King turned to the poor man's friend . . . the ill-fated London and

County Securities. London and County (A & D), one of the subsidiaries, was willing to lend King up to £2m. But he had to pay through the nose to get it. First he had to pay a massive £250,000 commitment fee, to be followed by interest at a phenomenal 5% above bank rate.

With stiff terms like these it's not surprising that only three months after getting the loan King was telling shareholders that he would like to "repay, or at least very substantially reduce the loan . . . well in advance of the due date in December 1974."

King has since been trying to get another loan—this time from the Government—at a much lower rate of interest. He hopes to borrow £850,000 interest free for one year, and at 7½% for the remaining two years. According to latest reports this has not yet been finalised.

After Gershfield had been paid, IPD was once again short of cash. Gershfield quickly saw this as a chance to make even more money. Why not let IPD have his spare cash in exchange for a few million extra shares to speculate with?

But there were problems. Because of Stock Exchange rules IPD could not simply print some share certificates and sell them to Gershfield.

One idea was for Gershfield to buy a company belonging to Gershfield and pay him with shares. Gershfield used two companies for the operation. Both happened to have the same name— Magenta Properties—but one was based in the Isle of Man and the other in Jersey.

First Gershfield's Jersey company took over his Isle of Man company. The Isle of Man company received £600,000 in cash from the Jersey company in exchange for its shares.

Magenta (Isle of Man) used the cash to buy up a few small property companies, bringing its total assets to over £1m. King's IPD then bought the Isle of Man company for £2,700,000 shares which were paid to Magenta (Jersey).

On the face of it such a deal was against the rules of 'good' business. But

the ever-alert Gershfield had found a neat way around the rules.

The problem was that Magenta (Jersey) belonged to Gershfield. Gershfield also owned 22% of IPD (as a result of the Clohurst deal)—which meant a potential clash of interest.

To avoid the clash of interest Gershfield brought in one of his front-men, an accountant called Michael Forrest. Gershfield "gave" the Jersey company to Forrest just before the takeover went through.

At this point Forrest could, if he had wished, have walked off with the company's money. But he proved to be a loyal servant and dutifully handed the company back to Gershfield as soon as the transaction was completed.

This meant that although Gershfield owned the Jersey company before and after King's takeover, he did not own it at the moment the deal was going through. Hence no clash of interest!

So Gershfield had got a hat trick! What with his profit on the sale of the factory, with his shares from the sale of Clohurst and now Magenta, he had made a million pounds or more.

Profiteering

Much of the responsibility for Gershfield's profiteering rests with Thorn, who sold him the factory in the first place.

And although King tries to give the impression that he got a good deal, things would have been easier for him and his employees without Gershfield.

In the local press, however, King's efforts to make the factory pay its way have been portrayed as a battle to tame a bunch of militant workers.

King himself once told the Daily Post he could run the factory without trade unions, and described them as "unnecessary".

It's surprising in the circumstances that he didn't direct his remark towards one of the least necessary people of all . . . . Ivor Gershfield.

May 1974

King's firm later collapsed and the government stepped in with a £3.9 million grant to set up a workers' co-operative.

A S A COUNTERWEIGHT to the more serious articles, we had a regular column of amusing snippets. Here is a selection.

BARNSLEY council's nuclear shelter has been wrecked by vandals.

● ● ●

THE SHOP inside Walton jail sells only one kind of chocolate biscuit: The one called "Bandit".

● ● ●

RED FACES at Chester when both Conservative and Labour parties chose Mr Tony Chilton as a prospective candidate.

● ● ●

WHEN a film on safety at work was shown at a factory in Preston one man had to have stitches in his head after falling off his seat.

● ● ●

EXTRACT from Liverpool City Council's theatre regulations, Section 14 (Dangerous Performances): "No person shall be fixed or hung from the flies in positions from which they cannot release themselves.

● ● ●

AMERICANS must not be eaten. There is more DDT in the average American's body fat than is allowed in food in Britain.

● ● ●

THE CAMPAIGN within the Tory Party to bring back hanging has nothing to do with the fact that Mr Anthony Barber MP is a former director of British Ropes Ltd.

● ● ●

BUTLER George Kelly and his wife often complained that after serving pheasant or venison to their master, Viscount Mountsarett, they had to eat fish fingers. Things came to a head when Mr Kelly served a new Stilton cheese at dinner. The viscount demanded to know where the crust was. Mr Kelly retrieved it from the dustbin and served it on a silver platter. Half an hour later Mr Kelly and his wife sacked.

● ● ●

AN OLD corkscrew has been sold for a record £125 at Christie's.

● ● ●

A NEW design of weapon has just been patented by the Ministry of Defence. The patent number is 1333558 and the weapon . . . an archery bow.

● ● ●

COUNCIL officials were among the unlikely visitors to the Watchfield pop festival. They spent the Bank Holiday weekend testing noise levels. Highest score — 93 decibels — came from a police helicopter.

● ● ●

IN AUSTRALIA a bus carrying 28 plump members of the Wagga Wagga weight-watchers club pulled up at a car park and sank 2ft into the tarmac.

● ● ●

THE MAYOR of Gloucester was bitten by an alsatian guard dog when he opened a security firm's new premises.

● ● ●

Afterword

Beyond the Free Press: recent developments in the radical press.
by Crispin Aubrey of the Minority Press Group

THE birth and death of the *Liverpool Free Press* spanned an important period in the development of alternative journalism in Britain. When it started, in 1971, local radical newspapers, mostly based on urban centres, were developing fast around the country (though rarely with such dramatic effect as the *Free Press*), and the national scene still included such titles as *Oz, International Times* and *Frendz*. Six years later, when it stopped, the local radical press had become more established, whilst at a national level the underground press of cultural rebellion had been replaced by a mass of magazines concerned with the fragments, and major slices, of the non-aligned left opposition. But to what extent have the ideas of the *Free Press* of using skills of traditional journalism in a radically different manner been important to this movement?

Several important elements are worth noting from the way in which *Liverpool Free Press* was produced. Firstly, the language in which its stories were written and the style in which they were presented was not dissimilar from a bright tabloid: bold, simple headlines, short, tight sentences and a fair sprinkling of journalistic words. Invariably, it was clear from the opening paragraph what the articles were going to be about. The page design was exceptionally clear and easy to read, with plenty of pictures of the personalities and places involved. All these were skills taken from the day-to-day journalistic practice of which the *Free Press* workers had direct experience.

Secondly, the journalists involved were concerned to investigate their stories to the full — digging out the facts with a thoroughness that it still impressive many years later. Though other articles were included, it was the exposure of scandals, whether in the private or the public sector, which involved the most time and energy.

But it is a third element which explains most clearly what made the *Free Press* different from its commercial counterparts. For one of the apparently confusing things about the techniques just described is that they are used equally by the national press. The *News of the World* is an obvious example, though its targets are more often than not people or organisations whose privacy many people would defend from door-stepping snoopers. Social security 'scroungers' are more likely to be the subject of exposure than a firm which refuses to pay maternity benefits.

But what about *The Sunday Times'* 'Insight', which has investigated many issues of much broader public concern?

The crucial difference here is in the area of news-gathering with which the *Free Press* was concerned and in the context with which those stories were presented. An investigation by 'Insight', for example into price rigging by soft drinks firms, sits uncomfortably beside articles which are little more than promotional puffs for consumer products. The overall image of *The Sunday Times* is of an affluent society finding its feet, and the effect is to lessen the impact of the investigation and to give the impression that such scandals are only rare interruptions in the otherwise smooth flow of commerce. The *Free Press* placed analyses of double-dealing and corruption at the centre of its news list and, persistently concerned itself with what affected working people in Liverpool, whether factory workers or council tenants. It's also true that the main news media in the city lacked any interest for investigative journalism.

There remains, nonetheless, a secpticism among the radical press towards employing the techniques of journalism, refined as they have been for the sensationalising and trivialising of the news. The concept of the scoop, the personal drama, a concentration on the individual event rather that the wider movement appear inevitably entwined with journalistic practice. What does it matter if one manager of a steel foundry was dipping into the till when the system which encouraged that action remains challenged only by implication? Journalism is also seen as largely an individual profession, where reporters vie with each other for the best story, ignoring any wider responsibility. The products of journalism, as seen on the news-stands, are equally interpreted as the only way in which journalists can produce the news, ignoring the fact that reporters, sub-editors and designers are dependent on their employers as much as in any other job, often poorly paid outside Fleet Street and frequently alienated from their work.

But these arguments ignore the fact that some basic elements of journalism are essential to a successful newspaper — the ability to write clearly and concisely, the skill of gathering information and presenting it in a comprehensible form, a concern for accuracy in apparently minor details, sympathetic and careful editing, the use and development of sources, as well as such basic skills as typing, layout and design. To say that these skills are neutral is inaccurate, since any journalist trained in traditional proactice will have employed them in a particular way. But there is no reason why they cannot be adpated to entirely different circumstances — and learned by non-professionals.

In fact, *Liverpool Free Press* is not the only example of a newspaper which has attempted that transposition, nor was it alone in being established by disillusioned journalists. At both a national and local level, numerous attempts have been made over the last ten years to create newspapers or magazines which carry *general* news coverage (as opposed to news of a particular interest or movement) aimed at a radical or labour movement audience. Many have had unfortunately brief lives, foundering on financial or political problems. But it's important to look at both the successes and the failures to place the *Free Press* in a broader context.

As we discovered during the research for *Here is the Other News** there are something like 80 papers around the country which provide 'alternative news' on a monthly or less regular basis. Inside London, these are usually based on a particular borough (*Islington Gutter Press, Hackney People's Press, Pavement* in Wandsworth or *Gnat* in Newham); outside London, on a town (*Leeds Other Paper, Sheffield Free Press, Brighton Voice, Durham Street Press*). Their circulations average around the 1,000 mark, though a few achieve more — for example, *Leeds Other Paper* sells 2,000-plus every week. Some have also been publishing regularly since before *Liverpool Free Press* started, and have achieved a loyal readership, an intimate knowledge of their area's politics and a focus for opposition to council or government policies.

In the south London borough of Wandsworth, for instance, *Pavement* has been publishing since 1970 with up to six broadsheet pages of news about both local and national campaigns against policies which affect working people in the borough. Housing, the police, public service cuts, racism, planning decisions and some industrial news are the most familiar subjects, as well as occasional longer articles explaining the current political scene from a socialist perspective. The paper has also established an excellent range of contacts both within the local council and among opposition groups, enabling it, for instance, to reveal the planned sacking of the council's chief officer over his reluctance to implement cuts, or to campaign for the removal of a reactionary magistrate. Though its circulation hovers around 1,000 copies monthly (one third are sold door-to-door on housing estates, the rest mostly to political activists), it probably has more influence than that figure suggests. Run as a collective, *Pavement* has about 15 regular volunteers who agree on two people to act as editors for the month's issue. It has been regularly attacked by the council and its stories taken up by other newpapers.

For many of these papers, however, the very process of providing a sounding board for local campaigns and pressure groups has limited their appeal to a wider audience. An enormous amount of energy is expended on democratising the actual production of the paper — ensuring that decisions are reached collectively, encouraging the sharing of skills, allowing access to its pages to those outside the production group — and not enough on what events the paper should be covering, what it should be saying editorially and who might eventually buy it.

**Here is the Other News*, Minority Press Group series, number 1.

Though no doubt people *will* buy it, it is enough to say simply that there's a lot of activity on the left?

Several other towns *have* produced papers with a similar approach to the *Free Press*. The most prominent example is *Rochdale's Alternative Paper* (*RAP*) which, though appearing like an alternative magazine rather than a newspaper, has concentrated on exclusive news stories about the corruption and hypocrisy of the local establishment. These are presented either as short 'gossip' items or as full-blown investigations into, for example, the links between a council surveyor and a building firm or the influence of members of the town's Rotary clubs. It also carries industrial news, a pubs column, a what's on guide, welfare rights advice and an 'open' column for political groups.

But the essence of *RAP* is that it is deliberately written in a snappy, readable way with a large proportion of articles angled towards the people involved as much as the issue. *RAP* boasts that an average issue contains information on 50 members of the town's bourgeoise. And it is this, the paper's insight into the other side of the town's life which doesn't appear in the commercial local press, which has pushed its circulation figures to impressive figures of 7,500. It is now attempting to raise finance for a weekly.

None of this has happened by chance. *RAP* deliberately decided to go for a popular format, to achieve wide distribution through an agreement with the local newsagents' organisation, to have a tight, professional organisation with an editor (originally two co-editors) and to build up an impressive information resource. The paper's files include 3,000 microfiched records from Companies House on all Rochdale's limited companies, press cuttings and shareholder's lists on the major firms, a card index covering 4,000 individuals and a similar one on property ownership. This has enabled *RAP* to produce, for instance, a house by house guide to one of the town's richest streets and to pass on useful information to local trade unionists. But it's also true that none of this would be possible without an important subsidy from *RAP*'s allied printing press, which prints a wide range of other radical publications.

RAP's formula has been followed by *Metro News* in Bury, which takes its name from the fact that Bury is a metropolitan district. Started four years after *RAP*, in 1975, the paper has a similar emphasis on investigations, council scandals and industrial news — for instance an imaginative report on Bury's twin town, Angouleme in France — and has reached a circulation of roughly 5,000. It also has two co-editors and sells exclusively through newsagents. A comparable approach has also been adopted by *Tameside Eye* in Greater Manchester, a bi-monthly launched in 1978.

RAP's style of producing a local monthly has not gone without criticism, however. An emphasis on journalism, in the sense of investigation and enquiry, is seen as too easily transformed into a search for the scandulous, without any analysis of what is important in terms of social change. At the irregular conferences held to discuss the problems of local radical newspapers, *RAP* has been distinctly isolated from the mainstream of papers, whose roots are most commly in the libertarian left. They see their job as primarily to report on the wide range of non-aligned campaigns and organisations in towns like Bristol or Brighton, from the women's movement through to the anti-nuclear campaign, and providing some of the evidence (of council housing policy or business exploitation) to support those group's arguments. This is undoubtedly an important function, but it's equally clear that there's been a growing interest in publishing newspapers which are firstly more regular in appearance, and secondly, far wider in their appeal. Interestingly, both Scotland and Wales have produced radical papers which, in different ways, have attempted to deal with those problems.

On the Isle of Skye, the *West Highland Free Press* is the longest-running example of a traditional-style weekly paper with a socialist editorial policy. Started in 1972, it is first and foremost a local paper, with news of council decisions and sporting achievements; but on to that has been grafted more aggressive reports of land speculation, oil exploitation and the swamping of the area by military bases, as well as a weekly opinion column of clear left-wing views. Run as a co-operative, the *Free Press* has sometimes been attacked for its stand, but still manages to sell over 8,000 copies in a sparsely populated region — and get an important income from advertising. One distinct advantage, however, is that there is little competition from other publishers.

The difficulty of trying to launch a paper for a wider audience, in this case covering, Scotland, was shown by the experience of *Seven Days* during 1976/77. Much of the energy for this project in fact came from Brian Wilson, one of the founders of the *West Highland Free Press*, who hoped it would achieve the 7,000-plus circulation needed to pay its way in the early stages. But though *Seven Days* did achieve a series of scoop stories, including the attempted recruitment of an Edinburgh student as a Special Branch spy and a record of the racist judgements by a local immigration adjudicator (leading to his removal), it was treated with suspicion by the trade union movement and suffered from severe under-capitalisation. After 18 issues it changed to monthly production and quickly collapsed. Looking back, Brian Wilson believes its mistakes were to go in at too high a market level and to place too much emphasis on investigations. (A paper similar to the *West Highland Free Press* based on the Inverness area, *Highland Link*, also failed to reach ita sales expectations and lasted for only a few issues during Autumn 1980. This was despite the support of an £8,000 grant from the Scottish Co-operative Development Board.)

Wales, on the other hand, has spawned one of the most successful experiments in radical investigative journalism. The magazine *Rebecca*, named after the *Rebecca* uprisings of the mid-nineteenth century, has published only 11 issues since 1973 — the infrequency being partly the result of dependence on one full-time journalist and partly the length of time needed to investigate stories thoroughly. But over that period it has exposed, among other things, the persistent corruption of councillors and businessmen in Swansea (resulting in a series of court cases), the relationship between James Callaghan and other Labour politicians with the Julian Hodge fringe banking firm, and the steady stream of small deals and fiddles which permeate the Welsh Labour Party. Many of these articles have been printed in special Corruption Supplements. They have also invariably been well researched, the complexities of personal and business relationships explained in understandable language and justify the magazine's argument that it has 'proved that ordinary people will read difficult articles provided they concern issues which affect their lives.'

Rebecca's sales have also reflected this interest; an average of 7,000 per issues, with 9,000 copies sold during 1980, though the magazine's comparison with the figures for other current affairs magazines in Wales (*New Statesman* 1,200, *Private Eye*, 1,800) is perhaps unfair, since these are a weekly and a fortnightly. But unlike *Private Eye*, with which it is often compared, *Rebecca* is firmly committed to supporting trade union and grass roots political struggles. It is also at present attempting to raise £40,000 to re-launch itself in September 1981 as a monthly, with a 15,000 circulation, broader coverage of Welsh politics and culture, a full time staff and a research library. One indication of the difficulties involved in such a venture is that *Rebecca* has already been turned down for funding by the Welsh Arts Council, after being intially accepted by the Council's literature committee. Instead, the grant went to *Arcade*, a more conventional monthly, a decision which *Rebecca*'s editor, Paddy French, claims was made for political reasons.

Rebecca's investigations were also instrumental in the emergence of *Alarm*, a Swansea-based weekly which for almost two years (1977-79) produced a steady stream of stories about what it called the town's 'Mafia'. Sold mostly in pubs, *Alarm*, was written in an aggressive, chatty style and charted the day-to-day corruption of local public figures. The very fact that it talked about scandals which were often discussed in pubs but never seen in print gained it a circulation of up to 4,000 — though admittedly at the extremely low price of 2p. But the lack of any focus for action resulting from these stories, apart from the apparently unending series of corruption trials, led those involved to consider other forms of involvement outside the paper. During a period when *Alarm* candidates actually stood in local elections (gaining several hundred votes in one case) and closer links were being established with such groups as tenants associations, the paper ceased publication through sheer lack of energy.

At a national level, the picture of the radical press is considerably more diverse, and less clearly related to the experiment at the *Free Press*. On the one hand, a wide range of magazines have appeared in the last ten years covering such areas of struggle and campaigning as the women's movement, ecology, education, fringe theatre, anarchism, scientific developments, fascism etc. *Spare Rib, Undercurrents, Community Action, Searchlight, Race Today* and *Camerawork* are some of the better known examples. The alternative distributors, Full Time Distribution (formerly Publications Distribution Co-operative) now handle over 80 such titles, mostly monthlies or less frequent in appearance, and their quality in terms of design and actual writing has improved enormously. Nonetheless, to achieve a circulation of over 10,000 is still considered a breakthrough. This figure is important because at that point the economies of scale begin to take effect, and papers can escape from the vicious circle of self-exploitation, undercapitalisation and a readership limited only to a left 'ghetto'. One of the newer magazines, *The Beast* (animal liberation, nuclear power and ecology), is a good example of the professionalism with which such issues can be approached, and includes some investigative material. But it has still not reached the magic 10,000 figure, in part because of the reluctance of the major commercial distributors to take it seriously.

Attempts to produce general news magazines from the same broadly left libertarian standpoint have proved less successful. Well before its Scottish namesake emerged, the London-based *Seven Days* (1971-72) was intended to be a left version of *Picture Post*, but never attained its expected sale. There was also the short-lived *Street Life* in 1976, a mixture of rock music coverage and radical journalism, whilst London's *Time Out* has only survived because of its clear market base as a comprehensive entertainments guide to the city — out of which has developed a radical news section.

One general news magazine which *has* kept going for over five years without any substantial funding from outside its committed supporters is *The Leveller*. This has managed to both deal in depth with a broad spread of issues of concern to socialists — from rape to nuclear war to the secret state — and maintain a regular flow of news reports and investigations. It has also shown that a collective structure can move to get a paper out on time, although they have had to abandon the idea of having no division of labour. But though sales of the fortnightly (launched in 1980) have not stayed above the 8,000 level, its main achievement is that the enthusiasm of those involved has kept it constantly controversial and lively.

All this, of course, ignores the fact that there is a range of newspapers and magazines much more closely allied to left political organisations, although all of them survive on subsidies from various sources. Among socialist groups to the left of the Labour party there is a steady flow of weeklies and monthlies, though only few consciously try to popularise their arguments for those not involved in the particular party. The two biggest sellers among these papers, the weeklies *Socialist Challenge* (International Marxist Group) and *Socialist Worker* (Socialist Workers Party), both employ popular tabloid-style format, dramatic headlines and strong, simple language in order to attract new activists. *Socialist Worker* in particular has an aggressive, confrontational approach — labelling the rich as greedy blood-suckers of the country's wealth — and has deliberately abandoned an earlier move towards more complex investigative articles.

There are also several weeklies which in different ways either support the Labour Party or criticise it from a basically sympathetic position. *Labour Weekly* is the official party newspaper and therefore limited in its approach. *Tribune,* though not directly allied to the Tribune group of MP's takes a comparable line, but the *New Statesman* has begun under the editorship of Bruce Page to develop investigative journalism in a way not expected from an established labour oriented publication. With this strategy they have begun to claw back circulation they had steadily been losing and it shows that it is possible to attract new readers to a style of journalism which is critical of both capitalism and the trade unions and therefore comparable to the local initiative of the *Liverpool Free Press*.

It is equally often forgotten that two left-wing dailies do exist — *News Line* and the *Morning Star*. The former is frequently dismissed because of its link to the Workers Revolutionary Party, and its small circulation. The *Morning Star*, while often presenting a view of industrial relations in stark opposition to the rest of Fleet Street, has become stuck in a predictable mould of design and coverage. It has also found it increasingly difficult to survive financially without either substantial advertising or a broad enough readership outside the Communist Party. Its current circulation in Britain is 19,000.

The fact that there is no national daily newspaper independent of a political party which effectively counters the largely Conservative — and conservative — products of Fleet Street proprietors has encouraged renewed debate about the possibility of establishing one based on trade union and labour movement funding. This is not an entirely new idea, one that has been revived intermittently ever since the death of the *Daily Herald* in 1964, and it has been given additional impetus by the recent press treatment given to trade unionists, in particular over such periods as the 1979/80 'winter of discontent' and the TUC's 1980 Day of Action. But though there is undoubtedly a need for such a paper, the costs of setting up the venture from scratch (estimates range from £5 to £20 million) and the potential arguments over editorial control, would be enormous hurdles to overcome. How, for instance, could it avoid becoming a mouthpiece for either the Labour Party or the TUC? The TUC has in fact launched a £40,000 feasability study for a new labour daily with a possible launch in 1982.

The experience of *Liverpool Free Press* is important in relation to this argument because it clearly shows that it is possible to establish a provincial market for a radical newspaper on comparatively small resources. One reason for this is simple: there is less competition from existing papers, usually only one local newspaper chain. But a town or a metropolitan area also presents more manageable problems in terms of advertising, finance and the development of a close relationship between the paper and local political groups.

In the past few years several attempts have been made to create new weekly newspapers which would firstly aim for a wider and larger readership than the existing local monthlies and secondly, try to work more closely with trade union and left organisations. The first aim is important in terms of the economics of such a project: a weekly needs sales in the 8,000 – 15,000 bracket if it is to maintain its cash flow ands draw in advertisers. But the second element is equally crucial: support from local political groups can provide initial funding, help with sales, and, most importantly, a grounding in the politics of the area. However, the experiences so far have produced conflicts in both these areas.

Hull News, for example, a weekly launched by Hull Trades Council in 1979, appeared just twice before a mass desertion of advertisers nervous at its political 'bias' cut income from this source to virtually nil. But it was equally clear that, even if it had survived longer, a deeper conflict between the expectations of the Trades Council and those of the part-time journalists, who were less in tune with the principles involved, would have emerged.

The *Dundee Standard*, by contrast, which appeared weekly between November 1979 and September 1980 had a much clearer vision of its role as an alternative to the DC Thomson-owned local press and, to start with, a good relationship with its supporters in the town's Labour Party and trades unions. At its peak the *Standard* sold 9,000 copies, two-thirds of those through union branches, received regular adverts from local business despite its left-wing views, and succeeded in blending the expected elements of a local weekly — sport, entertainment, personality stories — with some well written articles about council policies and business malpractice. This balance was achieved largely through the efforts of a handful of experienced journalists, but in the end it was a conflict between the paper's editor and the management committee, who wanted to cut costs, which led to the *Standard*'s demise — again ultimately through advertisers pulling out during a period of bad publicity.

What the *Standard* did show was that it is possible to produce a successful weekly without covering all the day to day events of council business, courts, fires, retirements and awards with which most local papers are packed. Instead, it concentrated on a limited number of investigative stories, though all of local interest. But it also benefitted from both a strong labour movement tradition and a history of similar Dundee papers in the past.

The latest attempt at a radical weekly, the *East End News* in London, differs considerably from the *Standard*. Not only does it provide a spread of news coverage much closer to that of a traditional

per but has made a determined effort to counterbalance the
power of the journalists to decide what goes in. The latter
achieved by the creation of a consumers' cooperative through which
representatives of local groups and parties can elect a management
committee. This in turn decides general policy for the paper.

Whether this exceptionally democratic structure can work long-
term in the context of a weekly deadline, with snap decisions to be made,
remains to be seen. The *East End News* originated primarily from the
energies of local journalists struggling against both closures and the
editorial bias of their proprietors, notably the closure of the area's most
progressive paper, the *East Ender*. But the idea was discussed over many
months at local meetings, £25,000 raised from donations (some from
national trade unions) and two pilot issues printed before weekly
production started in March 1981.

The only local weekly to have been launched in recent years with
trade union backing which *has* maintained publication is *Nottingham
News*. This has been produced since February 1979 by journalists
sacked from the *Nottingham Evening Post* during a long and bitter pay
dispute. Initially it survived on strike pay from the National Union of
Journalists but an appeal was launched last year to give it more
permanent funding. It is run by a workers' co-operative, sells about
12,000 copies a week, and though it has been criticised for not having
alternative news values, it does give fairer treatment to trade union
issues and supports the Labour Party to the extent of including the local
party's manifesto as a four page pull-out.

Finance apart — and *Nottingham News* would have great difficulty
without the payment of salaries by the NUJ — the issue with which all
these papers have to grapple is how to develop a popular weekly without
either imitating the existing local press or, at the other extreme,
alienating readers by rabble-rousing calls for the immediate overthrow of
the government. There is a place for papers which act as the vanguard for
the movement, promoting its struggles and debating issues; but if the
concern is to open out the press to a wider readership without being
beholden to any interest group then the Liverpool Free Press is a good
example of what can be done.